VANDER ZALM

VANDER ZALM
From Immigrant to Premier

Alan Twigg

Harbour Publishing

To Vicki Hall
for all our changes

CONTENTS

Harbour Publishing Co. Ltd.
P.O. Box 219
Madeira Park, BC V0N 2H0

Jacket design: Gaye Hammond
Front jacket photograph: Craig Hodge
Back jacket photograph: Paul Little

Canadian Cataloguing in Publication Data

Twigg, Alan, 1952–
    Vander Zalm: from immigrant to premier

    Includes index.
    ISBN 0-920080-30-8

    1. Vander Zalm, William N.   2. Prime ministers —
British Columbia — Biography.   I. Title.
FC3828.1.V3T85 1986   971.1'04'0924   C86-091505-0
F1088.V3T85 1986

Printed and bound in Canada by Friesen Printers

PUBLISHER'S FOREWORD

by Howard White

For those who have been following Bill Vander Zalm's bizarre and audacious course across the political stage, it will make perfect sense for a book to appear on him at this point, before he has well begun his role as premier of British Columbia, but others will no doubt find it strange. Since it was my idea, I had better try to explain.

Vander Zalm comes to the premier's job after 20 years of being the most controversial politician in BC. He has already been in politics longer and had more ink spilt in his cause than most premiers can claim for their entire careers. But this is not by itself the reason for this book.

Despite the attention Bill Vander Zalm has had, he remains a largely unknown quantity. He is still surprising people every day. No leading political commentator predicted his dramatic grassroots triumph at the Social Credit leadership convention in July 1986, and once he was in the premier's chair, no one could quite agree whether he was "the first Liberal premier of BC in 40 years," or a "right wing, redneck populist." Such divergence of opinion after so much time is in itself remarkable. But it is not an idle mystery. Although he is supposed to have avoided discussing policy during his amazing and triumphant return to politics in 1986, Vander Zalm said just enough to make it plain that, in his mind, everything is up in the air. He reopened the question of logging in provincial parks. He said he might put an end to subsidy programs for business. He said he might put schools on the voucher system, rewriting the book on education funding. He said he might redraw the province's political map, replacing school districts, regional districts and municipalities

1

with counties. He said he would like to redraft our "antiquated" parliamentary system. In Vander Zalm's hands nothing about British Columbia's immediate future can be taken for granted.

This makes the question, "who is the real Bill Vander Zalm?" of more than passing interest. Is it the man who called Quebec premier Rene Levesque a frog and said he wouldn't lose any sleep if Canada broke up, or is it the patriot who built a Canadian war memorial on his own property? Is it the miser who underspent his welfare budget by $100 million, or the prodigal who gave critics the brushoff when his experimental rapid transit system went half a billion over estimate? Is it the conscientious democrat who, during the 1986 election, said he wouldn't presume to decide policy until he found out what people wanted, or the stubborn autocrat who, as Municipal Affairs minister, spent two years trying to push through a controversial Land Use Act even his own cabinet colleagues couldn't stomach?

What does Bill Vander Zalm's record tell us, exactly?

Pulling together much of Vander Zalm's vast public record and adding extensive new information from his friends, relatives, enemies and from the man himself, this book allows the patterns that make up the Vander Zalm enigma to be unravelled for the first time.

1

NOORDWYKERHOUT
Formative Years

*"It isn't the specific experiences you have that dictate
your lifestyle, but the attitude you adopt to them."*

Bill Vander Zalm
to Lisa Hobbs in the *Sun*
April 4, 1976

"I was born in Noordwykerhout, Holland on May 29, 1934.
My most vivid memory at about age five was peeking from
behind the front room curtains and watching Nazi planes drop
firebombs to burn out Dutch soldiers hidden between the pine
trees."[1]

As a small boy, Bill Vander Zalm watched as German troops
efficiently captured his hometown of 10,000 people. Vander
Zalm, his mother, and six other children in the family were
forced to fend for themselves through five years of fear,
deprivation and degradation. "I had two older brothers," says
Vander Zalm, "but the Germans were always raiding the villages
for workers and they had been taken away, although fortunately
not out of Holland."[2] The older brothers were Nick Petrus and
Petrus Nick. His younger brother was Adrianus Petrus. The two
sisters were named Trudy and Alice. Another younger brother
died just after the war. Vander Zalm's father, as both good and
bad luck would have it, was travelling in Canada as a bulb
salesman when Germany attacked the Netherlands. "We didn't
hear from him for five years," says Vander Zalm.[3]

Zuid Holland, the area where the Vander Zalm family lived,
thirty-five kilometres west of Amsterdam, in the dunes of the
bulb growing district, only two kilometres from the North Sea,

was one of the last areas of the Netherlands to be liberated. (The terms Holland and the Netherlands are not strictly synonymous. Holland refers to the historic counties dating back to 1323, called Noord Holland, Zuid Holland and Zeeland. The overall country is officially the Kingdom of the Netherlands, established in 1831.) The deprivations endured in the province of Zuid Holland were unparalleled in other parts of occupied western Europe. "I remember my mother sending me to a neighboring farmer to beg him for a potato," he says. "He cut it into four pieces and gave me a piece."[4]

Bill Vander Zalm was born at 47 Dorpsstraat in a large and relatively new house on the main street of Noordwykerhout. His mother, Agatha (Warmerdam) Vander Zalm, was from a family of well-to-do dairy farmers. His father, Wilhelmus Vander Zalm, was a bulb salesman and partner in a prosperous company established by his own father, Nicholas Klaas Vander Zalm. Bill Vander Zalm's uncles, Theodore and Cornelius, were also partners in this company, N.C. Vander Zalm & Sons. Bill Vander Zalm's grandfather had worked as a local contractor, installing Noordwykerhout's sewer system, before starting his bulb exporting firm. The company of N.C. Vander Zalm & Sons still exists, managed by a Vander Zalm, and the house at 47 Dorpsstraat has been occupied by the widow of Theodore Vander Zalm.

Vander Zalm's self-professed "very Dutch" character is directly connected to the spirit and soil of the country. His first name, Wilhelmus, which he shares with his father, is also the title of the Dutch national anthem, "Wilhelmus van Nassauwe," a song about Prince William of Orange. Noordwykerhout, in the west coast province of Zuid Holland, is not far from Aalsmeer, home to Holland's most famous flower auction. Between Haarlem, only 17 kilometres away, and Lieden, birthplace of Rembrandt, is the country's principle bulb cultivation district, de Bloembollenstreek. Many Canadians assume the entire country is a bulb-growing district, and that it is only normal for a Dutch immigrant like Vander Zalm to have horticulture in his blood, but it is really not a leading industry. Bulb growing is only one of many agricultural activities, and agriculture overall provides less than 12% of the country's jobs. Steel mills, appliance factories and big banks are what give the Dutch economy its rosy cheeks.

Zuid Hollanders, according to native Jake Brouwer, a one-time Conservative candidate for the BC Legislature, are "basic people." He says, "People from that part of the country are pretty stubborn, pretty tenacious; and they had to be, to keep the water out for hundreds and hundreds of years. It's a pretty conservative area. You were either Dutch Reformed, who are Calvinistic in their outlook, or Catholic, and by Catholic I mean orthodox Catholic."[5]

Noordwykerhout, 80% Catholic, was an island of Catholicism in a strongly Protestant region. Bill Vander Zalm attended Saint Joseph Parish School, a strict school with large classes. The Catholic order administering the school also established the St. Bavo asylum for male mental patients within the village, and the St. Mary psychiatric hospital for female patients outside the town. These were the major institutions of Noordwykerhout. It was not uncommon for the inmates of the psychiatric institutions to be reported wandering about the district, only to be turned in by schoolboys who would receive a token reward for their help.

The church that dominated the town pervaded life in general. The North American tradition of keeping church separate from state has no parallel in Holland. Staunch Catholics might form their opinions by reading the Catholic newspaper, listening to the Catholic radio station, shopping at the Catholic store, while expressing their political will through the powerful Catholic People's Party. It was a different kind of religion than most Canadians have known, an out-in-the-open, every-day-of-the-week religion, demanding a say in every facet of life. It is the sort of background that stands between Vander Zalm and more secular-minded British Columbians when he frankly admits that personal religious belief shapes his policy thinking and refuses to tone down his enthusiasm for conservative church-inspired causes like the anti-abortion movement or religious schools.

The bulb trade dominated Noordwykerhout's economy. There was only one other industry of note, a small factory supplying parts to Dutch shipbuilders. In addition to N.C.

Vander Zalm & Sons, other exporting firms were Geerlings & Sons, Pennings Bros., Verdegaal and Van Noordt & Son. Noordwykerhout native Leo Van Noordt remembers the Vander Zalms. "They were a very well-known family," he says. Van Noordt's father, like Bill Vander Zalm's father, was a bulb salesmen stranded outside the Netherlands during the German invasion. Van Noordt's father returned.

"There was, at that time, several other salesmen who managed to return by way of Portugal and Spain," says Van Noordt. "They got back around Christmas of 1940. Portugal was still neutral. I don't think that my Dad ever regretted going back. I don't think so. Because if you were married and you have a family, I think that's the place where you . . . regardless of how miserable the circumstances were later on, you try to go back where you belong. Mind you, I'm not condemning Bill's father, Bill. He stayed in Canada. He didn't pursue, or he was not made aware of, that kind of returning."

Forced to fend for themselves, the Vander Zalm family relied primarily on the ingenuity and stamina of the mother. "She really deserves a lot of credit," says Pete Warmerdam, Bill Vander Zalm's second cousin. "She raised the family for about five years — the length of the war — by herself with those kids. She raised those kids and she did a good job of it. She's the type of woman . . . she still would frown on somebody wasting food. Because she knows what it's like to be without."

Frugality became almost instinctive with Bill Vander Zalm. His press secretary, Bill Kay, tells the story of the new BC premier staying in a BC Interior hotel with him. The hotel had supplied some complimentary fruit in the rooms, which was not eaten. When checking out of the hotel, Vander Zalm told Kay to grab the fruit, even though it was going bad. Kay balked at the request, but Vander Zalm insisted. On the airplane home, Lillian Vander Zalm urged her husband to discard the rotting fruit. "We can feed it to the parrots," he told her.

Vander Zalm gives credit to his mother for being "a strong, positive, determined provider,"[6] something he would become himself. "She ruled by respect," he remembers. "In teen years, when we went out late at night, if we came in late, we didn't fear coming home and, you know, getting a bang on the head or anything like that. What we feared really was hurting mother. Or, you know, having her scold us. You know it was sort of a respect for mother that probably brought us through and kept us on the straight and narrow."

"But they still had some relatives," says Warmerdam. "They still had some help. They were a typical family except for the fact that they had come through the war without father being there."

The Vander Zalms also had their bulb fields but there was little business to be conducted during the war. Minimal trade was restricted to Germany and Belgium and parts of France. Towards the close of the war, Bill Vander Zalm was sent to forage for food by his mother.

"Things were very tough," says Vander Zalm. "We had no heat, no electricity, no food. We ate tulip bulbs. By 1944 we were limited to wearing repeatedly made-over clothes and crudely carved wooden shoes. Our diet consisted of tulip bulbs fried, boiled, and even ground into bread. Occasionally we had sugar beets as a treat."[7]

An aunt of Vander Zalm's, Mrs A.J.C. Vander Zalm-Warmerdam, claims the family never had to eat tulip bulbs, and that the family didn't suffer that much.[8] Pete Warmerdam, raised in a nearby town, is also dubious, but they are contradicted by Van Noordt, a Noordwykerhout native. "Mind you, we never ate them outright." he recalls, "They were ground. Then they were mixed in with flour and then baked in rye bread, primarily." Bill Vander Zalm's brother Pete concurs. "She's [their aunt] probably feeling guilty that [her family] didn't help my mother more."[9]

"Vander Zalm's years in Holland have shaped him, I'm sure they have," says Gerald Bonekamp, editor of the national Dutch-Canadian newspaper, *Hollandse de Krant*. Bonekamp is Vander Zalm's age. "He was a young boy when the war broke out and those are years in a boy's life when he notices more what's going on around him."[10]

By British Columbian standards, the 27th premier of BC had a very abnormal childhood. Vander Zalm says this upbringing has given him confidence in himself and traditional Dutch values. Cleanliness, neatness and a love of physical order are Dutch traits every tourist can attest to. In the Dutch language, the word for "beauty" and the word for "clean" are the same. Vander Zalm, who spoke only Dutch until he was 12, obviously carries this cultural heritage in his blood. Since his first days in politics, reporters have noted the obsessive neatness of his appearance. Some visitors to his Fantasy Garden World find the emphasis on order and cleanliness to be oppressive.

After neatness, national traits get harder to agree on. Dutch society today is generally very progressive, although enclaves of blackstocking fundamentalists coexist peacefully within the mix. Today the Dutch church is in constant hot water with Pope John Paul II for being too liberal, but it is a commonly observed fact that immigrants of all countries in all times tend to cling to the way things were in the motherland when they left, and to become frozen in time, cut off from the progress that goes on after they emigrate. This accounts to some extent for the irony that Dutch immigrants of Vander Zalm's generation tend to be seen as a conservative element in Canada while their own countrymen back home support a system that remains very socialistic in spite of a swing to more moderate politics in the last seven years.

Political parties are myriad, representing every extreme. One quality most Dutch have a hard time denying is that they tend to harbour strong opinions, and are accustomed to vigorous and sustained debate at all levels of society. "One Dutchman is a temple, two a religion and three a schism," goes the saying.

Outspokenness has been Vander Zalm's trademark in politics, and it is possible some of what appears to be deliberately provocative in the subdued Canadian context would seem mild fare by Dutch standards. Another strong, though not quite so universal, national trait is mercantilism. Sometimes called the "Chinese of Europe," the Dutch burgher is an inveterate trader. As the great French philosopher Rene Descartes put it while exiled in Amsterdam in 1631, "Everybody here except me is in business and so absorbed by profit-making that I could spend my entire life here and never be noticed by a soul."

Of course, during World War II Dutch mercantilism was stifled. "The Netherlands in May 1940 had entered a nightmare that went on and on," historian Michiel Horn wrote in *A Liberation Album*. "It lasted more than four years in the three southern provinces, almost five years to the day in the eight provinces north of the great rivers."[11]

People of the major cities had to be fed by central kitchens. As the war progressed, and as gas and electricity were cut off, these "Bolshevist" kitchens, initially discouraged by the Germans, operated by necessity, distributing millions of meals daily.

It has been estimated that between 8,000 and 10,000 Jews survived by hiding indoors for the duration of the war. Many Dutch Jews died in Polish concentration camps. Of 60,000 Dutch Jews sent to Auschwitz, 500 survived. Of 34,000 sent to Sobibor, only nineteen returned to Holland. Relatively few Jews deported from Holland during the war, if they survived, came back to Holland to live.

There was a considerable Jewish-Dutch population in and around Noordwykerhout. "Many people lived in the fields," recalls Van Noordt. "They never lived in a house anymore." The Dutch Resistance was also very active in the town. "If there was some sabotage to annoy the Germans, you can be sure the next day they would retaliate," says Van Noordt. "You would have to help them build their fortifications or start building a canal or anything they wanted."

Violence and the threat of death were constant because the British Spitfires made almost daily raids on the railway tracks near the ocean. The Germans, in turn, were launching rockets from the outskirts of Noordwykerhout to attack England. It was not uncommon for these rockets to misfire and explode near the town. One of these errant rockets landed in a field owned by the Vander Zalms. British Spitfire pilots routinely took machine gun practice on Dutch windmills after raids.

German rule became more vicious as the war dragged the powerless country further into misery. From May 1940 to December 1944, 1,228 private citizens were shot. In the next four months, another 1,579 were executed. In the north, during the so-called Hunger Winter of 1944–45, when most citizens were forced to beg for potatoes, conditions became almost intolerable. By August 1944 the average daily caloric intake per adult was 1,500, far below the normal consumption of 2,500. Meat was almost unattainable. In November the daily ration of bread, potatoes and sugar beets fell to 1,040 calories. By late January it was 500 calories. This figure rose in March to 770, but fell in April 1945 to only 320 calories per day.

With several million Netherlanders living below sea level, there evolved a new daily hazard: death by drowning. The Nazis began flooding parts of Holland for military purposes. As well, it turned out to be an abnormally cold winter. Waterways froze, complicating the transportation of food. Desperate for fuel to keep warm, people burned their own furniture or tore the woodwork out of their homes. Trees were cut down in parks, bombarded buildings were stripped of wood and ties were torn from streetcar tracks.

With defeat of the Third Reich pending, chances of survival in Holland worsened. Shootings increasingly took place in public. Bodies were sometimes left where they fell. With the wood shortage, the Dutch used coffins made of cardboard. Then the cardboard ran out. One Amsterdam church was filled with 235 corpses, name tags on emaciated wrists, until they were finally wrapped in sheets and simply removed to a mass grave.

As one bitter joke of the time went, "Even to be buried you have to queue up."

Typhoid and rats appeared. Medicine was scarce. Standards of cleanliness fell. It was not unknown for hunger-stricken families in one-room dwellings to keep corpses as long as five weeks in order to obtain extra ration coupons for the deceased. People began to faint and die from hunger in the streets. Remarkably, the bureaucratic regulations of the Germans and the self-regulatory nature of the Dutch combined to prevent a collapse of social order or the disintegration of social life.

Dutch women and children foraged in the countryside for their food. Some of the farming population dealt fairly with the hunger trekkers but others were known to take ruthless advantage of them. Recipes were printed in the newspapers instructing the people how to make soup from tulip bulbs and dahlias. Family pets were not spared.

Historian Henri van der Zee was ten years old during the Hunger Winter, as was Bill Vander Zalm. He attests to the severity of the crisis. "The only thing that mattered was food, food and food again."[12] The economy was at a standstill. Some northerners dreamily took to wearing the spring's colourful crop of new flowers. Van der Zee tells of one man in Amsterdam who wrote, "Misery has hit rock-bottom and one approaches the stage of indifference. We buy flowers and we put them in our rooms, on the window-sill. We salute the new life that grows festively among the swollen bodies of the oedema victims, among the emaciated children and the garbage heaps in the parks." The same man later observed, on April 29, "Today I saw two children dying in the street. They looked like small dead birds in winter, so sad and helpless."[13]

Agatha Vander Zalm also lost one of her children—not that year, but immediately after the war, as conditions remained harsh. The small boy cut his foot while running about without shoes and contracted tetanus. With proper medication unavailable, he sickened and died.

One naturally assumes such experiences would have a profoundly sobering effect on the nascent premier of British Columbia, instilling in him an appreciation of human suffering that would ballast his character later in life. But one of the most unaccountable attitudes harboured by this often baffling man is his positive view of his whole war experience.

"I can't think of a disadvantage," he told me not long after becoming premier, "Even during those very difficult times...I was only a youngster. But it certainly sticks with you. And it makes one aware of how you can survive when things are tough if you'll somehow apply yourself. There's always a way through it. There was no welfare, there was no unemployment insurance, there was no food, there wasn't anything. And my mother was there with seven children. But she found her way through it. Now sometimes we had to go out and beg, you know. We ate things we didn't particularly enjoy. Tulip bulbs or sugar beets and those sorts of things aren't really good eating. So it was very, very difficult and very tough but we got through it. It's amazing. Even like with clothing, as I've mentioned so many times, mother could make things over six times. So it makes you conscious of the fact that you can survive if you work at it and there's always a way through. Nothing really need stop you...People were certainly much more law-abiding...We didn't like the enemy, and we were upset with the enemy, but the real fear wasn't there because we had, initially, the conventional German forces. And they weren't really that bad. It's the ones that came later in the black uniforms. And then we had the Mongolian soldiers coming in. And this is where the difficult part came."

I suggested to Vander Zalm that his tendency to look on the bright side of the war experience and of life in general could be developed to an abnormal degree in reaction to those dark times he went through as a child.

"To some degree," he replied. "Because even when I refer to those times, I don't refer to them as dark times. Knowing they were. I'm still, you know, looking at what the brighter side of what it was and saying, 'Ya, but during those times we did have order.' And things were principled."

During the Hunger Winter 18,000 Dutch citizens starved to death. The death toll for Dutch soldiers in battle was only 4,500.

An estimated figure for those who died in the Dutch Resistance is 23,000. Another 258 Dutchmen died in German POW camps. The toll for Dutch sailors was 1,500. In addition, over 100,000 Dutch Jews never returned from concentration camps. More than 5,000 Dutch citizens died in prisons. Another 50,000 Dutch died during the war simply because medical help was unavailable. Of the 550,000 Dutch men forced to work for the Nazis, 30,000 never returned. And it is estimated that some 23,000 Netherlanders died in air raids.

The liberation of Holland also took the lives of approximately 50,000 Allied soldiers. Of these, 5,700 were Canadians. The first Canadians marched over the German-Dutch border into Dinxperloo near Doetinchem on March 30, Good Friday, as the

Germans dismantled their last rocket sites near The Hague. Allied armies stormed through the east and north of Holland. The Germans held fast only in Noord Holland, Zuid Holland and Utrecht. The Germans declared this area "Festung Holland," or Fortress Holland.

Bill Vander Zalm was in Fortress Holland. One evening, after church and prior to curfew, Bill Vander Zalm had another experience he would never forget. "A jeep with strangely dressed men wearing berets drove into our village. Even though German soldiers with guns lined the sidewalks, the newcomers approached the worshippers, who recognized them as liberators, and without hesitation picked them up, carried them on their shoulders, shouted for joy, sang songs, and partied throughout the night."

Canadian soldiers had liberated Noordwykerhout.

The Canadian role in liberating Holland created a bond between the two countries, one Vander Zalm is well aware of. He would invoke it again 40 years later by adding a war monument to his tourist attractions at Fantasy Garden and bringing his aged mother in to dedicate it.

After the liberation, Wilhelmus Vander Zalm Sr. returned to Noordwykerhout with the help of the Red Cross, but it was not to stay. The rebuilding of the shattered Dutch economy would be a slow and unrewarding process, and the bulb business, in particular, was in shambles. The bulb supply around Noordwykerhout had been seriously depleted, machinery and tools were in short supply and two of Holland's major clients in years past, England and Germany, needed only enough flowers to place on their graves.

Jolly and plump Wilhelmus Vander Zalm Sr. announced he was taking the family to a better land.

2

FAMILY MATTERS
The "Consignment Bills"

"The Vander Zalm family image is coated in sugar."
Anne Fletcher
Sun family profile
August 9, 1986

It doesn't look like much. About forty yards back from a bumpy backroad, down a dirt driveway, hidden beneath overhanging trees, sits an old house, badly in need of a paint job. It's not worth a second glance unless you happen to know this old farmhouse at 27840 Inter-Provincial Highway in the Fraser Valley has a unique history.

This was the home of Wilhelmus Vander Zalm Sr. during World War II, when he began to develop the Fraser Valley Bulb Company, a pioneer in the BC bulb producing industry. It was also the house where Wilhelmus Vander Zalm Jr. grew up, learned English, developed his aptitude for hard work and began to emulate his gregarious father's flair for business

The house was built by Beryl Dospital's father, a "jackknife carpenter" from Saskatchewan, in 1934. She and her sisters helped in the construction when their neighborhood was being cut from the bush. "I remember cutting 75 trees for the foundation," she recalls, at age 82. "The house was set on cedar posts. They didn't use cement in those days." The tiny hamlet was so remote from the nearest store, in Bradner, that the area was given a name of its own, Lombard.

During World War II, Bill Vander Zalm Sr. came to Beryl Dospital's father and suggested a deal. In return for use of land owned by Dospital, Vander Zalm would plant bulbs and give Dospital a share of the business. Dospital agreed to let the

Dutchman use his land for free. The two men became friends. Vander Zalm jokingly referred to his Canadian partner as the Mayor of Lombard.

When he had enough money, Bill Vander Zalm Sr. bought the Lombard farmhouse where Beryl Dospital was living with her husband. The Dospitals remained for approximately a year afterwards and Vander Zalm moved in with them as an owner-lodger. Beryl Dospital often cooked Vander Zalm's meals and got to know him well during the war. "He was a very pleasant man. Lots of laughs. He was always so jolly," she says. Bill Vander Zalm Sr. told her if she named her son after him he would give the boy an acre of land when the boy turned 18. Beryl Dospital gave her son Jack the middle name of William, as they agreed. Dospital's husband fell off a ladder at Sam's Store in Abbotsford and died when little Jack William was only two years old. The boy could have used that acre. But he never got it.

Across the road from the Vander Zalms' old farmhouse lives Pat Brady, Dospital's brother-in-law. He was already there in the early days when Bill Vander Zalm Sr. arrived. "We used to call him Consignment Bill. He'd sell the Bradner bulb growers on three months' consignment. So there's no bloody way he was going to lose. He was a big guy, over 200 pounds. Easy to get along with. But he was a tough operator. He always came out on the good side."

The stranded bulb merchant was united with his family in Noordwykerhout at war's end. According to Noordwykerhouter Leo Van Noordt, it was known in the town during the war that Vander Zalm Sr. had been building a business somewhere in Canada. Vander Zalm Jr. disagrees: "No, we didn't know what he was doing the whole of that war period. When he left Holland just before the war he was a bulb salesman. He was caught over here. . . . He was in Vancouver at the time. And of course he had to take a boat back. Or he had to take a train back, then catch a boat in Montreal. There were no planes back then. It was impossible because you couldn't get across the ocean. There was another eleven hundred Dutchmen waiting on the dock when he arrived. So he was stuck over here. We didn't hear. And he had a tough time of it, too, for a good while. Because really his job, his expertise, was bulbs and he couldn't get any bulbs from Holland. So what he ended up doing was . . . buying bulbs that had been used in greenhouses which would normally be dumped and nursing these back. And he bought a piece of land in Bradner to do that. So he built a little business."

The Vander Zalms became the first Noordwykerhout family to emigrate after the war. Bill Vander Zalm Jr. seems to be confused as to his exact age at this time. He has written he was eleven years old upon his arrival in Canada. He has also written that he arrived in the Fraser Valley in April 1947, when he would have been twelve.

"After a three-week boat journey we arrived in St. John's, Newfoundland, proceeded to Montreal, and then drove across the country to British Columbia — enjoying wonderful new experiences like a first banana, first orange, real ice cream, and something called hamburgers."[1]

"We arrived on a Wednesday in April, 1947. On Thursday I was out in the field hoeing daffodils."[2] Undoubtedly his appreciation for the so-called "work ethic" is genuine. "I was brought up to work hard, not to squander, and if you wanted something you put out. I'm tied in, like it or not, with the old work ethic."[3]

By the time the entire Vander Zalm family arrived, later in the year, the business was already operational. Bill Vander Zalm probably hoed daffodils on Thursday; Friday he might have gone fishing. "When they started out here," says Pete Warmerdam, whose grandmother was Agatha Vander Zalm's sister, "they had some of the backing from Holland, but not that much. They were not well-off, but I wouldn't call it struggling either."

Warmerdam, a few years older than Bill Vander Zalm, came to Canada in 1949. He initially worked for the Vander Zalms in Bradner. "They've been instrumental in starting the bulb trade here. They were the first ones who were buying and shipping. There were a few people growing some [tulip bulbs] for greenhouse purposes but they were the first who came here and started to buy locally grown daffodils and marketing them in the east. The one thing I always thought was special about the Vander Zalms: they always were looking for good opportunities and when they would see one, they would utilize it."

Bill Sr., an extroverted go-getter, had made annual sales trips to Canada prior to the war. He had some contacts and clients within the country from whom he could collect money owing to N.C. Vander Zalm & Sons of Noordwykerhout. He had used the war years wisely, acquiring land and a home when prices were cheap. The Lombard home soon became the focal point for postwar Dutch settlers less fortunate than the Vander Zalms. "We had good times," recalls Warmerdam. "At one time, them being the first Dutch people out here, some of us emigrated and came out here. I know Sundays that home was open to all the people who knew them. I remember people coming in there Sundays and there was always a big pot of soup. They were good that way."

Warmerdam says the Vander Zalms were good people to work for, enjoyable company. "The Dutch were used to working hard so that was not a problem," he says. Everybody pitched in, helped out, and tried to put the past behind them. "All that crew worked hard," recalls neighbour Pat Brady. "He [Bill Sr.] had a ready-made work crew when he brought them over from Holland." The Vander Zalms were not tightfisted, especially when it came to helping emigrating Dutch.

"This gives you an indication what kind of people they were," says Warmerdam. "I know a doctor came out here about a year after they did. Probably that would be '48. He just came out from Holland. He happened to be in the bank. He needed some money to buy a car. This was Dr. Alberts from Abbotsford. It so happened that Bill Vander Zalm [Sr.] happens to be in the bank. He heard some of the conversation. Dr. Alberts says I'm here trying to borrow some money. Ah, Bill says, that was no problem at all. He went into the bank and signed the note. Dr. Alberts started off with a new car." *Vancouver* Magazine journalist Sean Rossiter maintains that Vander Zalm Sr.'s pioneer bulb business in Bradner, firmly established during the war years on the ground floor of an industry slated for rapid postwar growth, gave Bill Vander Zalm a running start in business, belying his image as a self-made millionaire who raised himself from the squalor of war-torn Holland entirely by his own efforts.

Post-World War II emigration was well organized and directed by the Canadian and Netherlands governments. From the small town of Noordwykerhout alone there are numerous families in BC, mostly involved in the horticulture trade. William Duvenvoorde of Aldergrove formerly managed the Art Knapp's franchise in Langley. Among others are the Heemskerks of Chilliwack and Langley, the Van Hages of Prince George, the Van Noordts of Langley. Two Dutch-Canadian wholesale bulb companies operate in the Fraser Valley besides Van Noordt's firm: Paridon Horticultural (Delta) owned by the Zanten family, and Pan-American Bulbs. The latter company purchased the Vander Zalms' troubled bulb wholesaling operation from Bill Vander Zalm in 1960.

It is not generally known that Dutch-Canadians constitute the sixth largest ethnic group in British Columbia. In 1981 they ranked only ninth among the ethnic-origin peoples in metropolitan Vancouver because only 5,000 lived within the political limits of the city. More than five times as many resided in the suburbs of Vancouver. The Dutch preferred to disperse into agricultural areas and have formed few visible community groups. According to the most recent census, there are over 75,000 people of Dutch extraction in BC.

Bill Vander Zalm Jr. officially became a Canadian citizen in 1952. The issue of how important his "Dutch-ness" is has been cause for national debate. Ontario-based novelist Margaret Laurence (who has discussed at length the significance of her own "Black Celt" heritage) has taken celebrity columnist Allan Fotheringham to task for calling Premier Vander Zalm "Willie Woodenshoes" in *Maclean's*. Laurence wrote the magazine charging that Fotheringham's language did "not seem very different from Vander Zalm's racism in calling Rene Levesque a frog," and that to ridicule Vander Zalm's political buffoonery as being part and parcel of his ethnic heritage was 'in effect a slur on the countless numbers of Dutch immigrants who have given so much to this country." Fotheringham countered, not a little deviously, "He is very proud that he is a Dutch immigrant. He mentions it every chance he gets and, in fact, used it extensively in his climb to the top—pointing out to the electorate how the free enterprise system could reward someone who never got past high school but worked hard, slogged head-down and made a million."[4]

As author Helen Colijn has noted in her book, *Of Dutch Ways*, "Once set on a course, they will stick to their goal with a determination that some call stubbornness. The long struggle against the water is supposed to account for this Dutch quality. They are persistent in their beliefs, too, and easily irked when they have to put up for long with dissenting opinions."[5] Bill Vander Zalm Jr. appears in many regards to be a stereotypical Dutchman, but he emphasizes that he is now a Canadian. "I still have an interest in the place [the Netherlands]," he told me. "And I've never forgotten my roots or where it was I initially came from. I keep in touch, I take an interest, I know what's happening. But I don't necessarily use that as an example. I don't get details on programs or approaches.

"I'm very Canadian. I'm not very Dutch. I'm very Canadian. But I've always said that if a person sort of runs down his homeland, and doesn't really appreciate where it is he came from, and the customs and the cultures he was born with, then he'll not make a good Canadian. Because he could develop that same disrespect and lack of interest in Canada."

At age twelve, Bill Vander Zalm spoke only Dutch. "We picked up English very quickly—we hadn't spoken a word of it—and especially enjoyed a game new to us called baseball."[6] He was forced to assimilate quickly. "In those days we didn't have special education classes set up especially for immigrants, which is why from time to time, the biases that I have developed about these programs may show in me."[7]

Bill Vander Zalm's own good luck as an immigrant hasn't prevented him taking a jaundiced view of immigration for others. "For a great many years, the Immigration Department has been operating like a social welfare agency, and I suppose this is defensible in many respects. Perhaps one could argue that we owe it to the world to provide for the underprivileged, but how much of that can we afford?[8]

"You can't cut off immigration—nor should you. If you get a scientist, a skilled tradesman, or someone who is willing to risk money to start up a new business employing Canadians, then Canada can only benefit from that. But when we allow large numbers of refugees in, who in turn sponsor all their relatives, then it becomes more of a social service program.

"And that is fine as long as it is recognized as such, and people realize that they will then have to dig into their pockets to give those people food, shelter, training—perhaps UIC or welfare. That is not to say I don't believe we have any responsibility for those who need help, providing it is realized that such responsibility is a cost item for the country."[9]

After the dreary years in Holland when productive and improving work was hard to come by, that first summer in BC must have been a relatively happy one for the reunited Vander Zalms. There was even some poetic justice in their emigration to B.C: The name Vander Zalm means essentially "of the salmon." (It is correctly pronounced Zalm as in palm, not Zalm as in ham.)

"In September I was ready to enter Grade Six," he says, "but I found many of my friends registering in Grade Eight. I had to make my first important decision. I had already discovered I was much advanced in math over the other boys and reasoned that I might just as well register in Grade Eight with them."[10]

The other children in the remote Lombard neighborhood near Bill Vander Zalm's age were Pat Brady Jr. and his younger brother, Bob; Raymond Van Skiver and his sister; Ivar and Lillia Vidman; and his own younger brother Art. At Lombard there were seven houses and nineteen people (including children).

"Wim and I used to go back and forth to school together," recalls Brady Jr. "We used to walk up the train tracks to Bradner, then catch the bus into Abbotsford. We'd leave at around 7:15 and get back around 4:30. I can remember him practicing one of his speeches on me for school. It was for a debate or something and it was about the Benefits of Free

Enterprise Versus Socialism. I can remember that because at the time I didn't know what either of those words meant.

"There were a bunch of us that used to hang out together. The boys used to go down to the creek to do our fishing and swimming. We used to call it the Ol' Bare Balls Club. Sometimes we'd collect cascara bark off the trees and dry it into pieces about the size of a quarter. That's how we got spending money. You could sell that dried bark to the local Buckerfield's for two bits a pound. They used it to make some sort of laxative. I remember we had some in our house. Really good stuff.

"Most of the time we couldn't go to school functions like dances and parties because we were too far away. One of the problems where we lived is that we didn't have any transportation. I remember when my Aunt Hazel got the first black & white TV. We'd all go over there and watch it. It was a big deal."

Brady Sr. recalls watching "Wim" Vander Zalm growing up. He describes him as "kind of a BSer who used to tell a lot of screwy jokes. They used to go to my sister-in-law's place and learn how to speak English, play cards in the wintertime because this was the boondocks out here. He used to tell my kids a lot of garbage about during the war when they were eating bulbs. They were starving...and hanging on the dykes, hiding from the Germans. They'd [Germans] come along with their spiked boots and step on your hands...telling my kids all this garbage. That's all it was."

He recalls Vander Zalm was a nice looking boy, always "putting on the dog," concerned about his appearance. He was a "sweet talker" with "a pretty thick skull—nothing bugged him." As Vander Zalm moved through his teens, both Brady Sr. and Brady Jr. had business involvements with him.

Brady Jr. used to work with his friend Wim at the Vander Zalms' vegetable stand in Whalley. "He was always pretty sharp on his feet and a real go-getter," recalls Brady, "nothing obnoxious though." Thirty years later, when Vander Zalm was BC's Municipal Affairs minister, Brady was president of the BC Teachers Federation. George Ferguson of Abbotsford was head of the Union of BC Municipalities. David Kendall of Abbotsford was president of the BC School Trustees. Brady, now a Prince George alderman and teacher, met Vander Zalm in Victoria. "I told him maybe the four of us should all meet back at the Bradner Store and have a few beers and solve all the problems. I told him we could do that if he was Education minister and not Municipal Affairs minister. He said don't hold your breath. But pretty soon after that he was in charge of Education."

Brady Sr. remembers Bill Vander Zalm as a businessman less fondly. Brady, a retired CPR assistant yard master, knew Bill Vander Zalm Jr. as "another Consignment Bill. He learned that from his Dad. He was well-coached from his Dad in the business. He got into consignment. You want to sell him anything in his store in Whalley? He says, 'Put it down. I'll sell it for you.' If he sold it, he got his cut and you got yours. . . . His Dad was so goddamned good at talking it just rolled out of him. The way I see it, young Bill, he had a good coach."

Brady Sr., at age 78, remains bitter about a deal with Vander Zalm Jr. when the family operated a wholesale bulb store in Whalley. "I remember one time, a year we had some nice dahlias," he says, "beautiful dahlias. I went to see him and asked if he wanted to buy them. He said, 'Well, they have to be dug and dried and tagged.' So, in the fall, my wife and I dug them up. They come in clusters like rhubarb root. We took them into Whalley.

"He said, 'Well, I can't sell them like that. You have to take them home and divide them all, dry them.' They're all interlocked like this," he entwines his fingers, "and then you had to take them out as a tuber and see that there was a little green in there. My wife and I, we done all that. We put them in this big bloody box. They were all marked and all that. So we asked him if he wanted to buy them and he said, 'Alright, just put them down. I'll see if I can sell them.

"So, two or three weeks later, we went back. I said, 'Oh, I see you sold all the dahlias.' He said, 'No, I didn't sell them all. I had to dump a third of them.' Dumping means get rid of them. And I said, 'Well, where the hell are they now?' He says, 'I threw them out. I couldn't sell them. I just have to pay what I sold you.' That was it. That's when I got screwed. I don't know where the other third went." Would Pat Brady Sr. trust Bill Vander Zalm Jr. again? "No bloody way."

Bill Vander Zalm was hoping to become a lawyer. Attending Philip Sheffield High School in Abbotsford, he was a popular student who stood out in a crowd with his good looks. According to one of his teachers, he was somewhat weak in French but appeared to be of above average intelligence. The fact that the Vander Zalm boys had to help their father hindered their academic work and participation in extracurricular activities, although Bill Vander Zalm did take part in school plays as an actor. The graduating class annual said he "likes to be surrounded by beautiful girls."[11] In a section of that school's 1952 annual dubbed Grade XII Prophecies, it was also suggested that one day Wim, with his stylishly slicked-back hair, would own a large modelling agency. He did not participate in many sports, except soccer, and he was realistically "thinking of becoming a bulb salesman."[12]

Realism interrupted his life far sooner than he expected. The first of two fatal and fateful heart attacks — one to his father and one to nurseryman Art Knapp — determined his course.

"Just before my graduation from Grade 12 my father had a heart attack," he recalls, "and again a family meeting decided that Wim (as I was then known) would have to take over the customer accounts from British Columbia to the Lakehead. At age seventeen, having just acquired a driver's license, I set off in the winter to travel through British Columbia, the prairies and northern Ontario. I called on greenhouses, florists and seed houses to sell bulbs. My success, partly because I was young and many felt sorry for me, was considerable"[13]

Being a salesman at seventeen, driving half the breadth of the second largest nation on earth, still learning the English language, supporting the family back home — clearly it was a challenging adventure. It was during this period in the 1950s that "Consignment Bill," who had passed his long Bradner winters playing hours and hours of card games, would become "a bit of a promoter."[14]

Years later, deputy premier Grace McCarthy, who herself had learned her political salesmanship building a string of flower shops, remarked of Bill Vander Zalm's grinning manner, "Bill is tremendously good-natured; no moodiness to him at all. He's always up; never up-and-down. That's neat—to work with people who are up."[15]

Bill was always up. He developed a regimen of rising at 7 A.M., mostly working until midnight every day of the week. Bran flakes for breakfast. A ham and cheese sandwich for lunch. White wine with a large dinner. At 5 feet 10 inches and 170 pounds, his weight would not change for twenty years. He would relax by working. He would not have time for books.

While Vander Zalm's mother had laid the groundwork for Vander Zalm's inner character—a keen determination, a rigid respect for inherited values, an appreciation for the importance of security—Vander Zalm had modeled his outer character during his adolescence—a gladhanding salesmanlike manner, a promotional spirit, a Dale Carnegie sense of values—upon the example of his namesake father.

At age 18 Bill Vander Zalm proceeded to market his most important product, himself, for the most important sale of his life.

While passing through Kelowna—the hometown in 1951 of the new premier of British Columbia, a former hardware salesman named W.A.C. Bennett—the energetic bulb peddler entered the Ferry News Stand and Gift Shop. Legend has it that he had just seen a photograph of an unknown local girl in the front window of a photo shop and he had told himself he ought to marry that girl. By coincidence, there she was eating dinner in the gift shop, wearing bobby socks, talking to her sister behind the counter.

The blonde in the bobby socks was 15-year-old Lillian Beatrice Mihalic. Lillian was, according to her mother, "a very good little girl. So pretty, I had to watch her—the boys were always after her, but she wasn't the girl to run around." Lillian's weakness was not boys, but clothes. "She was always crazy about clothes," says her mother. "Whenever she made any money, she spent it on clothes."[16]

To this day Lillian Mihalic remembers her meeting with Bill Vander Zalm very clearly. She was in pigtails. "And he was dressed in a charcoal black suit and pink shirt—yes, a pink shirt—and blue suede shoes. But he was so cute with that ruddy Dutch complexion. It was love at first sight. As soon as I saw him, I knew he was the one. He was just my type, clean, smiling and cheeky."[17]

Lillian's older sister, Betty, was working at the combination diner and gift shop at the time. Lillian was working in the hardware store during the day, and at the nearby Paramount Theatre selling candy at night. "He just stared at me," recalls Lillian. "My sister finally introduced us."[18] Lillian suddenly remembered she had to pick up two corsages that evening from the florist. "Straight out of the blue he volunteered to pick them up for me. I was in the powder room when he returned and he left, leaving the corsages with my sister.

"But when I left for work at the Paramount, there he was outside offering me a ride in his car—it was only one block but I went anyway."[19]

The romance was not without its complications. Vander Zalm was nervous when he came to Lillian's house courting. "I tried to give him tea and cakes," says Lillian's mother, "and he wasn't sure if he would take them. Lillian was shy, too."[20] When the couple began to correspond, Lillian addressed him as "Dear Vander."[21] She hadn't got his name right. "I quit writing to him. He was so far away. But I couldn't get him out of my mind so the next Christmas I sent him a card. The next thing I knew he was in Kelowna asking me to go steady."[22]

Love letters pleaded his case. "How did you like the idea of an apartment, sweetheart? Have you thought it over? Couldn't we be married this summer, darling?"[23] He was not a salesman who would take no for an answer. "Say yes, darling. I have to go to bed now sweetheart so I can get three or four hours sleep before I start work again. I'll dream of you, darling. Your love, faithful for always...Wim."[24]

Lillian agreed to move to the coast to stay with his sister-in-law. "It's funny," she says, "but I was never going to marry a salesman or someone who would always be away from home—I wanted him where I could spoil him."[25]

Lillian Mihalic, to put it mildly, had a conventional, 1950s view of marriage. "He asked me before we were married whether I was Catholic and luckily I was, but I would have converted anyway."

The attractive couple was wed at St. Peter's Church in New Westminster on June 27, 1956. It was a white wedding. There was a turkey and wine reception outdoors. The day was hot and sunny. The future was bright. Bill Vander Zalm was handsome as the devil and determined to get ahead.

Born on August 31, 1938 in Pine Falls, Manitoba, near Winnipeg, Lillian Mihalic was the fourth child in a poor family of ten. Her father, John, had emigrated from Yugoslavia at age 21 to work as a painter and a construction labourer. Her mother, Marie (living in a small and unprepossessing house in Penticton in 1986), was a child of Ukrainian immigrants. John Mihalic died at age 80 in October 1985 after a lengthy illness. Mrs. Mihalic is a longtime NDP supporter who thought Bill Bennett was "sneaky" and continued working for her favourite party during the 1986 election. "He's a good gardener and a hard worker but I don't know if I'm going to vote for him," she said. The story made front-page headlines for days. She told reporters she hadn't heard from Lillian since a call when the campaign started, telling her not to talk to the press. "I bet I'm going to hear pretty soon again, though," she added. "Oh, am I going to catch hell." When confronted with the story, the premier said it must be one of those wild rumours that get going during election campaigns, insisting Mrs. Mihalic was a member of the Social Credit Party. It turned out she was, but only because she had bought a membership the previous spring under family pressure.[26]

Lillian dropped out of school after Grade 7 to help supplement the family income. "I felt I saved my mother by going to work early," she has said.[27] She says she has always been happy, doesn't feel hampered by her lack of formal education, and believes, "I married the greatest guy in the world."[28] The press coverage of the Vander Zalms' marriage has almost uniformly perpetuated the impression that Bill and Lillian Vander Zalm still behave as newlyweds.

The first night of their four-day honeymoon in San Francisco was spent in Seattle. "Oh, it was just so beautiful, just to be with him."[29] The next morning, standing by a candy dispenser, Lillian mistakenly remarked, "I can't think what's keeping my boyfriend."[30]

Lillian Vander Zalm would display an unfortunate penchant for making similar gaffes with journalists, once causing a reporter to miss an interview with her husband, giggling brightly, "Isn't that funny. I thought today was Friday."[31] Her quotes in the newspapers have a tendency to appear banal. An unimpressed *Vancouver Sun* writer in 1986 chose to end her profile piece: "But she will admit to one form of idleness. 'I like a nice bath,' she says."[32] Add to this her much ballyhooed habit of wearing headbands, flogged at Fantasy Gardens as $5.95 "Vander Bands," and Vander Zalm's "Kennedyesque wife"[33] is easily viewed as a bubble-headed blonde.

In fact, Lillian Vander Zalm, like her husband, has good street smarts and keen business acumen. The woman who once said, "I never, ever wanted a career. I like being a mother,"[34] has taken a strong hand in managing her absentee husband's involved business enterprises for over a decade.

Before motherhood, Lillian Vander Zalm worked in her brother-in-law's store. When the couple returned from their San Francisco honeymoon they reportedly had less than $100 and were living in a one room trailer with a camp stove. When Bill sold plants and bulbs from the back of a truck, it was Lillian who often collected the money. "We did that all over the province," she says, "and little by little we saved."[35]

Lillian filled bulb orders at home. She took her firstborn child to the family store, placing him in a wheelbarrow for safekeeping. While maintaining her teenage love of clothes, Lillian evolved into a determinedly successful merchant in her own right, devoting nearly all her energies to business and family.

"I'm always too busy to read," she says.[36] She reportedly took three years to finish reading the last book she could recall, but couldn't remember either the book's author or title when asked by a reporter. She rarely has time for a movie, watches television and enjoys staying home in the evenings, ironing some of Bill Vander Zalm's twenty or so dress shirts. Her willingness to serve her husband became an issue in the 1986 election when Vander Zalm told reporters his wife was absent from the campaign trail one morning because she was washing his socks. Both the press and NDP leader Bob Skelly lamely tried to insinuate this remark reflected Bill Vander Zalm's condescending attitude toward women.

Although reporters delight in giving the impression she is lightheaded, she has nonetheless endured twenty years of marriage to BC's most controversial politician, remaining steadfast in her support. Sawdust has been dumped on her driveway. Eggs have been broken in her mailbox. Lamps have been smashed. Abusive threats have been made on the telephone and in the mail. "Lillian was always extremely supportive throughout all of those years," Vander Zalm told me in September 1986. "She pretty well decided that whatever it was I wanted to do, she would help me with it. And she always insisted I do it well. As a matter of fact, all my years in politics I had a listed telephone number. And because I was extremely well known, and my name was well known, I'd get more than my share of calls, obviously. And because I was often involved in controversial issues, I got more than my share of calls. And because I always responded to my calls...you know, if people phoned, I'd phone back...word got out fairly quickly. If you need a problem solved or attended to, well phone Vander Zalm you'll get a call back. So all of those years I had a listed telephone, my phone would ring off the wall during supper, breakfast, lunch, no matter what. And a few times I said to Lillian, we gotta get an unlisted telephone. We can't go on like this. But she'd say no, no, you looked for the job, you took on the job, now you just keep answering those phone calls. So she was a good guide through it all, too."

Vander Zalm telephones his wife, almost without fail, every evening when away from home. The couple, according to Reverend John Brown of the Precious Blood Parish in Cloverdale, have been "model parishioners," noting Lillian "didn't take on anything independent of Bill."[37] Although it appears that Lillian Vander Zalm habitually accedes to her husband's wishes, Premier Vander Zalm maintains that he would like to have accepted offers to buy Fantasy Gardens in 1986 but Lillian overruled him.

In 1985 the Vander Zalms swapped their sprawling $400,000 Surrey home for a $1.5 million shopping plaza—the Vedder Village Mall outside Chilliwack—that was a half-empty strip mall in 1986. The purchasers plan to transform it into a "Fantasy Village." Liquidators of the defunct Canadian Commercial Bank made the trade with Vander Zalm because they reasoned selling the palatial Spanish-style home would be easier than unloading a mall which had been in receivership for two years. Lillian gave up her 6,400-square-foot luxury home, complete with a sunken bath, jacuzzi, six bedrooms, a library, a recreation room, a triple garage, an underground sprinkling system for the four acres of grounds, a tennis court and a basketball court. In place of this Port Kells estate, she moved into a mobile home on the grounds of her Fantasy Garden development.

Although she has been made fun of in the media as a woman who advises her husband with ESP ("You can feel if people are with you or against you. If I'm with him and I feel something, I tell him"[38]), the fact that she has been handed the ownership of the $7-million Fantasy Garden World—which she renamed after they began to expand it—is in fact an appropriate recognition of the role she has played in building the business.

The Vander Zalms' first child, Jeffrey, was born March 13, 1957. "Jeff," says Jos Van Hage, who lived with the family and operated a nursery with the Vander Zalms' eldest son, "is a very friendly guy, a nice guy. But he don't want to be bothered with other people's problems. He never would step his foot in politics." Jeff Vander Zalm is married and content to own two Art Knapp's stores, in Kelowna and Vernon. "It's a fun business," he says. "I'm dealing with a clientele who's pretty happy about what they're doing."[39]

The Vander Zalms' first daughter, Juanita, was born July 23, 1959. Inheriting a musical aptitude from her maternal grandmother, she took Conservatory lessons on the piano and began to play at weddings with her English and Social Studies teacher from Cloverdale junior secondary, Ken Allison. Her brothers' friends then recruited her to sing for five years with their rock group, 14 Karat. Married at age 19, she became Juanita Evans, but was divorced three years later, no doubt disappointing her Catholic parents. She writes jingles and. campaign songs, and has played with ex-members of the once successful rock group BTO. She remarried in December 1985, to Scotty Moffat. She helps her mother at Fantasy Gardens.

Wim Vander Zalm was born August 20, 1961. "Wim, again, is a nice guy," says Van Hage, "[but] pretty stubborn. Very stubborn, to be honest, to work with. Maybe he can change because he's still young. He probably has the most from his father." Wim is anxious to enter politics. In September 1986 he took over from his father as the host of "The Garden Show" on radio station CKNW. He operates an Art Knapp's store in Port Moody and is young enough to recall the disappointment he felt when his father was not around enough during his teen years. His parents are trying to dissuade him from entering politics too soon.

Lucia Vander Zalm was born on December 31, 1964. She grew up working in the family business and, still single, has worked for her brother, Wim. Probably most affected by her father's frequent absences, Lucia says she stomped into her bedroom and slammed the door more than once after discussions with her mother over grades or neglected chores. The attractive daughter of "the most wonderful family man you could find,"[40] according to her mother, hopes for a career in modelling.

Queried as to whether or not he was aware that he had stereotypical views of women, Bill Vander Zalm was once asked if he would influence his daughters. No, he said, they could do as they wished, "Although if one said she didn't know whether to be an electrician or a music teacher, I would tell her not to be an electrician, that it would be far more suitable for her to be a music teacher."[41] Similarly when women rallied in Victoria on March 22, 1976, lobbying for equal job training opportunities,

Vander Zalm advised, "Women make the best cooks and housewives and should be encouraged in that role."[42] One of Vander Zalm's sons took a cooking course at school and "I thought he was crazy."[43]

The evident harmony in the Vander Zalm household seems to have been achieved with impressive ease, but it hasn't all been smooth sailing.

On Saturday, March 15, 1975 Jeffrey Vander Zalm was driving westbound on the Fraser Highway when his vehicle collided with a vehicle also westbound on Fraser Highway. The driver of the other vehicle, 80-year-old John A. Sauer of Surrey, died three hours later. Jeff Vander Zalm was not injured. No charges were laid. Later that same year Jeffrey's car was being repaired. He was subsequently charged, along with automobile dealership employee Reginald Nedo, with attempting to defraud ICBC of $609.21 by deceit, falsehood and other fraudulent means. The offence was alleged to have occurred between August 17 and September 6. The charges against Jeffrey were later dropped for lack of evidence by Surrey judge Douglas Reed.

According to Lillian, trouble at home with Jeffrey was one of the reasons Vander Zalm quit politics in 1983.

"Jeffrey was snapping at everyone and I could see he was ready to set up his own garden centre," she told *Province* reporter Holly Horwood.[44]

Bill Vander Zalm, entangled in numerous legal cases throughout his political career, has also been to court for private matters. In January 1978 Surrey contractor Robert Albers of Albers Furniture and Heartwood Industries completed the finishing of ten doors in Vander Zalm's pentagonal living room. Vander Zalm claimed the varathane used to treat the doors had cracked and he refused to pay the approximately $800 balance remaining on Albers' $15,000 bill for installing solid-oak panelling until adequate repairs were made to his satisfaction.

The case was ultimately heard by Judge D.E. McTaggart in New Westminster court on June 9 and August 15 1979. Albers had sued in small claims court for $901.88 and the court had awarded him $401.88. Vander Zalm's counterclaim for $200 was dismissed. Both men had appealed. In his final decision on this matter, heard on August 29, 1979, Judge McTaggart weighed the conflicting evidence and decided the issue was one of credibility.

Judge McTaggart assessed "the general integrity and intelligence of the witness, his power to observe, his capacity to remember and his accuracy in statement. It is also important to determine whether he is sincere and frank, or whether he is biased, reticent and evasive."

Vander Zalm lost.

The general perception is that Bill Vander Zalm is a winner in both public and private who leads a kind of charmed life. But Bill Vander Zalm is more correctly seen as a diligent campaigner who has advanced to where he is today not because he has had no setbacks, but because his stubbornness and resiliency have allowed him to overcome them. That, more or less, is the story behind his decision to get into public life in 1965.

He decided to run for office, he says, after a small group of neighbours asked him to help them prevent a local park in Surrey, which contained plants donated by Art Knapp's, from being turned into a gravel pit. The citizens' coalition lost their fight with the municipal hall, but more significant for British Columbia, a new municipal politician was born of the conflict.

Bill Vander Zalm first attempted to gain a seat on Surrey Council in December 1964. He polled 2,522 votes. The elected councilor with the least votes, Alfred Dainard, polled 2,609. In most summaries of his career, including his own, this defeat at the outset of his political history is overlooked. As a salesman he understands the importance of never admitting defeat, of never appearing to be a loser, of promoting only the good selling points of a product.

In the election of December 11, 1965, Bill Vander Zalm won a two-year term on council. He polled 4,702 votes, the second highest total of the five councilors elected. The man they would dub "The Ronald Reagan of Surrey"[45] was leaving family matters to Lillian. He was easily re-elected for another two-year term as a councilor in 1967, topping the polls with endorsements from 78% of the Surrey electorate.

Vander Zalm's mother had molded him in Noordwykerhout. Vander Zalm's father had molded him in Bradner. And his own family was providing a base of self-esteem and security in Surrey.

The group family photos with Vander Zalm in his Santa Claus hat convey a pleasingly relaxed camaraderie, and father acknowledges his family's strength and support through rough political times: "The kids took it very well. . .it's amazing. They really never, ever came home with it or complained about it. They just took it in their stride, it seems. They were pretty tough kids. They never really were too terribly upset by it all. I can't ever recall sitting around the table when it was brought up as a point that they were bothered with at school. It's amazing how they came through it. But I did have my regrets. . . .I've had moments when I could just about have cried, you know, because I'm reminiscing as to what I missed, or what it was I might have been doing with the kids. Fishing, hiking, doing things that I really missed out on. And if I could do it all over again, starting from square one, I'm not sure I would do it all exactly as I've done it. . . ."

3

BUSINESS MATTERS
Art Knapp's Connections

"He's a rather astute businessman...the kind who makes you want to check your gold fillings after he leaves the office."

Bill Jones
Jones Nursery, Richmond
July 16, 1986

One of Prince George's 70 taxicabs is waiting. There just happens to be a jingle for Art Knapp's Plantland playing on the taxi's radio. Prince George now has two Art Knapp's locations. The jingle is being sung by the woman who wrote it, Juanita (Vander Zalm) Moffat. We're on our way to see Juanita's former boyfriend.

At 32 years of age, Jos Van Hage is one of the most important Art Knapp's operators outside of the Vander Zalm family. He often decides where bulbs will be purchased in Holland. And he's also Bill and Lillian's unofficially adopted son. Together with his brother, Wil, Jos Van Hage operates a large Art Knapp's store on forty acres and a smaller store closer to town.

There are copies of *The Plain Truth* in the lobby. Outside stands a windmill—one of BC's two most authentic Dutch windmills according to Van Hage. It's exactly one-seventh the size of a Dutch windmill, built precisely to scale, with wooden gears inside. It is fully operational, turns with a faint breeze and is capable of grinding grain. It was built outside Noordwykerhout, where Jos Van Hage was born and raised, and purchased by him in 1984.

"I've been with Bill for a long time. He picked me up at the airport. He sponsored me. Outside of his own family, I probably know him the best."

Van Hage's father dealt with Bill Vander Zalm's father in the bulb business prior to the war. The Van Hages, like the Vander Zalms, were deeply affected by the German invasion. During the war Van Hage's mother had to cook for thirty to forty Germans on their farm just outside Noordwykerhout. Jos Van Hage attended St. Joseph Parish school and had two teachers who had taught Bill Vander Zalm.

At nineteen, he was sponsored by the Future Farmers of America to study agriculture with his uncle in California, who was married to an aunt of Bill Vander Zalm's. He spent six months in Denver and six months in California. Van Hage returned to over-populated Holland and realized he wished to emigrate. It was difficult to emigrate to the US so the California relative contacted Bill Vander Zalm, who agreed to help.

In 1969, Van Hage was met by Bill Vander Zalm at the Vancouver airport.

"I never seen him before. I'll never forget it. I come off the plane and I didn't know where to look. He comes to me. He says, 'You must be Jos. I can see it in your face. You look like your mother.' So he picked me up and we're driving through the tunnel and I remember he tells me the tunnel was designed by a Dutch guy.

"He said, 'One thing I have to tell you. I already know that you're here for a reason.' I remember that from day one. He said, 'You're here to work but also to start your own business. Otherwise you would be back working for your Dad at home.' "

Vander Zalm explained to Van Hage that now that he was in Canada, the laws were so loose he could go anywhere he wanted to as long as he had a sponsor. He could work in a logging camp and make three times the amount of money he would make working at the Vander Zalm's nursery. "But one thing you have to realize, when you want to start for yourself one day, when you need some help, just a little thing or whatever, I will be there."

Van Hage stayed with the Vander Zalm family. He became like the eldest son, three years older than Jeff. Van Hage often worked seven days a week. Jeff took care of the inside of their store, Van Hage took care of outside operations.

"I think he [Bill Vander Zalm] is the smartest man I ever

met," says Van Hage. "For instance I was sitting there one night and we were having a little disagreement. I'll never forget it. Friday night Bill comes home. We had supper always together. Talking about the business, how are things going. We were talking about a major thing and his wife Lillian was really involved because she really runs the thing when it came right down to it.

"And the phone rang. It was a reporter from the Vancouver *Sun*. While we were in the middle of the discussion, we were in the kitchen, having supper. So Bill goes to the phone and gives a major interview. It was about welfare or something. He did something and everybody jumped. In the mean time, we were so much into our discussion that we kept going.

"Bill hangs up the phone and he listened to the whole discussion! Not only did he give a major interview with the Vancouver *Sun* but he also listened to the whole discussion and he had all the answers. I couldn't believe it. Then I knew how smart the fellow was."

Van Hage also respects Bill Vander Zalm for his self-control and manners. "Bill always taught me from day one, and he's right: when you cannot say anything good about a person, don't say nothing. Just go around them or whatever. I never heard Bill Vander Zalm say anything bad about a person, really bad.

"For instance, in politics. I was there when he was in Municipal Affairs and Welfare and things like this. With all the things they were saying about him, he never came back and said, 'This Barrett, he should be. . .' He never really did, you know."

So why is one brother, Bill, so well known and his three other brothers are not? Van Hage doesn't know the answer, but he knows the brothers.

"Nick is the oldest. He's a very quiet guy. Laid back. Pete is outgoing, very outgoing. When we say today the wind is coming out of the south, he say, no, the wind is coming out of the north, just to get an argument going. That's his brother Pete.

"Art was a partner of Bill. You see, Nick and Pete were partners and Art and Bill were partners. They all were in the nursery business. But Bill, you know, he helped them all out. Because Bill had it. Everything. He can talk to people. He has the big smile, you know. Everybody likes him. When you cannot find Bill and you know he's there, you just look around and you see a whole bunch of women standing. You just go in there and find him in the middle."

Van Hage says the other brothers are more like farmers. But Bill has a gift. Pete Warmerdam agrees. "I would say one of the big things Bill had going for him was he was a real good merchandiser," says Warmerdam. "All the Art Knapp stores, have you ever been in one of them? At one time those nursery outlets, they were just a drab little thing. But they have gone out of their way to make it attractive.

"I think Lillian, she's outstanding in that. For a while there, when they were still operating the Lougheed Art Knapp outlet, she would go and buy, say pottery, you know, from Mexico and stuff. She had taste. She's got a real taste for something that will sell. I think they're a very good couple."

Vander Zalm's younger brother, Art, who runs a nursery in Port Kells, is, according to Van Hage, probably most like the premier of the three brothers. "A customer can come in with a dead tree, ready to kill the guy. That customer, and it doesn't matter how long it takes, but that customer walks out twenty minutes later with the tree and a smile on his face." Art and Bill, says Van Hage, are promoters. "They can promote anything and everything."

But Peter Warmerdam notes that for all his talk about shovels, Bill's younger brother was the one who ended up doing most of the digging. "Bill was more or less the guy who was taking over the selling or in the warehouse doing the office work," he says. "It was Art who was doing the field work.... Bill was the salesman."

After living with the Vander Zalms for five years, Van Hage bought forty acres outside Prince George. Bill's son Wim had decided to work with the family business.

"I went to Bill. He said, 'I hate losing you' but he said go ahead. I went to the bank and got a loan and he co-signed it for me. He never gave me money or anything, just co-signed that loan. That was the thing I needed."

Vander Zalm also gave Van Hage permission to use the Art

Knapp's name for his nursery at no charge. In 1984, Van Hage explains, Bill Vander Zalm sold his interests in Art Knapp's, but contrary to public perception, Vander Zalm never did have controlling interests in all the Art Knapp's franchises.

"Bill owned the name Art Knapp's. He bought Art Knapp's from Art Knapp. I know Art Knapp. He's still living. He's a friend of me. He became a friend. Because he was staying in Bill's place, too, when I was there. So Bill took that name and just gave it to his brothers and a couple of friends to use, you know. There was never any charge. Everybody was an independent owner." Van Hage says Bill Vander Zalm never took a cut from the independent operators.

Art Knapp's Nurseries Ltd. was formed on April 7, 1955. Vander Zalm bought Art Knapp's original business for $3,200 when there was no store. Plants were auctioned from semi-trailers. He kept the name Art Knapp's Nurseries Ltd. because the name was well known throughout BC and into Alberta and he wanted to maintain customer loyalty. Vander Zalm remarked in 1982 when his political fortunes were at a low point, "It's a good thing, now. I'd hate to be called Vander Zalm's garden shop. We wouldn't do any business."[1] There are eighteen Art Knapp's outlets in 1986. Long the president of Art Knapp's Nurseries Ltd., Vander Zalm sold his own garden shops in the early 1980s. It remains largely a family operation in that Vander Zalm and his brothers also have their children involved—Jeff Vander Zalm owns the Art Knapp's stores in Vernon and Kelowna. Wim Vander Zalm owns the store in Port Moody. A group managerial meeting is held approximately once a month. Van Hage says there are eight owners. Different owners specialize in different areas of purchasing. Van Hage arranges where to buy bulbs, then all the independent stores receive a preferred price, although the purchases are normally made separately. Similarly an operator who specializes in chemicals would advise the other operators where and how to buy chemicals. Or tools.

There is no main warehouse for Art Knapp's, although Bill Vander Zalm did some wholesaling in the early years. Each store is now usually individually billed and shipped, yet the operators have the advantage of collective buying power.

"That's how we make this business," says Van Hage. "It's a very nice operation. It's very loose. There are no strings attached. If I want today to take my name off, I take my name off. Nobody tells me I have to pay so much or whatever. It's like a family." So what are the legal complications to membership in the Art Knapp's fraternity? "Handshake," says Van Hage. "That's all it is. It's all a handshake."

Van Hage has run his Art Knapp's Plantland store for seven years. Other operators have been in business for twenty years. "Bill is never going to say, for instance, you have to take the name off. He's never going to say that. He realized he's not the only one who built it up. Together we did it."

The growth of the Art Knapp's collective into the major chain in the BC nursery business has not always been smooth, despite the harmony and hard work of its operators. Rules have been bent and laws have been broken.

In 1970, when Vander Zalm was mayor of Surrey, he was summoned to appear in Burnaby court for a Christmas tree bonfire on January 3, which contravened a municipal bylaw. It was a harbinger of things to come.

In 1977 Vander Zalm built an addition to his Art Knapp's store at 6250 Lougheed Highway in Burnaby without obtaining a building permit. Despite a warning on December 5, 1977 that he was violating a municipal bylaw, Vander Zalm did not comply. Burnaby building inspector M.J. Jones notified Vander Zalm "of unauthorized building alterations being undertaken without benefit of a building permit and the consequences of that." Vander Zalm could have been required to demolish the structure or suspend construction. The Human Resources minister was assessed the minimum penalty, and was subsequently issued a permit on February 8.

In 1981 Agricultural Land Commission staff began to make inquiries into how an outlet owned by Nick and Pete Vander Zalm was located in the Agricultural Land Reserve without proper permission being sought. The Highways Department noted the brothers had not submitted a request for access to King George Highway, something they were obliged to do. With a 7,000-square-foot building located on land zoned A3, the Surrey business was entitled to sell only agricultural products produced on the land, flowers, plants or produce. The store was also selling gardening implements, fertilizer, imported tropical plants, plastic swans, toys and furniture.

The property had been purchased on September 16, 1980 from Carlos Enrich for $190,000. Enrich maintained he had not sold products which contravened the bylaw.

Bill Vander Zalm, Municipal Affairs minister, personally intervened on his brothers' behalf. He wrote a letter on government stationery to Dr. M.F. Clarke, chairman of the BC Agricultural Land Commission, dated September 21, 1981.

"As MLA for Surrey and Provincial representative for all the people, including the principals of Mud Bay Nurseries, who happen to be my brothers," the letter began, "I was given a copy of an Order issued by you and dated September 9, 1981, a copy of which I enclose. My brothers, the principals of Mud Bay Nurseries, sought my advice on the Order before seeking further legal assistance, to gather all of the data required by you in the Order.

"I told them to stop spending their hard-earned tax dollars to defend your response to a newspaper article in the Vancouver Sun, dated August 22, 1981, A2. The article was inaccurate and biased but gave the Press little satisfaction as it appears the public may have read it for what it was. The only satisfaction the Vancouver Sun could hope to get from the article now is to stir your bureaucrats into badgering another taxpaying business into defending themselves against the unknown or unproven allegations of a 'mud-slinging' journalist who possibly could not make a living running a nursery because it takes honest hard work!"

Vander Zalm then dealt with nine questions raised by the ALR, saying that all sales in the nursery related to plants. The ALR's last request was for a legal description and use of other properties in the area owned by Mud Bay Nurseries or the principals of the firm.

"I guess this question upsets me the most," wrote Vander Zalm. "What business is it of any Government or Government Agency what property the principals own and where, as long as they pay their taxes? Is it illegal to own property or does your agency think maybe the amount of land a person can own ought to be restricted? I do not believe the principals own any other land in the area but even as MLA or brother, it is none of my business either."

M.F. Clarke replied on October 7, 1981, stating that Vander Zalm's concern that the Land Commission was reacting to a newspaper article was incorrect. The matter was on the Commission's agenda for August 18, 1981 and his staff had been involved in the matter prior to that date. He noted the Mud Bay Nurseries case was handled no differently than two other similar cases, both in Surrey at approximately the same time, and that the two other cases had both been resolved.

Surrey Alderman Garry Watkins, long a Vander Zalm foe, took the opportunity to blast Vander Zalm publicly for his action. "There's no historical precedent for a cabinet minister intervening like this on behalf of his relatives," he said. "I personally find it repugnant."[2]

Business competitors also had reason to resent Bill Vander Zalm's intervention on behalf of his brothers regarding the Art Knapp's franchise at Mud Bay. The manager of one rival Surrey garden centre says, "The way Mud Bay got there—it wasn't even commercial zoning and his brother Peter got away with opening a centre there. Then he [Peter Vander Zalm] put in an entrance and exit to the highway and the Department of Highways told them they couldn't. But they got to keep it anyway."

Also in 1981 concerns were raised about non-conformance to Agricultural Land Reserve stipulations at Jos Van Hage's new operation in Prince George. Van Hage was ordered to submit an application for relaxation of ALR restrictions because he, too, was selling more than agricultural products. Years later he would submit a request to the ALR for permission to construct a house on his 40-acre property and be denied.

Van Hage had first found his name in the BC news in 1978

regarding a confrontation involving two workers hired from the Downtown Eastside Residents Association.

DERA had complained about Human Resources Minister Vander Zalm's claims that able-bodied persons in low-employment areas of BC shouldn't collect welfare. "You know full well," DERA told him, "that there are no jobs for the vast majority of the unemployed, yet it has been your policy to malign these unfortunates."[3]

In 1978 Bruce Eriksen of DERA subsequently called Vander Zalm's bluff by leading a delegation of about thirty unemployed people to Surrey to look for work. Unsuccessful elsewhere, they appeared on the parking lot of Vander Zalm's Art Knapp's store. Van Hage said yes, they could use some workers. He showed Eriksen a large pile of manure. Eriksen, dressed in a suit, showed his DERA comrades how to shovel manure for the media. Tony Puddicombe and Andrew Halper were hired. About a week later Van Hage fired them, reportedly for trying to organize a union.

"We were discussing the labour code," maintained Puddicombe. "We weren't trying to start a union."[4] Lawyer Harry Rankin was quickly contacted. The dismissed workers filed a complaint with the BC Labour Relations Board. Nothing came of the charges. Van Hage recalls that graffiti about Social Credit and Vander Zalm began to appear on the walls of the store shortly after the two DERA-sponsored workers were hired.

"It was a family operation," he says. "When there was work, everybody worked very hard. And when there was no work, everybody laughed very hard.

"With these guys it changed very quickly. One day they were sitting on a table with dirty clothes and I asked them to get off the table. They said, okay, you can't boss me around at lunchtime. I said, 'You're still in the lunchroom and there are rules here.' I said, 'You have to get off the table.' He said, 'Why don't you fire me then?' I said, 'Okay, you're fired.' "

How this came to be construed as organizing a union seems open to question.

More serious was the conviction of Nick, Peter and Arthur Vander Zalm for illegally dumping pollutant. The brothers were charged September 10, 1980 under the Pollution Act with failure to have a permit or approval for a landfill of hog fuel in Surrey. They were charged in Surrey Provincial Court for dumping approximately 150,000 cubic yards of hog fuel at 125th Street and 113th Avenue in March of 1980 (Hog fuel, or wood chips, usually produced as a byproduct of brush clearing, becomes a pollutant when rain leeches a black tarry substance from it.) The three brothers pleaded guilty.

The three Vander Zalms were also involved in a legal dispute arising from the sale of property on King George Highway in 1981 for $850,000 to SGT Holdings Ltd. of Vancouver. The brothers and two realtors, James Donald Clark and Nirma Shergill, along with Phase IV Properties Ltd., were alleged by the buyer to have made fraudulent misrepresentations about the property involved.

It was claimed in a writ that defendants Clark and Shergill, as duly authorized representatives of the Vander Zalms, had told the prospective buyers that the total cost of making the property ready for sale as subdivided lots would be about $786,000. Clark indicated to SGT Holdings on a written cost-analysis that there was a potential profit of $473,000 to be made from the land. Clark said he had researched the property for several months and that the Surrey Planning Department had told him that Surrey was anxious to have the property developed and was willing to look at a condominium.

SGT Holdings was told that one commercial acre was already completely serviced and that the remaining seven acres for residential development could readily receive water and sewer services. SGT Holdings claimed they were told it would take approximately three to six months to get the property subdivided and ready to sell.

After purchasing the property SGT Holdings discovered they had bought a parcel of land that was, at least in part, a former garbage dump. Clark's cost-profit analysis had omitted the cost of removing the garbage from the property which, the writ claimed, the defendants knew or ought to have known was there. The subdivision of a former garbage dump was not allowed. The Municipality of Surrey required a soil permit prior to permitting subdivision. Replacement fill would be required to settle for approximately one year before the property would be approved for subdivision use.

In addition, the commercial acre was not completely serviced; water and sewer for the remaining acreage was not readily available; and the total cost of preparing the property for subdivision would be approximately $1 million.

Accused of dumping a garbage dump, the three Vander Zalm brothers, through their lawyer Ronald A. McKinnon, disputed the writ, claiming they themselves had made no false representations or promises of any kind. They claimed they did not employ any agents for the sale of the land and in particular did not employ the defendants Clark and Shergill or Phase IV Properties Ltd.

The Vander Zalms said they had executed an option for the sale of the land on January 12, 1981, an option which was exercised by the defendant Phase IV Properties Ltd. on January 27. The Vander Zalms executed all documents necessary to effect transfer to Phase IV Properties Ltd. on February 12 for the agreed consideration of $650,000. When Phase IV did not complete the option agreement by March 11, the Vander Zalms executed an Interim Agreement for sale of the land to James D. Clark, Nirma Shergill and Dr. Paramjit for $650,000 by May 11, 1981.

The case of the unwanted dump was dismissed by consent.

SGT Holdings Ltd. are not the only ones to raise objections to the business practices of the Vander Zalms.

Ralph Fisher, owner of Crestwood Farms, says "If you can't say anything good about a person, you'd better not say anything." Nonetheless Fisher notes that when he sold plants to Bill Vander Zalm when Vander Zalm owned his Kingsway store, Vander Zalm would attempt to buy everything that was on sale, cleaning out his specials and leaving nothing for other customers. " 'I'll take all of this, all of this and all of this,' he would say, but we wouldn't let him have it all because we needed some ourselves. And he was hard to collect [money] from."

Henry Kuypers, owner of Mandeville Garden Centre in Burnaby concurs. "If he saw anything on sale he'd buy up the whole stock, and not leave anything for the next guy." Kuypers has known Bill Vander Zalm for decades. "He got his training when he was young from Art Knapp. He worked with him for a few years. He was in the bulb business then, and he and Knapp would auction bulbs together. . . . He didn't make all his money in the nursery business, no sir. It may be good but not that good. . . . He bought and sold property and he had a good eye for what was coming."

Kuypers says Vander Zalm started in partnership with his brother Art but Art Vander Zalm eventually went into business for himself with his nursery in Port Kells.

Kuypers attests to Bill Vander Zalm's sharpness as a businessman. Bill Davenport, who was in the same class at school as one of the Vander Zalm brothers, bought the Kingsway garden centre from Bill Vander Zalm in 1960. He agrees that Bill has been the brother at the forefront of promoting and building Art Knapp's into a chain. "I drove truck for him," recalls Davenport, "and if you were feeling down he'd cheer you up. He's an optimist."

Van Hage says Bill Vander Zalm probably received his promotional talents from his father but received his managerial skills from his mother.

"They really watched their money," says Van Hage. "For instance, when you go to Agatha Vander Zalm, Bill's mother, she's very strict on the money. That's what brought 'em so far. They didn't waste money. They don't believe in waste. Like his mother, for instance, when she gives out a penny, she has to look twice [to see] if it is really penny, if it not a dime. They're not cheap. I'm not saying that. But they're very careful that there's no waste of money."

Van Hage says another valuable asset is Vander Zalm's ability to listen. "When there is a guy with an opposite view then he listens. He asks questions. That's the reason he is so far ahead than other people. For instance, I know some MLAs and politicians. They only listen to their own people. That's the biggest mistake they can make. Then there's Bill Vander Zalm. He's got time to talk to an NDPer, to a socialist. Because some of their thinking is right, too."

Another clue to understanding Bill Vander Zalm's success in

business is his ties to Dutch banking and even to the Dutch royal family. Princess Margriet of the Netherlands came to Langley on March 12, 1982 for the opening of Bill Vander Zalm's 30,000-square-metre lettuce greenhouse. The 39-year-old princess, fifth in line for the Dutch throne, whose family lived in Ottawa during the Second World War, was in Canada as the ceremonial head of a 25-member Dutch energy delegation. The greenhouse was built by a Dutch company, Kombi Greenhouse Ltd., and implemented Dutch computer technology. Vander Zalm, president and majority shareholder of Western Lettuce NOW Inc. at the time (he is no longer the major shareholder), told the Dutch princess and several hundred guests that "Canada's newest industry" would provide many jobs for BC residents and "make the province more self-sufficient in the produce market."[5] Vander Zalm's Langley greenhouse was built to produce as many as four to five million heads of lettuce a year. (BC in 1982 was importing two-thirds of its lettuce from the US.)

Because the technology for his lettuce company was from the Netherlands, Van Hage says, "part of it was financed from Holland. It was subsidized by the Dutch government...probably the company got a cut from certain taxes to come out here and build greenhouses." Dutch glaziers were also imported to BC to help build the greenhouse. The BC glaziers union protested. As well, some Polish-Canadian workers subsequently filed a complaint with the Labour Ministry after reportedly being unable to collect overtime for ten-hour days.

Jos Van Hage says Bill Vander Zalm is now favoured with invitations to visit with the Dutch royal family when he goes to the Netherlands. The cooperation between Vander Zalm and Dutch interests smoothed the way for Bill Vander Zalm to buy the Dutch Government's 1986 exhibit of Vancouver Castle in downtown Vancouver even before the exhibit opened to the public, although the deal later became hung up over the question of who would pay for transporting the structure.

Van Hage says Bill Vander Zalm knew when to liquidate many of his assets in the early 1980s partly by understanding the economic climate of Europe, by maintaining his links with the Netherlands and watching the investment scene there. He believes Europeans could sense a recession coming better than Canadians. "Five, six years ago, when times were so good up here, there was an end [coming] somewhere. It happened not only in Holland. It happened in Ontario. And up here. The people were blinded. They couldn't see that.

"Another thing, too, is these people went through the Depression. My father did, too. You know, the 30s. Here times have always been good and every year got better until it came to a stop a couple of years ago. My Dad was always telling me, 'Hey, Josh, don't go to the bank and put yourself in too heavy. Because this is artificial. Nobody can make a living on land where people are flipping.' You see, there is an end to that. And Bill Vander Zalm saw that, too. Because he had lots of land and buildings and everything else but he knew when to stop investing."

So Vander Zalm took his money and put it into his lettuce company. Is that where the money came from to build his reportedly $7-million Fantasy Garden World?

Van Hage scoffs at the lettuce investment. "Ah, lettuce. You know there's lots of things. Bill made a lot of money in real estate. You might as well face it. Sure, in the nursery business we made money year round. But that money he invested again in the real estate."

Van Hage agrees that Vander Zalm used his nursery as an economic base for his investments. As Bill Vander Zalm himself has noted, "It's sort of a recession-proof business in that people will always want to get out and hoe their garden."[6] Van Hage says Vander Zalm could make much "quicker money" with inflation in the real estate game. The Art Knapp's operation was good for Bill Vander Zalm's public image as a flower-lover, a man of the earth. Somehow the flowers lend all the money a nice smell. But Van Hage's view of Bill Vander Zalm is that his money has come largely from the less fragrant business of buying and selling of real estate.

"It is an old family joke," according to journalist Sean Rossiter who profiled Vander Zalm in 1983, "that Bill does the most menial jobs at Art Knapp's because he is there so seldom."[7] Nonetheless, Bill Vander Zalm denies that he has made more money from real estate deals than from operation of his Art Knapp's outlets. Although he says, "I really only owned a few of the stores," he maintains that those few stores have produced more profit revenue than his varied real estate holdings. "I've sold some real estate. And that probably helped in the process. It allowed me to put it back into the nursery or to rebuild or to improve or to bring in more and a better variety of merchandise. So it helped in that regard but, no, the money was made in the business."

"The Money" thus becomes a problem. Vander Zalm has encouraged the impression there is a lot of this money, and his selling of himself as a political leader has been underpinned by the claim that he is more than moderately successful in business. The idea has gotten around that he is, in fact, fabulously successful, a self-made multi-millionaire, and he does nothing to make people think otherwise. Only a week before the election the Vancouver *Sun* reported that he is "owner of one of the largest gardening chains in Canada . . . drives a Mercedes Benz, wears a gold watch and has gold neck chains, and most of his friends are millionaires." But he was never "owner" of the Art Knapp's chain, and the few stores he did own he sold in the early 1980s. Others in the nursery business, even within the Art Knapp chain, scoff at the notion that anyone could become a multi-millionaire from doing what they do, and Jos Van Hage avows Vander Zalm's venture into the lettuce business did not hit the jackpot either. Vander Zalm denies "The Money" came from real estate but businessmen close to him confide that is the only place he could have made it.

From Vander Zalm's unaudited disclosures, the picture that emerges is that of a small-time speculator, buying and selling single lots and small acreages at the rate of four or five a year. In 1976 he listed a half interest in ten acres at 8938 192nd Street in Surrey; one acre in Penticton, ten acres in Port Kells at 83rd Avenue and 196th Street; five acres at 19002 88th Avenue in Surrey; five acres at 18730 88th Avenue in Port Kells; one-fifth interest in ten acres at 2350 152nd Street in Surrey; and interest in a four-acre lot in Langley. This was a parcel Vander Zalm gained on when it was liberated from the Agricultural Land

Reserve. He was minister of Municipal Affairs at the time, but denied he used influence to have the land freed. In 1976 he also disclosed his shared interest in two Art Knapp's outlets and Nicola Copper Mines Ltd. Under creditors he listed the Canadian Imperial Bank of Commerce in Whalley.

In 1978 he still had his four acres in Langley but had moved several of the Surrey acreages, buying others. He now showed an association with only one Art Knapp's store at 8938 192nd St. This time he listed no creditors. In 1980, near the peak of the BC land boom, he was showing the acre in Penticton again, which he hadn't in 1978, and holding the same three Surrey lots with the one-fifth interest in the other. He had changed his Art Knapp's holdings apparently, now listing two different outlets, one at 6250 Lougheed and one at Fry's Corners. He was back in hock to the CIBC.

In 1981, he still had his the 16th Ave. property in Surrey; the Langley property on 216th Street, which he finally got out of the land freeze; the 85th Avenue property in Surrey, the acre in Penticton; associations with the Burnaby Art Knapp's store on Lougheed and his presidency of Art Knapp's Nurseries on 192nd Street; plus new acquisitions at 7092 Glover Road in Milner, at Fisherman's Circle in Parksville, and 36.9 acres in Qualicum, one of his larger land acquisitions. In May of '81 the bottom fell out of the market overnight, so this may not have been a happy purchase. He was still holding it in 1982, along with all his other 1981 disclosures, which by this time one would expect to have dropped drastically in value. If he had foreseen the land crash as Jos Van Hage suggested, it doesn't show on his disclosure forms. Another new holding in 1982 would not turn out too well either — BRIC shares. His presidency of Lettuce NOW Inc. at 19002 16th Avenue in Surrey showed up in 1982.

By 1986, Vander Zalm's three years in private life were having an invigorating effect on his business dealings in general. He listed associations with Vander Nurseries Inc., BCRIC, Impact Resources Inc., Little Bear Resources Ltd., Butler Mountain Minerals Corp. and Art Knapp's Nurseries (1983) Ltd. His property holdings were listed as three lots in Qualicum, one lot in Kamloops , four lots in Chilliwack, four lots in Penticton, two lots in Surrey and eighty acres in the Cariboo. He had apparently turned over most of his 1982 land holdings, although real estate values were still low. In mid-1986 he was reported to have traded his ostentatious 6,400-square-foot home in Port Kells (variously valued at over $400 thousand and under $300 thousand) for a small, bankrupt shopping centre in Vedder Crossing near Chilliwack. Setting apart the most significant addition to the 1986 list, Fantasy Garden World Inc., a whole story to be dealt with in a later chapter, there are none of the office towers, major shopping centres or big condo developments that might point to "money" the way multi-millionaires use the word.

Vander Zalm seems honest enough in saying "The Money" didn't originate this way—unless, of course, "The Money" is not as much money as people have been wont to believe. The second most significant addition to Vander Zalm's 1986 disclosure is a list of over 40 creditors, including a $2-million line of credit at the bank secured against the Fantasy Garden property. It all leaves one wondering about the exact state of the legendary Vander Zalm finances.

4

ASSUMING POWER
The Beautification of Surrey

"When I was mayor of Surrey, I was seen as left-wing."
Bill Vander Zalm
to Lisa Hobbs in the *Sun*
April 4, 1976

Bill Vander Zalm was elected mayor of Surrey for the first time in December 1969, beating incumbent mayor Bill Stagg. Vander Zalm had discovered Stagg started a building without a proper permit and, in a classic example of the pot calling the kettle black, he had made use of the issue. The final count was 5,898 to 3,678. "Mayor Stagg worked tirelessly at his job," said Vander Zalm, beginning a pattern of criticizing his political predecessors, "but his downfall was that he tried to do everything himself....He made all the decisions. He kept us in the dark about everything."[1]

The election also introduced an untried alderman, Rita Johnson. She would follow in Vander Zalm's tailwind to Victoria where over sixteen years later she would become the only other woman besides Grace McCarthy in Premier Bill Vander Zalm's first provincial cabinet.

Upon his election, Mayor Vander Zalm said, "I don't intend to make any startling changes."[2] In his inaugural address he announced a plan to develop Whalley and Guildford as "ultra-modern spacious cities," create a "space age" industrial centre for Newton, create a "Spanish theme" for Crescent Beach and develop the proposed Sunnyside townsite into an "old English" town. Cloverdale would be done over in the style of Dodge City. His wife Lillian later developed an indoor arcade of specialty shops with separate architectural themes for Art

Knapp's: Old West, Tudor, Carpenter's Gothic etc. The couple's Port Kells home, assessed at $434,450 in 1982, had a decorative Spanish theme.

His beautification projects to add character and charm to Surrey raised suspicions that business at Art Knapp's was benefiting. Vander Zalm said not all of the plants and shrubs used on municipal property directly benefited his nursery. "I never invoiced the city for any trees," he says. "They were all donated. But I promoted the whole idea of cleaning up the streets and beautifying the medians and this probably left me suspect to many people."[3]

Vander Zalm's "exaggerated take-charge complex"[4] quickly took charge. He established 34 new committees and commissions for himself and his eight aldermen, including a "Special Committee on Policy of Laying Charges for Violation of Municipal Bylaws." "We even had an advisory council that ruled on where the doors should be, the colour of the trim and of the houses," recalls Vander Zalm, who, once in charge, exercised the kind of strong control over developers he has spent much of his political career denouncing as red tape.[5]

"Some councilors thought it was socialist, contrary to freedom, but my argument is that individuals sometimes have to give up their rights for the over-all good of the community."[6]

He concluded his inaugural address to council in poly-ethnic Surrey with a plea. "Let us have true Christian understanding in our attitude...and we will never stand alone."[7] Local Surrey politician Garry Watkins testifies that Bill Vander Zalm never stood alone. "Vander Zalm was the first guy to bring party politics to Surrey with the help of a bunch of Liberal friends, for example, Bill Wallace of Wallace Neon," recalls Watkins. "They began the Surrey Voters' Association and the Socreds took it over in '73 and put in Bob Wenman. I brought Bill Vander Zalm to an NDP meeting one time. He was a young alderman. He's not an ideological person. We got the idea he was going to join."

On December 31, 1969, the last day of the sixties, Mayor Bill Vander Zalm first made big city headlines. The Vancouver *Sun* began to cover the case of Vander Zalm vs. the King George

Highway Hospital. This was an issue which was related to welfare policy. It was a harbinger of things to come in the seventies and is important because it reveals both Vander Zalm's tenacity in a fight and the extent of his desire for personal vindication.

The background is this: The King George Highway Hospital was built in 1967. The directors of this hospital approached Surrey with a proposal that 75 empty beds could be utilized by welfare recipients who required hospital care. Surrey agreed. In 1968, after the agreement had become operational, Surrey council received a letter from the hospital demanding that they increase the municipal subsidy rate for welfare patients within 30 days.

Surrey had been paying the standard provincial subsidy rate of $8.05 per patient per day. The hospital wanted a rate of $11.10 as of March 1, 1968. The owners of the hospital (two doctors, Robert Harper and Lewis T. Herberts) claimed costs were rising. The welfare patients would no longer be welcome if Surrey didn't pay higher rates. Soon after King George Highway Hospital confronted Surrey on this issue, three other private hospitals — Florence Nightingale, Scenic View and Cedarhurst — also started to send bills for the higher rate.

Prior to Mayor Vander Zalm's election, the doctor-owners had sued Surrey municipality and won. The Vancouver newspapers dutifully announced Surrey was ordered by the BC Supreme Court to pay its accumulated financial debt of $96,000. Mayor Vander Zalm was angry at this court decision. He decided he would rather fight than switch the rate, and took this test case for BC all the way to the Supreme Court of Canada. He urged a "ratepayer write-in" to Provincial Secretary Wesley Black asking for increased provincial aid. King George Highway Hospital sued Surrey again, on a separate suit, regarding another outstanding differential of 70 cents.

Vander Zalm argued Surrey had already helped the doctors by sending them patients in the first place. "That should teach us it doesn't pay to be a nice guy," he said.[8] Mayor Vander Zalm then attacked the provincial government of W.A.C. Bennett for touting itself as debt-free at a time when the cumulative debt for

BC municipalities had climbed 10% from the previous year to $2.6 billion.

Ultimately Vander Zalm's tenacity paid off. On May 10, 1972, Social Credit Rehabilitation minister Phil Gaglardi announced that BC and Ottawa were going to pay 85% of the more than $100,000 that Surrey now owed to the King George Highway Hospital.

For two and a half years Bill Vander Zalm had never let go of the first issue he tackled as mayor of Surrey. But a partial victory was not enough. Noting the Gaglardi agreement called for Ottawa to pay 50% and BC to pay 35%, he said the original judgment against his municipality had mushroomed to $130,000 when legal costs were included. He subsequently urged Gaglardi to pay 35% of total costs in this and in any subsequent claims. Meanwhile Surrey had steadfastly refused to send any more welfare patients to the four private care hospitals in Surrey throughout the duration of Vander Zalm's struggle.

The medical and emotional costs to welfare recipients requiring hospitalization were not appearing on anyone's balance sheet. Surrey welfare administrator Wallace Merner said the department normally placed eight welfare patients per month in Surrey private hospitals. This meant approximately 200 Surrey welfare recipients were forced to find alternate care or go without during Bill Vander Zalm's vendetta against the forces that plagued him.

One such case was Paul Kohler. In 1972, he was a 65-year-old man suffering from Parkinson's disease. He couldn't talk, couldn't feed himself and wore diapers. Because of the dispute over fees in Surrey, Kohler was unable to get the 24-hour nursing care he required. Kohler's wife, Anne Marie, at 55, was working a graveyard shift at Woodlands School, bringing home about $300 a month to support herself, her husband and her dead daughter's four children.

"I come home in tears," she told *Province* reporter Kathy Tait. "There's no place for him and I have four little ones to look after as well. I'm not complaining but I do pay taxes."[9] Outside care for the likes of Paul Kohler had been unavailable in Surrey ever since January 1970 when Mayor Vander Zalm first assumed office.

Bill Vander Zalm had fought on a matter of principle and won. Others had lost. The case of Vander Zalm vs. the King George Highway Hospital illustrates the dangers of Bill Vander Zalm's blinkered, Pollyanna approach to life. "My philosophy has assisted me a great deal," Vander Zalm says. "If a person does his or her best, with good intentions, then the result — whatever it is — was meant to be."[10]

But the aspect of this case which most makes the story worth telling is the aftermath.

Towards the close of his mayoralty service in Surrey in 1975, when allegations and rumours of land speculation were rife in Surrey, and everyone else had long forgotten about the hospital that beat the crusading mayor in court, Bill Vander Zalm slipped in for a private visit to King George Highway Hospital. Claiming to be alarmed by "the lack of staff and people not getting attention."[11] Vander Zalm turned a list of complaints in to the new NDP Health minister Dennis Cocke. An owner of the hospital dismissed Vander Zalm's charges as nonsense, balderdash and unjustifiable harassment, and when a *Province* reporter and photographer toured the facility the building was found scrupulously clean. Nevertheless, Vander Zalm succeeded in having Cocke launch an embarrassing government investigation into the affairs of the King George Highway Hospital.

It was the first recorded instance of the King George Highway Hospital Syndrome — Vander Zalm's seemingly chronic need to score the last blow against his adversaries — from the King George Highway Hospital owners to retiring premier Bill Bennett.

In his formative years in Surrey politics, Bill Vander Zalm was officially a Liberal. Not a friend of Victoria's in those days, he loudly cried foul when, in October 1970, Rehabilitation minister Gaglardi unexpectedly announced an increase of almost 40% for the municipal share of welfare costs. "We can't pay it. No way," he said. "Maybe we should just hand over the whole package to the provincial government. It's absolutely ridiculous. How can you budget if you don't know what's coming? I don't know what to do. I've loosened my tie and I'm in a cold sweat."[12]

Applauded by then Opposition Health critic Dennis Cocke,

Vander Zalm led a protest movement within the Union of BC Municipalities. He threatened to refuse to pay Victoria. He called the W.A.C. Bennett government "stupid" when Bennett decreed that municipalities could not raise property tax assessments more than 10%. In a burgeoning suburb such as Surrey, many property values had risen dramatically with major developments in place, legitimately calling for property tax assessments of more than 10%. What could Vander Zalm do? How could he offset the provincial government's squeeze on Surrey's budget?

It was at this point what some people might call Vander Zalm's mean streak came to the fore. Time and again he would strike out, not at the powerful in Victoria, Ottawa, or the Terminal City Club, but at the weakest members of his own constituency. He was not the only BC politician of the seventies to take this route, but the frequency with which he appeared in the role of scourge of the defenceless, of hippies, the unemployed, the sick, the young, displaced Indians, and the old made it his particular trademark, one cartoonist Bob Bierman would satirize by showing him pulling the wings off flies.

One little-known story which aptly reveals Vander Zalm's frequent lack of respect for the underprivileged was his attack on a political rival in Surrey because the man was not a landowner (even though Vander Zalm himself would later run for mayor of Vancouver without residing in Vancouver). "One of the saddest things I ever went through in my political life," recalls Garry Watkins, "was a candidates' meeting in Port Kells. We ran a candidate named Ron McClurg. He wasn't a landowner. He was a tenant. I felt so sorry for McClurg and so ashamed of the political process because Vander Zalm and his brothers were merciless with this guy simply because he didn't own property!" McClurg recalls the event today but Vander Zalm doesn't. "That's got to be wrong. My brothers never got involved in politics," he says.

On March 31, 1971, Mayor Vander Zalm charged Gaglardi had failed to sufficiently crack down on frauds within the welfare system. "Because the provincial government has been doing nothing about it, we decided to take the bull by the horns and act on our own. Our staff went on a blitz of welfare recipients and has obtained sufficient evidence to lay charges."[13] The man who has noted that his family never could collect welfare or UIC when the German Army occupied Noordwyker-hout began his vigilante approach to social service agencies back in Surrey.

Vander Zalm's military terminology masked an unspectacular raid: the "blitz" only yielded seven or eight potential welfare fraud cases. Meanwhile Surrey voted to hire a professional investigator, on a three-month trial basis, with a salary of $10,000 a year, to crack down on welfare cheats. Eventually two women and one man were charged with welfare fraud in one case which went to trial after the blitz. Then on June 1, 1971, Surrey tried to force single welfare recipients under 45 to pick berries in the summer. "I know the pay isn't very much," Vander Zalm said, "but a young person can earn $20 a day and that's enough to live on. I'm in the horticulture business myself and I know there isn't much money in it for a worker in the field."[14]

The purpose of the berry-picking scheme was partly to evacuate many welfare recipients in Surrey to other areas. "Cutting off the easy bread," Bill Vander Zalm once said, "should eliminate a few of the hippie communes."[15] He was particularly unnerved because sunny Surrey seemed to attract a great many transient youths. "When he was mayor there was a major fish kill in the Fraser [River]," says Garry Watkins, "and he said it was hippies dumping chemicals in the river to make farmers look bad. Then it turned out to be a company [that did it]."

On May 27, 1974 the Surrey council made the remarkable decision to take all employable adults under 35, without dependents, off the welfare rolls to do farm work. "I've had first hand experience in this," said Vander Zalm, "and that's made me tougher on this issue. I'm close to having no one working for me now and if I can't find help I'm going to close down my entire operation and import from the US."[16] Employers such as Vander Zalm were able to hire workers for $25 a day thanks to Surrey's anti-welfare scheme.

When this extraordinary May decision was reached, Bill

Vander Zalm was for the first time giving 278 welfare recipients the opportunity to, literally, pick up a shovel.

Surrey council planned to extend this mandatory labour scheme into the fall and winter. By 1975 the council was ready to vote in favour of cutting welfare payments to single, 19- to 45-year-old employables without dependents. Vander Zalm recommended Surrey double its welfare job-finding staff and triple its welfare fraud investigating team. An ambitious nine-point "job opportunity" plan was further approved by Surrey council, voting 7–0, on September 5. In November Surrey halved the period during which employable persons awaiting unemployment insurance were eligible for welfare.

Although Vander Zalm's scornful attacks on the habits of welfare recipients were unforgivable, he proved himself a capable manager of other municipal projects in his early years of office. After 1970 was designated as a difficult year that would "separate the men from the boys,"[17] Vander Zalm called 1971 "The Year of Initiation."[18] He oversaw the "Sunnyside Plan" and the "Newton Plan,"[19] increased recreational facilities, added a 20-storey senior citizens' home and provided overall garbage pickup. The lookalike grandson of the man who installed Noordwykerhout's sewage system in 1905 also commenced "BC's biggest sewer program."[20]

While W.A.C. Bennett was building highways and hydro dams, Bill Vander Zalm was making a name for himself as a builder of ice rinks and sewers. It was what Surrey residents seemed to want and need. Abbotsford teacher and Surrey School Board member Garry Watkins opposed Vander Zalm in the 1972 election for mayor. Watkins claimed the building of a new ice rink had been bungled; he opposed high density development; and he noted 2,000 residents had signed a petition of protest regarding garbage collection billing. Meanwhile Vander Zalm urged the removal of education and welfare costs from homeowners.

Garry Watkins was soundly defeated. He recalls, "Vander Zalm is a handsome fellow, he dresses stylishly, he has an attractive wife, a nice home, a nice family, he has all of this . . . the wealthy Kennedyesque appeal. . . .

"What I learned from him was how to make the most out of minor issues. You know, Surrey must be the only municipality in the world with a foreign policy and that's because of Vander Zalm. He was always making headline-grabbing announcements against nuclear power, marijuana or pornography.

"I'd say his prejudices are sincere—at least that day....He's a political animal. He's not in it to improve humanity. He switched from the Liberals to the Socreds without hesitation when it suited him. If socialism became popular, he'd be a socialist tomorrow. I think he's really rather shallow as a politician. I don't recall anything he did in Surrey that could be considered an improvement.

"He just reacted from crisis to crisis and got as much publicity as he could out of it but not many solutions."[21]

Following his encouraging re-election as a Surrey alderman in 1967, Vander Zalm had seized the opportunity to go swimming in a bigger pond. He ran federally on the wave of Trudeaumania for the Liberals, losing out to the NDP's Barry Mather. A chance in provincial politics arose when the 44-year-old leader of the BC Liberal Party, Dr. Pat McGeer, announced he was stepping down at a press conference on May 3, 1972.

McGeer and BC's four other Liberal MLAs, unanimously endorsed the 34-year-old Liberal MP for Esquimalt-Saanich, David Anderson, as their choice for leader. Anderson's ascent had been pre-arranged. The day after McGeer's blessing of Anderson, Vander Zalm prophetically said, "It has the appearance of old-time politics. I would like to see the leadership decided in the open on the convention floor. But I am not crying the blues. I am a fighting candidate and my strength lies on the convention floor. If I can't convince them on the convention floor, I'd just as soon not have it."[22]

McGeer, who had led the floundering Liberal Party in BC since 1969, said that before convincing Anderson to resign his federal seat and run, he had seen no suitable leadership material available. David Anderson was tri-lingual (French and Mandarin), had led the fight against super-tanker traffic down the coast, had a law degree, had assisted the Canadian trade commissioner in Hong Kong, had advised the Canadian contingent of the

Vietnam truce commission and had served on the China desk of Ottawa's External Affairs Department. He had also won a gold medal at the 1960 Olympics as a member of the UBC rowing team.

By comparison, Bill Vander Zalm was a hick mayor from Surrey with a Dutch accent. The only other potential leadership hopeful was Prince George brewer Ben Ginter. Ginter was opposed to a ban on liquor ads imposed by teetotaler W.A.C. Bennett. But Ginter delayed filing nomination papers and then found himself scurrying around the convention city of Penticton in vain, unable to garner the 25 required signatures.

It was between the suave Anderson and the gauche Vander Zalm.

Vander Zalm, at the Liberal convention, warned that soft political and social approaches would destroy society "morally, socially, economically, and lead us to certain rebellion or Communism."[23] He promised to cut off welfare to people under 19 years of age whose parents would still have them. Campaigning with cheerleaders and a two-man band, Vander Zalm failed to wow the delegates with strident literature which vowed he would "Whip-lash drug pushers, cut off welfare deadbeats, update education, crack down on wife-deserters and provide government-financed dental care."[24]

One Liberal in the audience raised his arm in a mock Nazi salute.

Vander Zalm lost for the third time in seven years. David Anderson, the candidate hand-picked by the retiring leader, tallied 69% of 559 ballots cast, defeating Vander Zalm 388–171. But the experience was ultimately more rewarding for Vander Zalm than Anderson. He gained practice in fighting a provincial leadership race. And in Penticton he met and mingled with three prominent Liberal MLAs: McGeer, Garde Gardom and Jack Davis.

In particular, Jack Davis, the Rhodes scholar and Pearson-era minister, would one day be useful. He recognized Vander Zalm's so-called "maverick" persona as being in common with his own plight as a banished intellectual on the back benches of the Bill Bennett administration. Davis later supported that brash

Penticton advocate of corporal punishment for drug dealers
when Vander Zalm wanted to return to lead the Socreds in 1986.

Mel Couvelier, too, met Vander Zalm in Penticton. As
president of the BC Liberal Party at the time, Couvelier did not
support Vander Zalm, the outsider, in 1972. Fourteen years later
at Whistler, when Couvelier himself ran as one of the outsiders
in the Social Credit leadership race, he became the only
contender to jump to Vander Zalm's camp after the first ballot.

Connections. Bill Vander Zalm made a few in the Liberal
Party that would be crucial in stopping the so-called "Anybody
But Zalm" coalition at the Whistler leadership convention in
1986. But back in Surrey, some of Vander Zalm's other
connections were threatening to destroy his political credibility
forever.

In his inaugural speeches of 1972 and 1973 Mayor Vander
Zalm was beginning to sound more like a developer. He praised
his council's own efforts in attracting shopping malls and
industrial plants. He cited "amazing"[25] accomplishments that
included a police building, urban renewal, a swimming pool and
sewers. The native of the Dutch lowlands also strongly urged the
development of flood control programs for Surrey and
appointed a dyking committee.

With Surrey's rapid growth came a very lively market for real
estate speculation.

There are many stories about awkwardly justified land
transactions in Surrey during the early 1970s. Here are just a
few, commencing with the case of the Missing Newton Dirty
Sewer Link:

On March 29, 1972, Surrey council asked municipal land
agent G.D. Higgs to start picking up options for some easements
for a proposed sewer line in Newton. Before the route of the
proposed line was made public on April 5, the land agent had
discovered that developers had recently preceded him along the
route. Mayor Vander Zalm asked his municipal manager Dan
Closkey to investigate. Was information leaking to developers?
After a conference with Closkey, Surrey's supervisor of zoning
and subdivisions, Bill Sullivan, resigned, calling himself a
"whipping boy"[26] and a victim of a witch hunt.

It was subsequently revealed that London Holdings Ltd. had purchased easement property on March 27 (two days prior to the land agent's receiving his purchasing orders). Other properties along the Newton trunk line had been secured by Link Developments. London and Link shared the same address in Vancouver, 1102 Wolfe, the residence of real estate developer Walter Harvey Link. Several other individuals were involved in easement options which connected back to Link's address. The chief suspect was, however, Surrey alderman Ed McKitka, chiefly because he had worked for Link as a construction project manager in the past. A man who had once worked for McKitka as a loader operator, Robert McEwan, claimed to have evidence to verify wrongdoings by McKitka.

Surrey council conducted its own enquiry to find the Missing Newton Dirty Sewer Link. A transcript of this enquiry mysteriously vanished in August. More documents disappeared in December. Ed McKitka was re-elected in an aldermanic race at the end of 1972. The RCMP in Surrey had searched McKitka's house, taken some of his papers and failed to lay any charges. Mayor Vander Zalm ultimately requested Municipal Affairs minister James Lorimer to launch an enquiry into the Newton land transactions on May 10, 1973. The NDP's Lorimer agreed.

"There's been a cloud hanging over the municipality for months," Vander Zalm said, welcoming the Victoria probe because morale in the municipal hall was suffering.[27] "It will clear the air," responded McKitka. "I'm sure people will be surprised at some of the big names that will be dragged into it."[28]

Vander Zalm was dragged into it at first simply because the Commission of Donald S. White, upon the urging of McKitka, looked into the books of Surrey's two main municipal voters' groups, the Surrey Voters Association (SVA) and FAST (For All Surrey Team). McKitka's books had been searched so why not theirs? Ed McKitka was the lone independent, non-aligned member of Surrey council. He maintained large corporations could control the voters' associations. "Certain people have made millions of dollars out of this municipality," he said, "and some politicians are attached to them."[29]

McKitka, who later was convicted of wrongdoings in Surrey, said he wanted to see corrupt politicians impeached. Vander Zalm defended his integrity by saying his land holdings consisted simply of his home, two parcels of land owned jointly with his three brothers, and another owned jointly with his wife. He said since taking office he had also sold 100 acres of greenbelt and one commercial property. He was above suspicion. According to a report at the time, Vander Zalm said he didn't know where campaign funds were raised, and was unaware of the details of expenditures.

On November 26, Surrey council voted in favour of investigating Bill Vander Zalm on conflict-of-interest charges. The vigilante was now being scrutinized. And he didn't like it one bit.

"There are no facts here whatsoever," he said. "You're asking for an inquiry on suspicion."[30] Vander Zalm suspected Alderman Don Ross was spearheading a personal vendetta. Ross accused Vander Zalm of voting in favour of a mobile home development in return for campaign funds. He also claimed that Vander Zalm, when approached for information by a developer about land potential in Surrey, directed this developer to his own 57 acres in Hazelmere. The developer then tentatively agreed to buy this property from Vander Zalm for $75,000. This was the case of the Hazelmere Smear.

The case of the Hazelmere Smear stole the limelight away from the case of the Missing Newton Dirty Sewer Link. To make the turnabout of their positions complete, Alderman Ed McKitka was then named Chairman of the Surrey municipal enquiry into Vander Zalm's affairs, slated for December 11. "I understand the mayor is a little upset about it," said McKitka.[31] Vander Zalm, in fact, was so upset that on the appointed day he refused to testify. "I will not subject myself to a biased, kangaroo court."[32]

Bill Vander Zalm knew that under the Municipal Act only the mayor had the legal power to subpoena witnesses. He said he would be willing, however, to submit to an enquiry to be conducted by Donald S. White. Alderman Ross agreed to this plan. "I have been accused of sour grapes in this matter," he said, "but that is not so. I have no political ambition. I am not prejudiced in this matter. Information was given to me and I had to act on it."[33]

Municipal Affairs Minister Lorimer in Victoria would later have reason to resent Bill Vander Zalm, citing a period in late 1974 and early 1975 when the NDP opened a new transit depot near Guildford, and Surrey refused to shoulder its share of expenses. ("Vander Zalm's was one of the few communities in BC which wouldn't widen the streets for buses or put in shelters. They were very non-cooperative on transit.") But Lorimer was reluctant to re-convene White's Commission to investigate Vander Zalm in 1973.

At the next council meeting Vander Zalm blasted Ross for dragging the good name of Surrey through the mud. He claimed Ross was conducting a smear campaign against him. "It's worse than Nazi Germany and Russia," Vander Zalm said.[34] The Hazelmere Smear case took a twist in Vander Zalm's favour. The purchasers of the Hazelmere property sent a letter to Surrey council saying that Mayor Vander Zalm had only agreed to sell the 57 acres at their urging. "There is no truth to the charge of wrongdoing," they wrote.[35] Surrey council then reversed its position and voted 6–2 to drop the enquiry into Vander Zalm's affairs.

But the suspicions about Vander Zalm's real estate investments did not disappear. Vander Zalm was the president of a widely active and loosely connected consortium of relatives. When his brothers got into hot water, none of the trouble ever seemed to spill on Vander Zalm. For instance, he escaped, unstained, from the Manning Kless Mess — a very simple case compared to the convolutions of the Missing Newton Dirty Sewer Link or the Hazelmere Smear.

According to an inter-office memo from the Corporation of the District of Surrey, dated March 21, 1975, the Manning Kless Mess began in early November 1974, when Mayor Vander Zalm, Alderman McKitka and municipal land agent Lance Jefferson met to discuss the feasibility of purchasing a property in the Bridgeview area of Surrey. Jefferson completed a title search and appraisal. The owner, who was rumoured to be in financial difficulty and therefore might be eager to sell, was contacted by land agent Jefferson on November 20, 1974.

This owner was Manning Allen Kless. With his wife, Jean Kless, he had purchased their property on October 1, 1973 from B & F Holdings Ltd. for $80,000. B & F had provided the buyers with a mortgage for $60,000. The Klesses then sold their property for $195,000 to JBK Investment Ltd. on March 28, 1974. The secretary of JBK was Manning Kless. The president of this company was Jeffrey B. Kless, hence the company name.

After the Surrey land agent made contact with the Kless family in November and determined their willingness to sell, Lance Jefferson dutifully commenced financial analyses for the municipality. By February he had completed a draft of a commercial feasibility study. By March 3, 1975 he had completed his final report on the Manning Kless property. On March 12, Jefferson submitted his final report to Mayor Bill Vander Zalm, Alderman McKitka and the Surrey manager.

On March 17, 1975 Alderman McKitka gave land agent Jefferson a very surprising piece of news. He had just learned that the Manning Kless property had been purchased for $195,000 on January 30, 1975. Surrey was too late. The bargain had been snapped up months before, while they continued to spend taxpayers money investigating it.

The unforeseen purchasers of the Manning Kless property were Nick, Pete and Arthur Vander Zalm.

Defending himself in the case of the Manning Kless Mess, Bill Vander Zalm said, "I'm not in business with my brothers."[36] He claimed his brothers had acted independently after being approached by a Block Brothers agent around Christmas. Vander Zalm maintained he had not given his brothers any special treatment over the Yuletide season.

The time was coming for Bill Vander Zalm's departure from Surrey politics.

On May 15, 1974, Vander Zalm said he would resign rather than comply with the NDP's new Public Disclosure Act, new legislation specifically designed to protect the public from political conflicts-of-interest. Vander Zalm had argued that he could not comply with the Disclosure Act because his salary as mayor was only $19,000. (In the aftermath of the Hazelmere Smear Vander Zalm had agreed to a 10% salary cut for himself as mayor. In August 1973 he had turned down a $3,000 cheque for a retroactive pay increase, after council moved to increase his annual salary to $21,000.) Vander Zalm argued that disclosure would be too expensive for him. He said it would require a second annual audit of his company, Art Knapp's Nurseries Ltd., and this could cost him up to $10,000. To comply with this new legislation would cost him almost as much as his annual take home pay after tax and expenses. "It would cost more or as much as my net indemnity," Vander Zalm said, "so there is absolutely no point in my continuing."[37]

In effect, Bill Vander Zalm was now telling the electorate of Surrey that his only reason for acting as mayor of Surrey was to get the salary.

On May 31 Social Credit Party leader Bill Bennett made the surprise announcement that former Liberal Bill Vander Zalm, the mayor of Surrey, had just joined the Social Credit Party. It was news. A Liberal had converted to Social Credit. A sudden transformation.

But the real drama might have been going on inside Bill Vander Zalm's mind. He had been expecting that the deadline for resignation from elected municipal office without disclosing an audited list of business interests would be May 31. He had also been anticipating a Disclosure Act that would specify that any municipal politicians who resigned after May 31 would be forced to comply. In a surprise move, the NDP had announced changes to the Public Disclosure Act on May 29—just two days before Bennett's announcement—saying audited statements would *not* be required after all.

Bill Vander Zalm subsequently complied with the NDP's amended Public Disclosure Act which required him to make only an unaudited statement. His disclosure statement in 1975 shows that he owned Art Knapp's Nurseries Ltd., and Art Knapp's (Port Kells) Ltd, plus shares in Nicola Copper Mines

Ltd. He also owned twenty acres scattered throughout Surrey, four acres in Langley, one acre in Penticton, a total of six acres in Burnaby and was a part-owner of twenty additional acres in Surrey.

Anticipating trouble over the Manning Kless Mess, Vander Zalm then chose to go public on August 25, 1975. He again denied he was involved in the purchase, but admitted the issue might appear "wrong" and be "touchy" in future elections. He wanted to clear up the matter. Eight months after the Manning Kless property had been purchased by his brothers, suddenly Bill Vander Zalm, in all honesty, was making a clean breast of it. Prior to seeking the premiership of British Columbia at Whistler in July 1986, he would employ much the same tactic, volunteering information about his highly controversial Fantasy Garden World dealings before others volunteered it for him.

The public bought Bill Vander Zalm's forthright confession about Fantasy Gardens in 1986. The Surrey electorate also seemed to be satisfied, by and large, with Vander Zalm's sudden urge to be open about the Manning Kless property in 1975. As Bill Vander Zalm once said, "Show me a man who doesn't cause any controversy and I'll show you someone who isn't doing anything."[38] It's clear that Mayor Bill Vander Zalm did a lot in Surrey.

Vander Zalm's years as a Surrey politician are recalled in a National Film Board documentary, *Some People May Have To Suffer*, which is available to the public. This film is but one more piece of evidence that the patterns for Bill Vander Zalm's behaviour as a politician were started in Surrey. While touting himself as a liberal, he devised redneck policies. He preached the need for teamwork and openness while delivering a climate of divisiveness and distrust. He accused others of conflict of interest while he busily carried out a number of controversial real estate deals himself. And he had done it all for the people, ending his 1974 inaugural address with a ditty:

> People are all everything
> All it has ever been,
> All it can ever be.

5

HUMAN RESOURCES
The Most Hated Man in BC

"I want to make the British Columbia human resources program the most innovative, the most forward-thinking and the best in North America."

Bill Vander Zalm
to Paul Mann in *Metro*
July 29, 1977

"One of the problems with a person that has my personality, my approach to things," Bill Vander Zalm once said, in a rare moment of introspection, "is that it is difficult to turn down a challenge. Everything is measured in challenges."[1]

Following the election victory of the Social Credit party on December 11, 1975, newly appointed Human Resources minister Bill Vander Zalm set for himself the immediate challenge of compensating for the errors of his predecessor, the NDP's Norman Levi.

The active and imaginative Levi, trying to rebuild after two decades of Socred stinginess, had overspent his budget by $98 million in one year. Premier Barrett, on September 18, 1974, had been forced to make an embarrassing announcement: "An unidentified person in the Human Resources Department has made a clerical error... of $102.8 million in this year's budget."[2]

The uproar that ensued for the Opposition lasted until the 1975 election. Premier Dave Barrett, himself a former social worker and roommate of Levi, had "tried to be a giver in a stagnant economy."[3] It became relatively easy for the corporate sector of BC to mount a persuasive propaganda blitz to convince the BC public that the NDP was, and would continue to be, irresponsible and dangerous in all fiscal matters. The prevalent bumper sticker on BC streets in 1975 was "Welfare. BC's #1 Industry."

No public outcry had accompanied the earlier announcements of major overruns by Social Credit's Phil Gaglardi in each of the three years he had run the equivalent of the Human Resources portfolio. He had gone over his budget $16.7 million (19%) in 1969–70; $37.1 million (34.3%) in 1970–71; and $11.9 million (9%) in 1971–72. In terms of 1974 dollars, Gaglardi's second overrun would have amounted to approximately $50 million, and he was not pioneering unpredictable new programs as was Levi.

Even though the NDP might have cut some good records in 1974, the airwaves were mostly controlled by the corporate sector. By 1975 everyone was hearing the blues. *Barron's*, the leading American business and financial weekly, described the NDP regime as "the Chile of the North."(This was before General Pinochet's CIA-backed coup made Chile once again safe for Wall Street.) *Time* magazine picked up this catchphrase. The consensus about the only socialist government on the North American continent at the time was that Dave Barrett was orchestrating "legislation by thunderbolt." The NDP, the airwaves claimed, was doing far too much far too fast.

This was probably true.

The NDP's first year in power doubled the average number of days the legislature was in session, to 140, and brought forth 400 bills to the House, 300 of which were important. Under W.A.C. Bennett's direction, the legislature had usually received 40 to 50 bills per session, with less than 10 of these being important.

On December 11, 1975 "fat little Dave" Barrett's NDP administration went down to a humiliating defeat. The Social Credit under Bill Bennett tallied almost 50% of the popular vote, something his predecessor father never achieved in 22 years of power.

Bill Vander Zalm, the dashing, sideburned young man from Surrey, was selected by Bill Bennett to refute the angry claim once levelled by social worker Barrett, that "Money is the only known cure for poverty."[4] As an immigrant in the Fraser Valley,

as a businessman, and as a mayor in Surrey, Bill Vander Zalm
had felt the best cure for poverty in the province of British
Columbia was simply hard work. He would ride the white horse
of restraint and save the taxpayers over $100 million. But where
to start? Where could he look for extravagance?

In World War Two the downtrodden Dutch had fooled the
Germans by obtaining ration coupons for comrades already
dead. Upon attaining power as a cabinet minister in BC, Bill
Vander Zalm made the charge that Pharmacare cards belonging
to dead people were being used to collect free prescription drugs.
A month after making this charge, Bill Vander Zalm told the
legislature there was no evidence of abuse after all.

He'd only been Human Resources minister a few weeks before
he decided to stop the distribution of vitamins through the
provincial Pharmacare program.

"I was told of a girl who would die without the mega-vitamins
she had been getting on Pharmacare and I was being held
directly responsible for the life of the girl. Now we don't know if
mega-vitamins can cure these illnesses, nobody does. I wanted to
go out and pay for the girl to get treatment myself but I couldn't
make a blanket ruling that these vitamins should be distributed
to everybody because of this one case. I had to be sure that these
mega-vitamins were a treatment that would work without
building up false hopes."[5]

Vander Zalm decided to institute a study into mega-vitamins.
(By 1977 he was still waiting for this study to appear sometime in
1978.) As in the case of Vander Zalm vs. King George Highway
Hospital, there was a principle involved. Vander Zalm stated
that he couldn't let the "wholesale distribution"[6] of vitamins be a
burden to the taxpayers of BC.

"It was one of the most difficult decisions I ever had to make,"
recalls Vander Zalm. "I was put in the position of withholding
the remedy for a critical condition like multiple sclerosis when
nobody knows if these mega-vitamins can cure multiple sclerosis
or not. And of course the people with these illnesses wanted to
believe that mega-vitamins would cure them. It only added to
the emotionalism of the argument."

No one knew, but most were prepared to err on the side of

hope. Vander Zalm stoutly refused. He afterward avowed this was an awkward time for him but, "Otherwise I sleep great."[7] "Really, you know, underneath I'm very soft-hearted. When people are in trouble I'll bend over backwards to help."[8]

One of the many remarkable qualities of Bill Vander Zalm's personality is that he seems to genuinely believe his own advertisements for himself. It is precisely this rock-ribbed self-confidence and self-righteousness that frustrates and defeats critics. Many feel they can't get at him; they can't get through to him. As if Bill Vander Zalm has somehow constructed a fantasy world of his own goodness around himself, justifying his actions by believing he is only doing his best to rectify the failings of others—namely, in this case, the NDP.

These two early decisions marked the beginning of a pattern in Vander Zalm's policies as a cabinet minister from 1975 to 1983, a pattern he had tested in Surrey—the pattern of equating high moral standards of government with a government's ability to preserve funds. His philosophy for conducting his Human Resources portfolio is well summarized in his own words. "Good government today...shouldn't be measured on how many programs they have. The measure of good government today is how do we resist the many demands that are upon us."[9] He had signaled his agenda for Human Resources on the very first day he had assumed the portfolio.

On December 22, 1975, after his swearing-in ceremony, Human Resources Minister Vander Zalm was sipping champagne when he made the most important remark of his political career, "If anybody is able to work, but refuses to pick up the shovel, we will find ways of dealing with him."[10] (This quote was also recorded as: "If they don't have a shovel, they should get one, because otherwise we're going to give them one."[11])

Vander Zalm said he did not know what criteria should or would be used to decide who was employable. This was clearly one of his haphazard, off-the-cuff remarks. But the press eagerly picked it up and went looking for responses. Alderman Darlene Marzari, vice-chairman of the Vancouver Resources Board, half-jokingly wondered if Vander Zalm might consider building "internment camps for single employable males."[12]

Vander Zalm took no steps to defuse this situation.

He did just the opposite.

Bill Vander Zalm ordered hundreds of tiny sterling silver shovel-shaped lapel pins. He sprayed short-handled shovels with gold paint. He proceeded to auction these "shovel packages"[13] to add to the Social Credit Party coffers. The shovel would become his emblem, his totem.

Like the merchandiser who uses a logo to distinguish his product from all others, Vander Zalm, with his training in sales, seized upon the shovel as a selling tool for himself. Soon shovels of various shapes and sizes decorated his office. The shovel, a symbol of unpretentious hard work and contact with the earth, a symbol of Vander Zalm's own past and his success in industry, was the perfect symbol for Vander Zalm to use in reaching out to the grass roots of the Social Credit Party.

He began to sign notes, "Happy Shovelling." His campaign for self-promotion was based upon his instinctive marketing knowledge that the secret of propaganda is repetition. In years to come shovels auctioned by Bill Vander Zalm at Social Credit functions would sell, in some cases, for almost $1,000.

The Happy Shoveller proceeded to claim as much as $80 million had been issued in fraudulent Human Resources cases under Norman Levi. He claimed this fraud comprised "20 to 39 percent" of expenditures at some Human Resources offices.[14] But the Happy Shoveller hadn't dug very deep. He was shovelling propaganda, not facts. Two months later he admitted in the House, "We really don't have any figures available to us right now."[15]

Vander Zalm established a welfare fraud squad and said he wanted police experience on the squad "so they could look at a file and determine very quickly as to whether it was worthy of further investigation. They're gonna turn up piles of fraud."[16] They didn't. Vander Zalm admitted in Hansard on April 6, 1977 that in 1976 just 80 convictions were obtained involving $148,623. That figure represented about one-tenth of one percent of the Income Assistance budget for 1976–77. The 80 convictions compared with 72, 59 and 74 convictions during the NDP years of 1973–75.

Bill Vander Zalm decided to create a $70,000 project called the Provincial Rehabilitation and Employment Program. Nicknamed PREP, its object was to find jobs. Vander Zalm appointed a coordinator who boasted he could find jobs for half of BC's 24,000 employable welfare recipients in the program's first three months.

Vander Zalm's PREP was patterned upon a PREP program he had developed in Surrey. PREP's director Ron Stew, reportedly a former encyclopedia salesman, had directed PREP in Surrey. The main thrust of PREP was a Surrey-inspired program to have welfare recipients patrolling schools at night, armed with flashlights, on the lookout for vandals. This scheme had started in Surrey after Vander Zalm had said welfare collectors must pick berries and do farm work in the summer. After that, stones had started flying through the windows of the municipal hall at night. Mr. Stew had suggested hiring welfare watchmen. The provincial program was called Operation Vandal Stop.

One of the main problems with Operation Vandal Stop from the beginning was that Vander Zalm announced it without holding discussions with school boards or with unions representing school janitors. Ottawa was understandably wary of forcing welfare recipients to go to work, essentially, for the state. The Canadian Union of Public Employees was, to say the least, reticent.

But Vander Zalm sensed a challenge. He had learned that $12.3 million worth of school property was damaged or destroyed by vandals in 1976. School boards maintained that to hire guards would cost twice that amount. So, Vander Zalm concluded, why not use welfare collectors in the same way that idle welfare recipients in Surrey had been used to supply cheap labour for businessmen such as himself?

The plan was to have 1,500 welfare recipients in the schools from sunset to sunrise, 40 hours a week. Single clients would receive $650 a month, those with families would get $100 extra. "Everyone will benefit with this plan," said Stew. "I estimate an $80 million saving through stopping vandalism and taking people off welfare."[17]

When PREP failed miserably to live up to its director's rosy prediction at the outset, Vander Zalm said, "Ron was foolish in setting such a high figure as his goal."[18] Then an internal government memo surfaced. It urged that jobs on road crews be given first to welfare recipients in order to swell PREP statistics.

Watching PREP unravel, Education minister Pat McGeer diplomatically said he'd leave it up to the individual school boards to decide if they wanted to hire the welfare vigilantes. Bill Vander Zalm had given a whole new meaning to the term PREP school. But somebody wasn't doing their homework. The PREP program never graduated into permanence.

The man the Opposition dubbed Brutus Vander Zalm started to get tough. He began to tighten auditing requirements for welfare offices and organizations receiving grants from his ministry. He also tried to eliminate welfare payments to employable people in 175 BC communities during the summer season. He suggested that social workers rouse lazy people out of bed and pack their lunch buckets if that's what it took to get welfare recipients off the dole.

Vander Zalm also threatened his own staff. He warned that lazy workers would either be retrained, relocated, or else "dealt with under the terms of the union contract."[19] On February 17, 1977 he further alienated much of his staff by announcing that tests, conducted within his ministry, showed the productivity of some civil servants amounted to only three days worth of work each week. Vander Zalm complained that tight job security for civil servants made them poorer employees. "Anytime you provide so much security to make it difficult, if not impossible, to remove people, you have that problem."[20]

Of Vander Zalm's three cabinet posts, the Human Resources Ministry was the one in which he received the most widespread and vehement opposition. But as usual, none of that got through to him.

"I was supposed to be a hard liner when I was [Human Resources minister] but it was my most enjoyable ministry. I think I had a good rapport with those involved..."

Moving further afield, he advised native Indians in Vancouver to return to their reserves. This remark temporarily created almost as much press coverage and indignation as his shovel remark. On April 12, 1976, *Sun* columnist Lisa Hobbs wrote, "Mr. Vander Zalm's penchant for saying the wrong thing is, apparently, as entrenched as his pathetic inability to see why it is the wrong thing."[21]

Undeterred, he kept auctioning those shovels. The faithful kept buying his $9 silver shovel lapel pins. He himself sported a gold one.

Vander Zalm said that "young people should be denied assistance because they have more mobility to find jobs."[22] He began to cut off welfare for 16- to 18-year-olds. Initially he said he hoped to work closely with the Attorney-General's Department to develop help programs for juveniles. Asked if this might involve locking up juvenile delinquents in closed facilities, he admitted that "offhand my attitude might be somewhat different"[23] to that of the NDP who had believed in having delinquents remain in their own communities. Vander Zalm also suggested a two-month cooling-off period for people planning to get married. Initially he wanted people applying for welfare because of marital problems to be referred to family court. He labelled the federal government-sponsored International Year of the Child a blatant waste of taxpayers' money.

Throughout heated responses to these policies, Vander Zalm remained convinced he was often misunderstood. Not unlike the father who takes off his belt to discipline his children, all the while assuring them that the beating he administers hurts him as much as it hurts them, Bill Vander Zalm would nevertheless assure the people during his three years at Human Resources he was himself remaining a deeply sensitive man. "I'm as soft-hearted as all get out,"[24] he said. "I'm not as hard-nosed as people make out. But I do establish goals and will not be distracted from achieving them without good cause. . . . People who know me well know I'm a bit of a softie."[25]

Unfortunately those British Columbians who were most adversely effected by Vander Zalm's emasculation of the 1976–77 Human Resources budget didn't get to know hard-headed, soft-hearted Bill.

When spending figures were tallied for Vander Zalm's first year in Human Resources, he had scored a victory, at least in his books: Norm Levi's overrun had been officially tabulated at $98 million for one year. Bill Vander Zalm's undercutting of his own budget was officially tabulated at $108 million. 108 minus 98? Human Resources was $10 million to the good.

His $108 million surplus included an unspent $61 million in welfare payments.

Vander Zalm attributed his remarkable surplus after his first year as Human Resources minister to a mild winter, his PREP program and a general "tightening up." Looking back on the Human Resources years after gaining the premiership, Vander Zalm told me, "I came into government and immediately got into Human Resources. I had to sort of turn one very permissive attitude, as evidenced by...my predecessor, Norman Levi, to where we really had to tighten up and change it. And it had to be done very quickly. And much of what I was able to accomplish in Human Resources was not by tough laws or hard lines—although it may appear that way—it was really because of attitude. A changing of attitudes."

While the strong stands in Human Resources, that marked this change in attitude, undoubtedly created hardship, he spoke with sensitivity on behalf of the handicapped and favoured a $9 million per year family support program for remedial care, daycare, counselling and homemaker services. "There should be more help for those in their 50s who've lost their jobs," he said, "and why should a mother on her own with three children get $370 a month while a couple aged 62 with maybe better means gets $530 a month?"[26]

As well, Vander Zalm claimed responsibility for establishing the Community Living Society for the mentally handicapped and for arranging the continuation of medical coverage to assist the handicapped to gain independence after leaving income assistance, thereby encouraging them to seek employment in the community. In 1977, Vander Zalm also provided the first welfare raise for single people since 1974. Amongst his other achievements Vander Zalm lists his proclamation of the GAIN Act (a centralization procedure from 1976 that combined all the province's welfare legislation into one statute and increased the discretionary powers of the minister), introduction of an internal audit team and introduction of the inspectors' program for the prevention and detection of fraud.

The next fiscal year the Human Resources budget showed a surplus of only $25 million.

But the longer he remained in charge of Human Resources, the more Zalm became a four-letter word in British Columbia, and the more he received direct opposition from both the NDP and the public.

Vander Zalm, in fact, received numerous threatening letters and phone calls. At one point he asked the RCMP to keep a close watch on his home in Surrey. "No one likes receiving threatening phone calls or letters, but personally I don't mind for myself. It's very difficult when these come to my daughter, or son, or my wife, and this is unfortunate."[27] Apparently Vander Zalm's family was becoming "somewhat accustomed to it. They've received crank letters or crank calls for so long that really, they're beginning to become somewhat like me. Your shoulders broaden, things run off, and you don't take them all that seriously."

The buffer zone between himself and reality—his steadfast belief in his own good intentions—held firm. As Human Resources minister he said cowardly protesters at loud demonstrations didn't bother him. "They really aren't the type that would take you on particularly."[28]

On the evening of November 23, 1977, during the Social Credit convention at the Hyatt Hotel in Vancouver, a young woman, later described as "a hippie-ish sort of person,"[29] moved quickly through the gathering and hit Human Resources Minister Vander Zalm in the face with a pie. The attacker promptly fled. News cameras clicked. "I'm very grateful it's banana cream," said Vander Zalm. "It's one of my favourites. . .except it's on my suit."[30] The Anarchist Party of Canada (Groucho Marxist) claimed the direct hit. But it was self-assured Bill Vander Zalm, gentlemanly and good-humoured, who scored the victory.

Grinning, Vander Zalm announced that his fleet-footed assailant needn't worry; he wouldn't send the cleaning bill to Human Resources. He then expressed his concern that, in her haste, the young Groucho Marxist had left behind her belongings. The young woman left behind a plastic briefcase containing a note. "We chose Vander Zalm because of his liquidation of the Vancouver Resources Board and because of his consistent attacks against welfare recipients, single mothers, mental patients, the hospitalized, native people and Quebec."[31]

Bill Vander Zalm behaved as if he was glad to be chosen and brilliantly turned a potentially embarrassing situation into a triumph.

The most severe opposition he received in the media was a devastating cartoon in the Victoria *Times* by Dutch-Canadian Bob Bierman. This cartoon showed the Human Resources minister gleefully picking the wings off flies. Bill Vander Zalm's subsequent lawsuit against Bierman and the Victoria *Times* is discussed at length in Chapter 14.

The most significant and consistent political opposition to Bill Vander Zalm came from NDP MLA Rosemary Brown after Bill Vander Zalm began his move to abolish the Vancouver Resources Board in June 1977. Vander Zalm's initiative to remove the "luxury"[32] of the Vancouver Resources Board was Bill 65, a piece of legislation that prompted a 15-hour filibuster from the Opposition Human Resources critic Brown.

The Vancouver Resources Board had been allowed to continue, on a one-year trial program, after the Social Credit government had eliminated the province's other 23 community resource boards. The VRB was the last vestige of the NDP's attempts to decentralize social service planning. When pressed to explain the reasons for Bill 65, Vander Zalm said, "Each time that I have cited an example [to support the VRB's dissolution] it has been disregarded as insignificant. And I agree, by and large, on the surface they may appear to be minor. But when do a series of nickel thefts become an outbreak of crime? When do smoldering cinders become a fire? When do minor skirmishes become a riot?"[33]

A rally protesting Bill 65 drew 2,000 in Vancouver. A petition with 27,000 names was presented to the government. Vander Zalm was unmoved. He said the VRB was not scrupulous enough in hiring personnel to investigate possible fraud cases, and was not effective enough in preventing family break-ups. He believed that the VRB board members were "little more than puppets for a manipulative administration."[34] He wanted social workers to be more accountable to himself.

When Vander Zalm first eliminated the 23 other community resources boards around BC in February 1976, Brown had reacted with sadness. "I know how much these services are used and with one sentence he wipes them out. It's a tremendous, tremendous loss to my constituency and it leaves me feeling really frustrated and impotent."[35]

At 47, Rosemary Brown was an articulate black Jamaica native known for her "energy, talent, charm, brains and money."[36] Educated at McGill, she received a masters degree in social work from UBC and married a psychiatrist. A dedicated feminist who had tried for the national leadership of the NDP in mid-1975, Brown was in many respects the polar opposite of Bill Vander Zalm. She would stand like Custer in the legislature, the doomed last hope for widespread opposition to Bill 65.

After Bill Vander Zalm introduced the bill, 250 protestors paced slowly outside the legislature on June 28. They paced slowly because many were old and crippled. The president of the BC Association of Social Workers, Marilyn Callahan, said Bill 65 ran counter to national trends towards community-based programs. Understandably opposed, Norm Levi compared Bill 65 with "the kind of midnight fascist legislation that took place in Germany 30 or 40 years ago."[37] The VRB chairman Ron Fenwich simply said, "We cannot find any support for this bill."[38]

Conducting a survey of Vancouver's Fairview-Mount Pleasant area, UBC social work professor John Crane concluded the Vancouver Resources Board had been functioning efficiently and well. The main complaint about the system that Crane could uncover was that "many clients find the social assistance budget to be barely above a survival level."[39] Some 60 community groups formed a "Save the VRB" offensive. Marching from the Pacific Press building to the Orpheum Theatre, approximately 2,000 Vancouverites were given an opportunity to hear protest songs and speeches from Brown, Alderman Marzari and Alderman Rankin.

"All of this banner-waving is silly as far as I'm concerned,"[40] said Vander Zalm on July 25, the day after the Vancouver gathering. He firmly contended that direct, vertical management by Victoria would produce cost savings and program efficiencies.

"It is not beyond the realms of possibility," editorialized the *Province*, "that Mr. Vander Zalm simply became antagonized with not having absolute control, with not being able to make a command and see it go all the way down the line. No questions asked. No messy, public boards."[41]

Stung more by media carping than human protests, Vander Zalm rose in the legislature and explained why he had to eliminate the Vancouver Resources Board. "The bureaucracy in Vancouver is running itself. Not only does it often determine its own policy but, I suggest, coerces board members into believing the kind of nonsense that is fed them."[42] The board was "being led down the garden path into a wonderland crawling with elusive, grinning Cheshire cats."[43]

With throat spray and lozenges, Rosemary Brown carried stacks of files into the legislature on Tuesday, September 20 and spoke for four hours in favour of the VRB. The next day the legislature was reduced to less than 20 members and Bill Vander Zalm reportedly snoozed through Brown's musings about the merits of what the press had dubbed "Rosemary's Baby." Brown wore a black t-shirt with white lettering saying "Kill Bill 65." She called Bill Vander Zalm a bully. "The only thing that ever came out of the minister is abuse, abuse of the poor."[44] After seven hours the house adjourned for dinner.

Thursday she was back. Her week-long filibuster ended just before Friday's noon adjournment. "I just want to say, Mr. Speaker," Brown concluded, "that I tried."[45]

Bill 65 was proclaimed law on October 3, 1977. Vander Zalm's deputy minister, John Noble, replaced the seven-member Vancouver Resources Board.

Speaking of her opponent, Vander Zalm, Rosemary Brown has said, "He doesn't make many speeches, you know. He does most of his talking outside, attacking the people he's supposed to be supporting. There may be more to him than meets the eye. He may be a good husband and father. But he's a terrible minister of Human Resources. My concern is that he's using the people of this province, whom he's supposed to be serving, to achieve his goals.

"I think if he ever became premier it would be disastrous for BC."[46]

6

MUNICIPAL AFFAIRS
Democrat vs. Autocrat

"The application of democracy sometimes gives me trouble."

Bill Vander Zalm

As Human Resources minister, Bill Vander Zalm had made himself without doubt the most hated man in British Columbia. His collection of bad headlines had made him a political liability in the Ministry of Human Resources, and with an election coming up, the premier moved him to Municipal Affairs on December 4th, 1978.

Less in the public eye, this was a posting where Vander Zalm's image as a right-wing zealot might well have been expected to cool down. He had already served as chairman of the Greater Vancouver Regional District's Planning Commission, and as a former mayor of one of the province's largest suburban municipalities, he ought to have been somewhat in tune with the needs of municipal officials.

The rate at which Vander Zalm racked up angry headlines hardly slackened. Initially he alienated local politicians by proposing that maximum salary levels be fixed according to population figures in their areas. He ruffled more feathers by saying he wanted to amend the Municipal Act so they couldn't vote on their own salaries. He would prescribe the same medicine for the BC Legislature.

But this was just the beginning. Following a narrow re-election victory in Surrey in the spring of 1979, Vander Zalm stubbornly strove for three years to introduce a radical rewrite of BC's provincial planning policies to centralize planning for Municipal Affairs.

Vander Zalm moved in January 1979 to jettison BC's 28 regional districts, established by his own party over a decade before. On October 31, 1978, a Regional District Review Committee report to the Ministry of Municipal Affairs had recommended, after 287 pages, 366 briefs and 395 witnesses, that regional districts ought to be retained. But Vander Zalm mused aloud that he thought regional districts should be abolished. He was not in favour of red tape. "It's costing this province tens of millions of dollars in lost development," he said.[1] While the fate of regional districts hung in the balance and hiring freezes went into effect, Vander Zalm limited spending increases for BC municipalities to 5%. He tackled regional districts again in his 1981 Land Use Act.

Vander Zalm then proceeded to step on the toes of Human Resources minister Grace McCarthy, the minister responsible for the Insurance Corporation of British Columbia (ICBC), by leaking information on proposed changes to automobile insurance rates. Vander Zalm was forced to retract his ICBC remarks as erroneous. Reporter Alan Garr claimed he told members of the press McCarthy was "stupid" following a cabinet argument over ICBC, a claim Vander Zalm now calls "a fabrication." (Vander Zalm's intrusion into ICBC affairs was largely prompted by his ongoing campaign to eliminate "no-fault" insurance. Years later he still insisted, "I see the issue of no-fault insurance as sort of the foot-in-the-door and that no-fault insurance simply means more decisions by bureaucrats."[2])

In 1979 he was criticized for ignoring his ministry when he did not respond to Vancouver City Council requests to clarify legislation regarding grants to cooperatively owned housing projects. Then in 1980 he was castigated severely for introducing a bill that would have given corporate tenants the right to vote in municipal elections, regardless of whether they actually lived in the municipalities in question. One *Sun* columnist called this "a regressive, hopelessly transparent attempt to stack the deck in municipal elections in favour of conservative interests."[3]

However, Bill Vander Zalm's two major controversies in Municipal Affairs still lay before him.

While visiting Prince George on February 1, 1979, he made a little-noticed remark that he was considering a new planning act for BC. He provoked the ire of the Union of BC Municipalities by airing some of his proposed changes. Some critics gleefully lunged to take advantage of this supposed "rebirth" of the old Vander Zalm.

"His proposed Planning Act is an exercise in centralizing power that probably would draw applause from Joseph Stalin if he were with us today," overstated Allen Garr of the *Province*.[4] No doubt such opposition to his scheme only fueled Vander Zalm's determination to see it instituted.

"I know I get accused an awful lot of being a bit of a centralist," Vander Zalm says. "I feel that democracy has been interpreted to mean that somehow you could make things more democratic by spreading out or diluting the responsibility of any one person.

"My type of democracy would require a lot less government. The more people who get involved, the more a program gets lost and ends up as part of somebody's budget. Implementation gets delayed. You call for a whole lot of studies. And by the time it's declared it isn't doing what it was supposed to do."[5]

Vander Zalm's proposed Land Use Act was introduced to the legislature on December 2, 1981. He described it not as an attempt to centralize power but rather as "a consolidation of some power" that "shifts some power away from regional bureaucrats."[6] The act, as expected, removed the regional districts' power to influence municipal planning, and called for the creation of regional planning committees, appointed by the provincial government, to develop broad planning objectives.

To eliminate red tape Vander Zalm proposed strict and uniform guidelines for municipal development. Community plans would have to include the location, amount and type of commercial and industrial development; ten-year projections of housing needs including locations, types and densities; redevelopment proposals; location of sewer and water lines with ten-year projections for their expansion; projections of school needs and plans for land acquisition; and anything else "required by the minister."[7]

Vander Zalm stipulated that if a municipality refused to alter plans to suit the minister, the Municipal Affairs minister of the day could restrain the municipality from issuing building permits or approving subdivisions. Any personal amendments he made to a plan would not be subjected to public hearings. The minister would also have the power to step into local land-use disputes and directly eliminate bylaw obstacles faced by land owners at his discretion.

Only the City of Vancouver, which operates according to its own charter, could ignore most of the 165 sections of the act. Technically, the changes proposed were many. The act allowed the minister to designate transit facility benefit areas and impose levies on new construction in those areas to help offset the costs of the Lower Mainland's developing commuter rail system (thereby helping to pay for the coming ALRT); provided for vertical zoning and allowances for increased densities when negotiating with builders; allowed municipalities to issue residential variance permits so that dwelling units could be established in non-residential areas; and allowed municipalities to issue agricultural permits to set conditions for farmers to establish controlled livestock and poultry operations within city limits.

Vander Zalm, ever the salesman, called his Land Use Act "a one-stop development shopping concept."[8]

Former NDP Municipal Affairs minister Jim Lorimer called it "a fascist document."[9] The NDP's Municipal Affairs critic Charles Barber said Vander Zalm's Land Use Act would take municipalities back to the days when all the decisions were made by the Colonial Office in Victoria. "This bill proposes a radical restructuring of local government. It will concentrate enormous power in the hands of the minister."[10]

In his own defence, Vander Zalm noted there were about 500 different bodies of government in BC. Duplication and red tape naturally occurred. He wanted to reduce the "discretionary authority of local governments"[11] and concentrate more veto powers in his ministry.

Members of Bennett's cabinet were squeamish about, among other things, Vander Zalm's desire to abolish the Islands Trust, the elected body empowered to preserve and protect the 11 major and 500 minor islands in Georgia Strait and Howe Sound from large-scale real estate investment. The possible abolition of the Islands Trust brought protesters to Victoria. While the public could not easily fathom the intricacies of building bylaws and residential variance permits, it was plain enough that Vander Zalm's Land Use Act was going to open the treasured Gulf Islands to ruinous exploitation.

Vander Zalm was forced to present his Land Use Act several times to his Socred colleagues and each time he was forced to revise it. First tabled in December 1981, the final draft appeared in July 1982.

The government of Bill Bennett ultimately decided to drop Bill Vander Zalm's Land Use Act. After three years of preliminary work it was left to die on the order paper when the legislative session ended July 27, 1982.

"The government was not strong, but gutless," Vander Zalm charged. "I'm terribly disappointed the government did not proceed with the bill. I thought it was a gutless measure to in fact drop it now when in fact we should have proceeded."[12]

But Bill Vander Zalm refused to consider himself beaten. He stood by his "gutless" quote, saying he was a fighter, not a quitter. Later, when he was taking a sabbatical from politics, he said, "My greatest disappointment was in not getting the Land Use Act adopted. There was a lot of opposition to the act, particularly the elimination of the Islands Trust. . . . I regret deeply that I didn't approach things differently and get that act passed, even if not to the same degree I had originally wanted. Because I still think that was the best piece of legislation that could have been put forth for the people of British Columbia."[13] And later still, after gaining the premier's seat, the Land Use Act came up in a conversation with me.

"I still think it's great legislation. That's not to say there aren't some things in that I would have changed today. Because nothing should ever be static. But the funny thing is, one of the criticisms used by some of the people opposed to it was centralization. Even though most local government people were supportive of it, they [the press] searched out some of those who were opposed and they were naturally the ones who were most often quoted — there's no use getting somebody to quote that's in agreement with you so they searched out the ones that were opposed. . . . And one of the criticisms was centralization.

"Centralization, not decentralization. I don't know whether that was a deliberate attempt to try and kill the legislation, or whether in fact it was a misunderstanding. The legislation was not centralist. It was quite the opposite. I was streamlining the approval process in Victoria so that instead of a person dealing with eight different ministries in government, you were dealing with one. It was centralization in that respect. But it was centralization at that particular point to get it through the process. So it was a misunderstood piece of legislation. Partially because I took it around the province so many times, presenting it to so many groups, that I think people got tired of it.

"It was around a long time. And the bureaucracy in Victoria did everything to kill it, and I think perhaps they may have aided the process by putting the bug in the right ears. Because they

were really very uptight about it, the bureaucracies, because it meant them losing a lot of power.

"Now we don't have as much red tape because now we are faced with a time when municipalities are sort of encouraging development, seeking development, because it creates employment, it keeps people going. It's a little different from the hard-nosed, bureaucratic obstacle route that was there a few years ago. That was the sort of atmosphere that I brought the Land Use Act legislation forth in."

Before he made his second major move within Municipal Affairs, Vander Zalm analyzed his defeat at the hands of his own colleagues. "It was the bureaucracy that fought and killed it."[14]

Bill Vander Zalm's next major policy decision entailed the expenditure of over a billion dollars to implement a rapid transit system in the Lower Mainland. The minister-in-a-hurry, as he was dubbed in this period, began work on the project on July 9, 1979 by introducing legislation to establish something called the Metro Transit Operating Company. The public was not deeply interested. Critics of the scheme asked, "Why is he in such a rush to force it down everyone's throat?"[15] Basically this was a separate transit commission for Greater Vancouver in case the Greater Vancouver Regional District (GVRD) refused to join an Urban Transit Authority.

Vander Zalm was having trouble with the GVRD. One problem was that he couldn't convince the directors to support an unspecified transit system without guarantees that the provincial government would refrain from using higher property taxes as a source for financing major transit debts.

His other problem with the GVRD was that it had been doing rapid transit studies for years, and favoured a conventional bus system. In October 1980 Vander Zalm's Urban Transit Authority noted, "conventional bus transit is labour-intensive and, as such, is subject to inflationary pressure."[16]

Vander Zalm unveiled tentative plans for a quiet elevated system which would not be labour intensive because it would be driverless. As early as June 1979 he'd stated preferences for an elevated monorail like Seattle's. "The most expensive part of light rapid transit is acquiring the right of way. With an elevated monorail you don't have to worry so much about that. And of course there's no problem with ground level rail crossings."[17] Originally he'd conceived a monorail along the median of the Trans Canada Highway. "The motorist could see the thing whizzing by during rush hour and it wouldn't be long until they started using it."[18]

Vander Zalm got his plans firmly on track on December 6, 1980. He announced he'd opted for a $650 million "people mover" called the ALRT.

ALRT (Advanced Light Rail Transit) was BC's name for Ontario's ICTS (Intermediate Capacity Transit System). Engineers of Ontario's Urban Transportation Development Corporation had refined German plans (since dropped by the Germans) to make driverless cars with linear induction motors running on a ribbon of elevated concrete known as a guideway. Of course critics, such as Vancouver mayor Mike Harcourt, correctly noted the ALRT would require expropriations, would invade privacy and was basically untried. "We're buying a pig in a poke," he said.[19]

Undeterred, Vander Zalm and his BC Rapid Transit Committee chairman Jack Davis (who would be "re-elevated" to a cabinet post when Vander Zalm became premier) maintained the ALRT would spawn 11,000 housing starts, spark $256 million worth of commercial construction and receive a $60 million contribution from the federal government. Some 1,700 people would be needed to build the ALRT and about $400 million of BC manpower and materials would be used.

The price? In 1980, citizens were told that Vander Zalm's first leg—a 22-kilometre section linking New Westminster with Vancouver in time for a proposed "Transpo 86" world's fair—would cost British Columbians $290 million. By 1984 this estimate had somehow jumped to $854 million. But as Allan Fotheringham noted in a column about Vander Zalm, "Newspaper readers—voters—can't analyze wild figures in headlines."[20] The *Globe & Mail* called the ALRT decision "a bolt out of the blue."[21] To this day it remains a mystery why the normally thrifty and conventional Vander Zalm would select an untested and costly system like ALRT. When asked about the

ALRT, Vander Zalm told me, "I know it's a very costly system . . . But I still maintain that it would have cost more to put in the conventional system. . . . That was purely my decision. But purely my decision based upon the information that I obtained from the ministry, and from the people of Ontario [Transit], and from people elsewhere in North America. It wasn't purely based upon my own calculations. It was something with a lot of backup." (Some guessed the ALRT system had been brought to BC by high-ranking civil servant Norman Spector, who had brought a sales pitch with him from Ontario in 1980.)

At the time of Vander Zalm's announcement, the GVRD, an organization slated to pick up one-third of the costs, was in the middle of a $30,000 study evaluating the Ontario system. When the GVRD grumbled about Vander Zalm's presumptuousness, the Municipal Affairs minister vowed to build the ALRT system with or without the GVRD even though technically he could not do so. The Urban Transit Authority he had established was building the system, not Municipal Affairs. "If the minister is going to operate UTA as a department of his ministry," said Burnaby board member and mayor Dave Mercier, "then there's no use for this board."[22]

The release of the GVRD study of ALRT showed that Vander Zalm had overlooked several details, approximately $100 million worth of them, in his eagerness to make the December announcement. "Possibly I'm a bit impatient," he told a reporter in 1983.[23]

Details, details.

In 1982, Des Turner, a retired engineer and chairman of Citizens for Rapid Transit, claimed BC taxpayers had been hoodwinked. "I think that one of the most significant initial items about ALRT was the name change," he said. "The proper name is Intermediate Capacity Transit System which doesn't sound particularly glamourous. UTDC's own president wrote in December, 1976, that ICTS was 'a system for smaller cities.'

"When they found in Ontario that they couldn't peddle the system to anybody . . . when the Ontario government got pretty desperate about selling this system, having spent $70 million plus, they decided that one way to sell it was to change the name."[24]

Criticism of ALRT was also mounted by civic officials. GVRD transit commissioner Jim Mansbridge noted, as did the *Globe & Mail*, that other provinces did not usually entrust the coordination of such major transit decisions to Municipal Affairs. Former GVRD appointee and Vancouver alderman Walter Hardwick took roundabout aim at Vander Zalm. "I think one of the problems we've had over the past decade," he said, "is that provincial people don't sit down very frequently with the regional and municipal people. You need some imagination, and you need some leadership, and you need coordinated leadership, and we haven't got coordinated leadership."[25]

It was originally predicted the ride from New Westminster to Vancouver would take only 26 minutes. By car, the trip takes an hour. When the system was installed, various journalists delightedly proved that a motorist could beat the train's trip time.

Vander Zalm had specifically stated his preference for a quiet system. By 1986 BC Transit Chairman Stu Hodgson had to spend another $1 million in the hope of lowering the noise level to its promised maximum of 74 decibels. Experts said the contact between steel wheels and rippled rails was causing an ear-splitting noise at 80 decibels. A citizens group called Homeowners Against SkyTrain Effects insisted the noise levels were increasing.

Vander Zalm held to his elevated position. He did not respond churlishly to his critics. In fact, he seldom responded at all. Jack Davis did most of the talking. When news surfaced that Ontario's UTDC was trying to sell its system to a second client by assuring the city of Scarborough that the bugs in the system would be worked out by experimentation in Vancouver, Davis defended the Terminal Avenue demonstration line in Vancouver as being "as much public relations as anything else."[26]

These public relations manoeuvres, Davis said, would help everybody decide about colour schemes, seat arrangements, things like that. "It's not a test track," he assured. "A test track exists in Kingston, Ontario."[27] Early runs nonetheless produced some problems. Twice ALRT cars jumped off rails while on manual operation. Eventually, on September 16, 1985, two trains collided due to human error. Worst of all, a driverless ALRT train hit and killed a 15-year-old Surrey youth, Aaron Furssedon, on August 8, 1985. By this time Bill Vander Zalm was out of politics, developing Fantasy Garden World.

The major problem with the ALRT, beyond technical matters and administrative coordination, was clearly money. With Transpo 86 evolving into a full-fledged world's fair called Expo 86, the rapid transit system was turned into a more expensive but less celebrated second fiddle. Who wanted to pay a billion dollars to hear a screeching second fiddle?

Victoria amended the BC Transit Act to exempt the ALRT line from property taxation, but the burden of ALRT costs strained the conventional transit system in Greater Vancouver. Fares were raised as service decreased. "That's the real problem with this new transit system," commented the *Globe & Mail.* "Quite possibly it could destroy a transit system that is now working reasonably well. ALRT doesn't solve problems. It creates them."[28]

"It's an awfully expensive system and it will cater to only a few," said Edgar Horwood, a professor of civil engineering and urban planning at the University of Washington. "The per-ride costs will run at $12 to $16 a ride if you include interest costs."[29]

Few Greater Vancouverites were interested in interest rates when the Social Credit government announced free rides for the public during the last week of December 1985. These free rides would cost, some said, as much as $1 million. The cars were decorated in Social Credit colours and had been officially christened by Grace McCarthy, the new minister responsible for ALRT, as the "Skytrain."

A comparable 24-kilometre system was slated for completion in Portland in 1986. In 1984, Professor Horwood had noted this line would probably cost Portland only $212 million. The project manager of Portland's more "conventional" system, Gerald Fox, said the "philosophy of light rail transit is to keep costs down and to not turn the community upside-down."[30]

Bill Vander Zalm's ALRT, by comparison, was light-duty transit with a heavy-duty pricetag. When she announced that

the ALRT deficit would be paid for over a 30-year period, Grace McCarthy said, "This way the cost will be shared with future generations of users."[31]

Bill Vander Zalm was not present on December 11, 1985, when Premier Bill Bennett and Grace McCarthy officially garnered the credit for Skytrain. "I planted the seed and someone else nurtured it to fruition," said Vander Zalm. "I don't begrudge them the glory."[32]

The lessons Bill Vander Zalm learned in Municipal Affairs would have repercussions in his next cabinet post: He had tried to play democratically with his colleagues in the formulation of his Land Use Act and he had lost. He had played autocratically with the ALRT and he had won.

------------------------------ 7 ------------------------------

EDUCATION
Schools & Hard Knocks

*"Intelligence you learn in school and from books;
being smart is making the right decisions. Sometimes
people who are intelligent are so sheltered they've
never had a chance to become smart. I like to think
I'm reasonably smart."*

Bill Vander Zalm
to Sid Tafler in *Monday*
December 2, 1982

When Bill Vander Zalm was shifted to the Education portfolio
in 1982, the prevailing political wisdom was that Premier
Bennett was enacting a "double punishment" ploy. Bennett,
who had reached the peak of success after a modest schooling in
Kelowna, was showing his disdain for the value of formal
education. At the same time Bennett was punishing BC's present
teachers for their increasing radicalism and left-wing orientation
at the executive level of the BC Teachers Federation (BCTF).

But it was triple punishment. Vander Zalm's sideways
demotion to the unglamourous Education portfolio was
Bennett's way of adding insult to injury. Bill Vander Zalm's
pride had already been injured by Bennett's refusal to accept his
Land Use Act. Bennett, on the other hand, was not the sort of
man who could easily forgive or forget Vander Zalm's "gutless"
charge. The two men continued to jockey for power within the
Social Credit hierarchy. Bennett threw the teachers at Bill
Vander Zalm — and Vander Zalm at the teachers.

According to *Province* analyst Barbara McLintock, it was all
part of Bennett's master plan for restraint. He had simultaneously shifted Bob McClelland to Labour and Jim Chabot to

Provincial Secretary. "All three ministries are key to the restraint program," she wrote, "and all three are now headed by tough, persistent streetfighters who won't back away from any confrontation, no matter how unpleasant."[1]

Vander Zalm, however, appeared to accept the position with grace: "You know, I didn't expect to be handed the Education portfolio.[2] I am the first non-academic minister.[3] But having been on the job for six months, I hope never to leave it."

As the new kid on the block, streetfighter Vander Zalm was introduced to the Education neighbourhood by local gang leader Larry Kuehn. As president of the BCTF, Kuehn sent Bill Vander Zalm a telegram of welcome and congratulations upon hearing of Vander Zalm's appointment — in French.

Not to be outdone, Vander Zalm fired back his own missive — an unoffended reply in Dutch.

So it was clear from Day One in August 1982 that Bill Vander Zalm and the BCTF were not going to speak the same language. Like two leaders of opposing street gangs, Kuehn and Vander Zalm would taunt one another personally with all the frustration of two rock-throwing youths who never got close enough to inflict any serious injury.

"I can understand why some of my staff might be a little fed up with the BCTF, Larry, and I think you and I and a whole group of us should get together and say, 'Look, it's the pupils we ought to be concerned about, the people, not the teachers or the politicians.' Let's bring it together. Why always politics into everything that's done in the school system?"[4]

Kuehn pleaded innocent. There was order in the neighbourhood before Vander Zalm arrived. Vander Zalm was a bully hurling rocks indiscriminately, just trying to get everybody's attention. "It got to a point where I could almost predict when I'd get a call from the press," Kuehn recalls, "If it was a slow day for news, I could be fairly certain that Vander Zalm would try and find something controversial to say."

The new minister's opinions on the province's educational system and standards made the headlines almost daily, and his comments raised the province's teachers, and many of its parents, to fury:

You know, I get a lot of calls from parents who have brought their children in from education systems in other countries. They say they can't understand how it is that BC children do not really get going in school until 9:30 A.M. and are already starting to pack up by 2:30 P.M., with recesses and lunch break in between—and then no homework.[5]

Everybody gets passed. You don't have to know anything to pass your grade.[6]

Well, I think a person has to be able to write good, read, spell, arithmetic—those basics I think are very necessary for no matter what you do in life today.[7]

There has to be more discipline and it can be provided in a variety of ways. For example, I believe I've said that if people were found writing on the school walls they perhaps could be required then to clean the school grounds.[8]

There's no easy answer but I've spoken with one teacher in Revelstoke who has an idea. She has her pupils write out lines.[9]

When I went to school, I must confess I found the strap fairly effective.[10]

I think the public itself is basically in agreement with me that the educational system has strayed off course—that there is too much emphasis on recreational and social activities and not enough on basics like Math, English and the Sciences.[11]

I've gone into schools where the school was half-empty because everybody was out someplace on a mountain. That's not what the educational system is for. The taxpayers shouldn't pay for that; that's up to individual parents.[12]

We tend to concentrate too much on those courses which lead people at the end of it all taking political science, sociology or psychology. We're not producing enough that are qualified to take engineering or to become a doctor or a dentist.[13]

I believe sincerely there has been far too much emphasis on swimming, on field trips, on all these sorts of things.[14]

I don't think we need a course to teach a new housewife how to tell what amount is in a ketchup bottle.[15]

[As to books] there's a lot of garbage gets into the schools, and hopefully we can weed out far more effectively than we did in the past.[16]

I think examinations should start early. Maybe at grade 3 or 4 they should take tests, and then again at 6,7, or 8.[17]

I think it's only fair to the child that we provide either some additional tuition before they graduate, or fail them and have them take the grade again. Which is harsh, no doubt, in today's society but on the other hand, what is the option? You can have a youngster graduate through school and find out, following their leaving grade 12, that they really have no place to turn because they really weren't taught the subjects. We have to have a measure as to what their ability and a minimum required.[18]

Right now there is legislation providing for the opening of class with the prayer and it's been the policy of making this optional at the school board level, and in the end to be left up to the teacher. My position is very favourable to school districts being positive to this. I view it as an opportunity to introduce a level of respect and order and discipline.

I'm also in support of the flag and having students stand to sing *O Canada* in assembly.[19]

I've always maintained the Lord's Prayer can be said by a Christian person, a Jewish person, a Moslem person. It doesn't matter, because it only speaks of "Our Father, Who art in Heaven," so it could be applicable to practically any faith.[20]

Sex education is nothing new. In California, they led us by a long shot, and they've got more 11-year-old pregnancies in California than they have anywhere else in the world.[21]

Sex education has been put on hold [here] for some time.[22]

Vander Zalm's comments about the BCTF itself were no less provocative:

I don't want to say that they're a bunch of sheep, nor do I think they're a bunch of sheep. But, you know, it's human nature...When they call their meetings now to have a vote, there's all these hard-hitting speeches, and there's all this bashing of the government and Bill Vander Zalm the minister, or whatever, and then they have a few singsongs in between to stir them up real good, and that, you know, really throws it. And people go to these meetings and vote one way, and after they've done so they'll come out and say, "Why did I do it? Really, what is it all about?"[23]

The BCTF — their executive at least — has to wave that NDP flag and they have to keep fighting things in a political way, which makes it very difficult.[24]

[Some teachers are] being bamboozled and bullied by some people in ivory towers in Vancouver.[25]

Nor were the province's professional educators thrilled when the intrepid Minister began offering ungrammatical tips on how they could improve their performance:

Sometimes (for instance) we don't do a good job of teaching youngsters to read well. Then we bring in a new program called remedial reading, which brings in more teachers and entrenches the bureaucracy.[26]

You can walk into many a school and find they've bought a computer or photocopier there, four years ago and the next year another salesman came along with a slightly better product and out goes the old one. They're just too loose with the public's money.[27]

It's a top-heavy system. For every teacher in the classroom, we have some professional or teacher that's not in the classroom. These are coordinators, these are superintendents, principals, vice-principals, and this is what is adding tremendously to the costs.[28]

I don't believe our principals are managing sufficiently. They're a part of that team, they're a part of the union, they tend to be much involved in group management. I think we do need some fairly good management in the schools as you would in any other business.[29]

Over the last number of years we've come to think that somehow the classroom size must forever be reduced in order for the teacher to be effective, and I don't think that's necessarily proven out.[30]

Philosophically, I think the size of a class is not as important as the quality of the teacher, and the quality of a teacher is not only determined by the amount of education received, but partially by how we permit the teacher to function.[31]

Education in BC is very expensive, not too productive and a relatively easy row for the students to hoe.[32]

The BCTF's Kuehn became Vander Zalm's most vocal critic. "We took a 1,000-teacher reduction without a confrontation," he complained in August, "and then they brought in the second level of budget cutbacks. And then they threw in Vander Zalm. The threat to the system by putting him in is incredible."[33] Previous Education minister Brian Smith had introduced his Education (Interim) Finance Act in April of 1982 giving the Education minister new power to reduce any school board's budget to whatever level was deemed necessary.

Vander Zalm quickly fired off telegrams to all the school boards warning them that the government's ability to pay salary increases would determine teachers' salaries. Layoffs would invariably result. Teachers immediately branded him Public Enemy #1. But years later Vander Zalm would feel himself victimized, too, seeing himself as the tough kid sent to fight alone without any backup. "When I was minister of Education, the team was wanting me to concentrate strictly on restraint. But as a practical person, I knew it was dynamite politically."[34]

The teachers picked up Vander Zalm's assertion that children should learn to "write good." "Stop Vanderlism in the Schools" joined the BC bumper-sticker war. Vander Zalm's supporters ordered hundreds of buttons saying "Back to Basics in

Education. Learn to Write Good. Bill Vander Zalm" — to be sold at $10 each. The two sides left few stones unturned. Whenever Vander Zalm spoke on radio programs or at meetings, the teachers monitored his speeches, copying down quotes as if they were propaganda rocks which could be tossed back at him.

"The majority of teachers understand the need for restraint," Vander Zalm told a Social Credit nominating convention in Delta, "and they will cooperate. But all the flak and all the hollering and all the screaming and all the press and all the publicity has come from Larry Kuehn, the BCTF. Because for them, hopefully, it might elect some NDP candidates and if it does, then hopefully those NDP candidates, if they're members of government, will somehow again feed the public service even more and more."[35]

The streetfight *was* along political lines. Smith's Interim Finance Act had given Vander Zalm the means to effectively scuttle the independence of the NDP-dominated school boards. Vander Zalm also wanted to initiate a new program for evaluating teachers. Bad teachers would be weeded out. He

publicly compared the efficiencies of BC school districts (calling Trail's the worst). And he took measures to find poor administrators with an administration cost commission. He would also boast he had reduced the staffing level within his own ministry by almost 20%.

But as *Monday Magazine*'s Sid Tafler noted, Vander Zalm's restraint in Education was as much philosophical as it was economic. Sometimes the philosopher didn't get his numbers right. The battleground was usually teachers' salaries.

> To my mind, the two most honest people in our society, in terms of their integrity, should be our judges and school teachers; judges because they have the last word and teachers because in many ways they have the first word.
>
> Following this point of view, it is logical that they should be amongst the best-paid in the public service, and I think they should. So you can see that it is not my desire to beat teachers down in regards to their pay packet.[36]

> [But] BC teachers have received salary increases in the past few years which far outstrip the public sector average and are significantly ahead of the private sector average.[37]

Left-wing critics later gathered statistics for salary scales showing that between 1977 and 1983, pay scales for BC teachers increased by 82.2% while the Canadian Consumer Price Index increased 86.3%.

The teachers felt they were being unfairly treated as recession scapegoats. "The man has a few grains of truth in a vast desert of ignorance," charged Richmond Secondary School principal Hal Lindsay, after 34 years of teaching.[38] "He is continuing to make statements without getting in and finding out what schools are all about," said BCTF vice-president Doug Smart.[39]

Having inherited a punitive mandate to force BC's 75 autonomous school boards to slash $60 million from their operating budgets in two phases before March 1983, and then cut another $55 million in the rest of that year, horticulturist Bill Vander Zalm had been handed a hot potato by Bennett. These teachers were articulate and organized. Collectively they were not patsies. So he would sometimes attack them individually.

A grade 7 teacher in Prince George once had students write Vander Zalm letters of criticism. Vander Zalm responded by having an assistant mark the grammatical errors in the sloppiest compositions. The corrected compositions were sent back. Vander Zalm also sent a letter of admonishment to the teacher, saying he wanted to get the chairman of the local school board to test the writing skills of the class. Vander Zalm claimed many of the teachers were his friends. Kuehn claimed nearly all of the teachers were fearful of Vander Zalm.

In Smithers, a grade 8 teacher mistakenly allowed her students to see a questionnaire on sex that was meant only to inform teachers of the kinds of questions that teenagers really have about sex. The minister handed a copy of the questionnaire over to the press, along with a copy of his personal letter of rebuke to the teacher.

> Words cannot express my revulsion towards this incident. The teacher should be suspended without pay for a reasonable period of time. The material delves into sexual techniques and goes well beyond what anyone would consider the sex-education needs of a 13-year-old.[40]

As the recession rolled on, 62 of 75 school district contract talks ended in arbitration. Meanwhile the proportion of the total provincial budget allocated to public school funding was declining from 14.7% in 1977/78 to 11.72% in 1983/84. Both the teachers and Vander Zalm found themselves mired in a stagnant BC economy, slinging mud.

"I would invite the minister to sit down with the boards if he wants to change things," said Gary Begin, president of the BC School Trustees, "These continual comments through the media do nothing to further dialogue. He needs to change his approach; instead he's shooting in the dark, firing from the hip. I don't know where he gets his information but he's operating outside the professional staff that work in his department."[41]

Rather than take Begin's suggestion to sit down with the

school boards, Bill Vander Zalm was considering abolishing their independence and replacing them with a county system.

The county system envisioned by Vander Zalm bore striking similarities to his spurned Land Use Act. Instead of having a municipal council, a school board, a board of health etc., Vander Zalm would have one county council of approximately 12 or 15 members to serve a given region.

"I know in the process of my being here, I'll get the reputation for being centralist, " he mused. "It's not my desire to try to run the show, but if decisions are not made at the local level I'll move in and see to them myself."[42]

"The great man scared the daylights out of the teachers with his talk of instituting his county system," recalls *Province* education critic and North Van school trustee Crawford Kilian (author of *School Wars*), "School trustees understandably hated the idea. The county system could put the schools at the mercy of people with no interest beyond filling in potholes and sprucing up the local shopping mall. School and municipal administrators would be endlessly battling one another over jurisdictional and budget issues."[43]

Vander Zalm was not in the Education neighborhood long enough to organize these jurisdictional fiefdoms, but he did manage to introduce a "deregulation discussion paper," implement a commission to monitor school district administration costs, and reintroduce provincial government exams Administrators and children would continue to feel the effects of Education Minister Vander Zalm long after he had passed along on his way to the quieter pastures of Fantasy Gardens.

During the era of the poisoned Tylenol scare in the US in 1982, Bill Vander Zalm received his ministerial equivalent to the banana cream pie he had received in Human Resources. Some extra-strength Tylenol capsules and a gift of dead flowers were left for him at a BCTF rally.

Larry Kuehn apologized for the Tylenol and dead flowers, saying the BCTF had no association with the gesture. But there was never a cease-fire declared. It would always be tit for tat. The next month Vander Zalm was quoted in the Vancouver *Sun* saying BCTF leaders like Kuehn had "turned to union work to get their kicks because they may not be as effective in the classroom as they should be."[44] Kuehn threatened a lawsuit. And it was Vander Zalm this time who was forced to write a formal letter of apology.

W.A.C. Bennett once described politics as war. Bill Vander Zalm was at war with the teachers of British Columbia for eight months before he decided it was time to retreat from politics and lick his wounds. He had produced a remarkable record of offensives in a very short period of time. He went home and told his daughter Lucia the news. She could hardly believe it. She said it would be nice to see her father without having to turn on the TV set. "Dad," asked Lucia Vander Zalm, "are you going to run again?"

"I don't think so, honey," he said.

Lucia put a writing pad in front of her father. "Write that down and sign it."[45]

Bill Vander Zalm did.

8

ON SABBATICAL
The Parable of the Saint and the Rat

"We pray every night, usually when we're in bed."
Lillian Vander Zalm
Vancouver *Courier*
April 17, 1979

April 1, 1983 was a rare day in BC history.

Bill Vander Zalm was on the radio saying he was leaving politics, saying he wanted to spend more time with his family. He was telling the listeners of Gary Bannerman's CKNW open-line program how to control aphids, as usual, but he was also saying that after eighteen years of political life he needed to take what he called a "sabbatical."

April 1, 1983 was Good Friday, one of the most meaningful dates on Bill Vander Zalm's Catholic calendar. His use of the word "sabbatical" came naturally to him. He was a politician who was very much at home with both religious terminology and the concepts of redemption and resurrection. Beginning a sabbatical on Good Friday was good timing.

April 1, 1983 was also, of course, April Fool's Day. It was a rare day indeed. And Bill Vander Zalm was on the radio making a pitch to the BC public that almost no one was buying. Vander Zalm's adversaries were as suspicious as they were relieved.

"Are you sure this isn't an April Fool's joke?" asked Kitty O'Callaghan, president of the Vancouver Elementary School Teachers' Association.[1] "He's a politician and I don't believe him," said cartoonist Bob Bierman. "He's playing some kind of strategy. He's used to the limelight and he couldn't possibly stand being out of it. He's got something up his sleeve. In the typical Vander Zalm way, he's planning something. Personally, I think he's after Bennett. He wants the leadership."[2]

Bill Bennett's cabinet had been pushing Vander Zalm to take a hard line with education, and Vander Zalm had complied. But those "gutless" colleagues in Victoria had not given him the public support that Vander Zalm felt he merited. It was time to repay the cabinet in kind. Publicly Vander Zalm said he was going on sabbatical for Lillian's sake, to help her run his nursery business. Privately he was disappointed with his teammates and was taking his bat and ball home.

There was also the matter of a forthcoming Surrey Social Credit riding association nominating meeting. In 1979 he had narrowly won his seat in the two-seat Surrey riding. The two NDP candidates had actually polled over 1,000 votes more than the two Social Credit candidates. At present the riding was split between Vander Zalm and NDP MLA Ernie Hall, but the NDP organization in the riding sniffed a two-seat victory.

By making his announcement on April 1, Vander Zalm said he was giving his riding association plenty of notice before they selected their candidates — on April 11 — prior to the forthcoming general election.

If, as many were predicting, the Social Credit restraint policies were to result in a defeat for Social Credit, Bill Bennett would probably resign rather than face ignominious years without power, squirming under the wit of a returned Premier Barrett. Political observers reasoned that Willie Woodenshoes would then be able to step in to fill William Woodenwit's vacated place.

That was the accepted theory: Bill Vander Zalm was not retiring simply because his wife had been working seven days a week. He was not a prodigal Prince Charming. He was just a rat deserting a sinking ship.

Naturally the press asked Bill Vander Zalm, the "maverick minister," if he could be convinced to terminate his sabbatical if the captain of the good ship Socred went under.

"Given the opportunity at the right time," he said, "I'll certainly not forgo the challenge. If somehow the present leader was to step down at some point simply because he had enough of it, or whatever it is, then obviously I would probably be in there pitching along with a number of others."[3]

Several Social Credit cabinet ministers would never forgive Bill Vander Zalm for this sabbatical. His desertion at a time of trial did little to boost his popularity with faithful warhorses like Bob McClelland, Jack Heinrich, Jim Nielsen and others. Three years later when Bill Vander Zalm became premier these men would resign from the Social Credit cabinet.

But besides the friendship of inner cabinet members, Bill Vander Zalm had little to lose by deserting the government. Bill Bennett would not hand Bill Vander Zalm his leadership mantle, even if Vander Zalm continued to toil in Victoria. It was better to wait outside Victoria for his chance, working for himself. There was little percentage in remaining much longer as a scorned hired gun who did Bill Bennett's dirty work. "I'm grateful to the premier for giving me three tough portfolios," he said.[4]

Vander Zalm said he would remain a member of the Social Credit party and support the party in the next election. Queried about his long term commitments he said, "Nothing is for the rest of my life, nothing. My options are open."[5] He admitted that his colleagues in Victoria had taken exception to his style. "I like to say what I am thinking," he said.[6]

Bill Bennett was not a man who liked to say what he was thinking, and he wasn't saying much now. Some of Bennett's cabinet would later agree that the famous "gutless" charge was not unfounded. The Bennett cabinet agreed to take a hard line then left Vander Zalm "out on a limb." Far from being a rat, it was possible to view Vander Zalm as the saint of restraint, forced to take a sabbatical, without honour, after a cleanly-fought fight for all.

The Vander Zalm-as-rat scenario and the Vander Zalm-as-saint scenario were both true.

And so Bill Vander Zalm went off on his sabbatical in the right wing wilderness.

"I know I'll be frustrated not being in politics," he said. "I'm a realist and I realized full well that I can't stay out of this game forever. I'm going to probably be back in the not-too-distant future."[7] But for the present, "I'll be concentrating more on the franchise end of the business," he said, "which was permitted to let go while I was in politics all those years."[8] He had a target of establishing 40 Art Knapp's franchises by 1986.

Only three days into the wilderness and already the rat was groomed by the press for his resurrection role as a saint. Barbara McLintock, Victoria correspondent, wrote, "There seems little doubt that if only the current members of the Social Credit party had votes to cast, Vander Zalm would win an immediate leadership convention.

"Some party polls have even said he might beat Bill Bennett if he chose to challenge him directly."[9]

The sabbatical was going well. Journalists came to him. He was asked tough questions: how did he view the results of his eight months as Education minister? "Our education system has not suffered at all," he said. "We have a very healthy system which has not suffered one little bit."[10] He said he wasn't bitter at the teachers for the little incident involving the dead flowers and a bottle of Tylenol. He said he had many friends amongst the teachers. "It's too bad that they've taken some shots at me which might have been avoided had we sat down together."[11] His main regret? He wished he could have legislated a no-increase contract for teachers for 1983.

In the tradition of Canadian Social Credit founder William "Bible Bill" Aberhart, the Alberta premier whose "Sunday Bible Hour" had garnered the highest ratings of any Alberta broadcast in the Depression, Bill Vander Zalm endeavored to use his sabbatical as an opportunity to broadcast his opinions and raise his profile on radio. A freelance agent, Peter Kosick, went around to radio stations offering them a radio garden show that would be sprinkled with politics.

Eventually, Vander Zalm was hired by CKNW. The saint out in the cold had a hot line to the public.

Bill Vander Zalm also brought out a book of his gardening columns and seasonal advice with publisher David Hancock. "He came out one day with hundreds of his newspaper columns," says Hancock. "He knew exactly what he wanted."

The way Hancock tells it, the idea was Vander Zalm's; Vander Zalm says Hancock came to him.

The Northwest Gardener's Almanac, by Bill Vander Zalm, reinforced his image as an authority on gardening. Illustrated with photos of himself and Lillian, it has sold well. The book is a fixture in the Fantasy Garden World gift shop. Autographed copies are available. The inscription, in bold handwriting, says, "Good Gardening & Happy Shovelling." Hancock says he would happily do another book with Vander Zalm. "I quite admire him. Some authors are orangutans but he was good to deal with." Hancock, a right-winger, says he now counts Vander Zalm as a friend. "Now I'm just hoping he's not going to be like Trudeau. Trudeau was all right wing in his advertising and he turned out to be all left wing in his actions."

A third course of media exposure for Vander Zalm during his sabbatical was his series of gardening columns which appeared in — and suddenly disappeared from — the Vancouver *Sun*.

The *Sun*'s acting Home section editor, Ros Oberlyn, approached Vander Zalm with a proposal to contribute a weekly

gardening column to appear on Saturdays. The first column, titled "If You Love A Plant, It Will Love You," appeared July 2, 1983. "This will be the first of what I hope will be a continuing column in the Home section," he began. This opening column asserted, "If you love a plant, it will love you in return. Have you ever noticed how kind grandmothers grow the very best African violets, or how beloved grandfathers grow the very best vegetable crop? A philodendron thrives much better in a cozy home or pleasant office than in a cold, sterile, commercial complex. Like people and animals, plants have feelings, instincts and even brain-like sensory organs (which we call roots)."

Vander Zalm was "pretty easy to deal with," Oberlyn says, and the *Sun* did not edit his copy a great deal. "The reason that we wanted him as a garden columnist at the *Sun* was because of his style. It seemed a little silly to take all the colour out of it, to make him sound like he's not himself." But the *Sun* did resist Vander Zalm's wish to end his columns with his personalized slogan, "Happy Shovelling."

The smiling face of Bill Vander Zalm, the happy gardener, suddenly disappeared, without any explanation, after nearly two months.

There was a story behind this mysterious disappearance, and it goes like this: A column by Bill Vander Zalm was slated to appear on September 1. This column was entirely about Vander Zalm's tour of Bota Gardens in Richmond. He gave Bota Gardens a rave review: "It is a pleasure to see a garden that is neatly trimmed and very colourful at all times in every season."[12]

Oberlyn read the column, containing instructions on how to get to Bota Gardens, and passed it to a typesetter. The typesetter read the column and asked Oberlyn if she had heard that Vander Zalm had just bought Bota Gardens. "I thought, 'It couldn't be. Vander Zalm wouldn't pull this on us,'" Oberlyn responded. "The column didn't state his connection to the Gardens; it didn't say anything about the fact that he owned it. The *Sun* would look like fools if we ran that."[13]

The incident provides an insight into Bill Vander Zalm's ability to adjudicate conflict-of-interest situations. When

Oberlyn called Vander Zalm, he said yes, he owned Bota Gardens, which was to become better know under the new name Lillian gave it, Fantasy Gardens. "He was surprised that I thought it was a conflict," says Oberlyn. "He didn't see it as a conflict at all. He didn't think there was a problem. He didn't understand why I did."

Vander Zalm reluctantly agreed to rewrite the column to placate Oberlyn's concern. Oberlyn told him to include the fact that he owned Bota Gardens, and also to include his views of other public and commercial gardens. She told Vander Zalm to give these other gardens equal emphasis. Bill Vander Zalm wrote, "We, in BC, are fortunate to have so many show gardens. Among the many, Butchart Gardens, Van Dusen Gardens, Minter Gardens and Bota Fantasy Gardens are the best known. Just before the weekend, as I often do since the family purchased these recently, I took a stroll through the Bota Fantasy Gardens."[14]

The rest of Vander Zalm's column was unchanged. Oberlyn checked with the *Sun*'s managing editor Bruce Larsen for his opinion on the matter. Then she called Vander Zalm again. "The result in the end was he decided, 'Well, if you don't want to run the column the way I'm writing it, I don't want to write for the paper.' So he quit writing for the paper," says Oberlyn.

This parting of the ways was not openly hostile at the time. Vander Zalm was more mystified than irate. *Province* columnist Mike Tytherleigh, a consistent Vander Zalm supporter, subsequently wrote in the rival paper that Vander Zalm had quit on a matter of principle. "Miffed about the pruning of his words, he picked up his spade and quit."[15] But three months later the King George Highway Hospital Syndrome would incite Vander Zalm to write a letter-to-the-editor accusing the *Sun* of "spewing its venom" on him.

"I realize, and always have, your position as far as Bill Vander Zalm is concerned. I appreciate that was aggravated by my refusal to continue a garden column when I was told by an editor that I could write about public (tax-supported) gardens but not privately owned gardens."[16]

Spurred by his own version of the truth, Vander Zalm

concluded his indignant counterattack on the *Sun* with an inference that the paper was contributing to a climate amenable to totalitarianism.

"If one day there is only one newspaper, no election, and no need to advertise, you can probably take pride in having been responsible for it, but you will not have the means to say it."[17]

Bill Vander Zalm's indignation was righteous. He had just pulled off a much greater media coup than hosting a radio show, publishing a book or contributing a column to the *Sun*. As a Socred saint in exile, Bill Vander Zalm had received the Good Catholic Seal Of Approval from none other than the pope. He was to use his talents as a promoter to organize what he later referred to as "the largest single gathering in the history of British Columbia."[18]

Hosting a pope was a tough job but somebody had to do it. Bill Vander Zalm was chosen by Vancouver's Roman Catholic archbishop, the Right Rev. James Carney, to oversee a huge public mass — the main event in Pope John Paul II's September visit to Vancouver. (As a youth, Vander Zalm had been one of the archbishop's altar boys.) A member of the Vander Zalm family told the *Sun* in February 1984 that Vander Zalm had been selected for the job "four or five months ago."[19] If Vander Zalm had known about the papal plum as far back as April 1, it would add meaning to his use of the word "sabbatical."

The proposed public mass was tentatively set for the Pacific National Exhibition grounds. It was expected to draw 300,000 people.

Organizational plans to promote the pope's visit drew fire from Father Jim Roberts, co-chairman of the Solidarity Coalition, who argued that Vander Zalm's selection was "not without a political message."[20]

The choice of Vander Zalm as promoter was defended by the managing director of the archbishop's papal visit committee, Ben MacDonald, former president of Chevron Canada. "Tell me who else has the get up and go, the energy and courage and time to do that job on a voluntary basis?"[21] Vander Zalm was a logical choice. His skills as a promoter and a marketer were unmatched in BC politics.

Criticism of the archbishop's organizational committee was more correctly levelled at the composition of that committee overall. Besides Vander Zalm and Ben MacDonald, the committee was weighted in favour of big-business nominees. Other pope promoters were C.J. Conaghan, former president of the Construction Labour Relations Association; Zachary Clark, general manager of Air Canada; Ron Longstaffe, executive vice-president of Canadian Forest Products Ltd.; Denis Foristall, general manager of the Westin Bayshore; and George O'Leary, chairman of the board of Scott Paper Ltd.

Ironically, the strongest objection to Bill Vander Zalm did not come from overlooked labour and disgruntled left-leaning priests. It came from one of the five brothers who owned J.C. Kerkhoff & Sons Ltd., the union-busting construction company that has been at the forefront of dismantling union strength in the BC construction industry. Maarten Kerkhoff of Chilliwack attacked Vander Zalm in a letter to the *Province*, calling the pope "the anti-Christ" and the "Whore of Babylon." Kerkhoff wrote, "I feel the Roman Catholic doctrine is totally wrong."[22]

Doctrine, schmoctrine. The chance to hobnob with the pope was also a chance for Vander Zalm to present a once-in-a-lifetime extravaganza. When the decision to stage the public mass at the Abbotsford Airport had been made, Vander Zalm went about ordering 2,500 toilets for the 1,200 acre site. The religious celebration would also have 33 concession stands. Tacky pope souvenirs would be the order of the day, not prayer books.

Pope John Paul II landed at the Abbotsford Airport in a helicopter on Tuesday, September 18, 1984. He was accompanied by Archbishop James Carney. The man who escorted the pontiff to his "popemobile" for his 2.5-kilometre tour through the crowd was Bill Vander Zalm.

Vander Zalm was ecstatic. "It's almost like a miracle — people dropping from the skies."[23] Afterwards he would give praise to his own organizational efforts. "The roads are clear and the people are here. I never guessed it would be this smooth."[24] He'd managed the mass for all of British Columbia. "What's so beautiful about all this, and I hope it lasts when it's all over, is that we've had the opportunity to show that British Columbians can get together when the cause is there and pull together."[25]

One of the reasons the Abbotsford show ran smoothly is that far less than the anticipated crowd of 300,000 showed up. The only calamity in the pope's visit to British Columbia occurred in Abbotsford, where over-zealous security guards delayed the departure of six helicopters for 40 minutes. These helicopters were scheduled to fly bishops, a cardinal, Lieutenant-Governor Robert Rogers, Premier Bill Bennett and federal representatives back to Vancouver behind the papal aircraft.

The delay in Abbotsford left Premier Bennett "fuming."[26] Because dignitaries were kept longer than planned in Abbotsford, two rented limousines had to race through Vancouver and screech to a halt outside BC Place Stadium, turning dignitaries into indignitaries. The opening remarks of the lieutenant-governor were cancelled from the program at BC Place. According to Bennett aide David Harris, director of protocol for the visit, "It upset the premier. He's following it up."[27]

"I was terribly chagrined about the whole affair," said visit director Ben MacDonald. "We held the program back as long as we could. I extended apologies to the people concerned and I'm trying to call the premier as well. It was the only glitch in the whole visit."[28]

For a man who had quit politics to help his wife, Bill Vander Zalm was having a very busy sabbatical. But no matter how busy he was, Vander Zalm took time to go to church every Sunday. "I don't think he ever missed once," says Jos Van Hage. Vander Zalm's Catholicism is not only important to him personally ("Through my church I have spiritual peace and I am happy in all I do"[29]), but is also significant on several political fronts.

While it is true that Bill Vander Zalm chose to distance himself during his leadership campaign from the financial bigwigs who constitute BC's so-called "Top Twenty Club" (i.e. large corporations), he was less likely to disregard the advice and influence of some very influential and powerful Catholic businessmen outside the confines of Vancouver's Howe Street. Vander Zalm is a member, with his brothers, of the Knights of Columbus. There are approximately 12,000 Knights in BC, and

1.6 million members internationally in the US, Canada, the Philippines and Mexico. They form a vast and economically intricate Catholic men's group that operates extensive RRSP programs and retirement packages, while maintaining the tenth-largest insurance company in North America. For several years the organization has been giving money to the Vatican in order to refurbish the facade of St. Peter's. The Knights of Columbus originated over 100 years ago as a service association which started the first American blood donors group. It is now near the forefront of anti-abortion lobbying.

Vander Zalm is forthright with his opinions on abortion and hankers to create policy changes. "I'm a pro-lifer. I am against abortions. With me, it's a religious conviction." he has said.[30]

"I admit I am a pro-lifer and I am alarmed that the percentage of abortions to live births is so much higher in BC than in other parts of Canada."[31]

"I am a pro-lifer and I make no bones about it."[32]

In September, 1986 he told me, "This is probably what's happening — abortion is being used as a means of birth control. . . . If I had my way completely, I would not have abortions. You can't be a pro-lifer conditional-upon, conditional-upon, conditional-upon. But I also know what the law is and I realize we have to stay within what the provisions of the law are. And I appreciate, too, that not everybody holds my view."

One of Vander Zalm's strongest supporters in his Richmond community is the Richmond councilor and anti-abortion lobbyist Tilly Marxreiter. During the Social Credit leadership campaign, Marxreiter and others helped Bill Vander Zalm win 21 delegate spots in Richmond, the riding of Jim Nielsen, former Health minister and a rival leadership candidate who had resisted pressure to have abortions banned at Richmond General Hospital. Nielsen was described as a murderer in anti-abortion leaflets. After the Whistler convention, he announced his intention to retire from politics in mid-September. (Nielsen doesn't attend church but says he is a Christian. "I'd like to see some people actually read the Bible rather than quote from it," he says.)

Bill Vander Zalm's Catholic peers expect their candidate to uphold his views on abortion and he has steadfastly done so to an extent that he has raised questions about the management of abortion procedures in BC. As the *Province* noted during the Social Credit leadership race, "Anti-abortionists appear to have rallied around the camps of former cabinet minister Bill Vander Zalm and Progressive Conservative MP Bob Wenman."

But abortion is a federal matter. More significant are Vander Zalm's religious concerns as they touch on education in BC. When he was Education minister he tried to encourage use of the Lord's Prayer in the school system. Since becoming premier he has repeatedly voiced his intention to introduce some experimental form of public funding for independent schools in BC. This is an issue of extreme importance to the Catholic community.

"I would personally stack a youngster who has received an education in an independent school against my own or any others who had received an education in public school,"he says.[33]

"Some of the independent schools possibly offer far greater opportunities for learning than some of our much larger, much better equipped public schools."[34]

"Frankly, as one who is and always has been extremely supportive of independent schools, I have a tremendous fear of what could and would happen to the independent school programs if somehow the socialists gained control."[35]

"I do believe in a competitive school system," he reaffirmed in conversation after becoming premier, "where you have both the good public system and a good independent system. And where people, in fact, have the choice of the type of education they want for the children by being able to choose between a public system that operates in a certain way or a private system that provides the educational opportunities yet has another approach to certain other aspects of life."

Bill Vander Zalm attended an independent Catholic school in Noordwykerhout. Since 1917 the Dutch government has subsidized any school parents ask for, provided enough pupils attend. As a result, 70% of all Dutch elementary school pupils and 60% of secondary school students go to a "bijzonder" or special school.

Vander Zalm has proposed to introduce a trial program in BC whereby tax vouchers will allow parents to spend their portion of the schools budget in any manner they see fit, although during the '86 election campaign he backed off on the idea somewhat, saying he might start by testing it in a limited area first. Vander Zalm maintains parents are more likely to become directly involved in the education of their children if they sense they are making a direct financial contribution to a particular school — in effect purchasing their children's education. He also claims the cost of educating a student in a private school is less than the cost of educating a student in a public school, so taxpayers will derive benefits from the new program.

Although politics and religion are not generally linked openly in Canada, in the Netherlands there is a separate Catholic political party and major Catholic newspapers. The habit of being forthright in one's religious convictions within the spectrum of politics has come naturally to Vander Zalm. He told me of the guidance his religion offers. "I rely a great deal on prayer. I pray often. I'm often sitting at a table involved in a very difficult problem and I may quietly be praying to myself."

He is even willing to exhibit his religion — literally — to supplement the profitability of Fantasy Garden World by building a $500,000 biblical garden.

Near the beginning of 1986, millionaire realtor Henry Block approached Bill Vander Zalm with an offer to donate a number of life-size statues of Christ, depicting Christ's life, from a large religious display erected on Block's 108 Mile House land development in the 1970s. If Vander Zalm agreed to put them on display for Expo 86, Block was willing to share them with Fantasy Gardens.

Vander Zalm made plans to display Block's statues, with sound systems explaining the significance of each statue, amid a garden that would contain the 232 plants and trees mentioned in the Bible. There would also be a miniature River Jordan, fed by a miniature Sea of Galilee. The water in the garden and the rocks lining the path came from the Holy Land via a Seattle entrepreneur.

"A man who lives in Seattle came in one day and looked over the garden and asked if we'd ever considered putting in a biblical display," says Vander Zalm. "Well, I told him we had. We didn't want it to be too religious but we had thought of putting in the plants and trees mentioned in the Bible.

"He had visited the holy lands and brought back ten tons of rock from the areas of Capernaum, Jerusalem, Tiberius, Nazareth and Bethlehem. He'd collected ten large containers of water from the Sea of Galilee and the River Jordan. They were all in a warehouse in Seattle. He'd planned to break up the rocks and put the water in phials and sell them off. But it never happened. So he offered it all to us."[36]

Vander Zalm expected 400,000 visitors to Fantasy Gardens to see the biblical statues during the Expo summer. "When I think about how it will all come together," he said, "I think there must be a higher authority at work."[37]

The higher authority must have taken a few months off. Embroiled in dicey negotiations with the Agricultural Land Commission—negotiations which could jeopardize the economic viability of Fantasy Garden World and which threatened his chances to replace Bill Bennett as premier—Vander Zalm, still on his sabbatical from politics, did not complete the proposed biblical garden as promised.

Bill Vander Zalm, the politician who smiles and hints at divine intervention, once mentioned to a reporter that he might someday join a mission to help teach trades to underprivileged people in the third world. He has continued to keep in close touch with his religious impulses in 1986. While addressing the Kamloops Chamber of Commerce in March, Vander Zalm referred to the recession as a blessing from God. He said the economic recession helped people "appreciate the way things are now—I think God sent it. It was needed. It was necessary and it had to happen when it did."[38]

9

VANDER ZALM
vs. HARCOURT
Give a Man Enough Rope

"I'm an ambitious person. There's no doubt about that. It's in my nature."

Bill Vander Zalm
to Paul Mann in *Metro*
July 29, 1977

In the big fight between Bill Vander Zalm and Mike Harcourt for the heavyweight championship of Vancouver politics, it is not unfair to say the challenger lost just about every round.

In retrospect, this fight was a mismatch. No candidate for mayor who resided outside the city limits had won a Vancouver mayoralty bout since Fred Hume was elected from North Vancouver in 1952. After squeezing by incumbent Jack Volrich in 1980 by a margin of 3,000 votes, Harcourt had easily whipped the Non-Partisan Association's Jonathan Baker in 1982 by 34,000. Vander Zalm would make many tactical errors in his campaign, but his biggest error was stepping into the ring in the first place.

A blow-by-blow analysis reveals Vander Zalm's corner failed to mold the challenger's approach beyond a strategy of misguided opportunism. Bill Vander Zalm hoped to be mayor during Expo 86. "I think it's an opportunity for a good profile and I think I can do it," he said.[1]

Vander Zalm's involvement in Vancouver municipal politics began as far back as 1982. While he was still Municipal Affairs minister, Vander Zalm was severely criticized by Mayor Mike

Harcourt for failing to respect the democratic wishes of the Vancouver electorate by blocking the implementation of a ward system.

In 1978, 51.7% of Vancouver voters had backed a referendum calling for the city to discontinue electing aldermen-at-large, and to change to the ward system used in most other major Canadian cities. Mayor Jack Volrich ignored the issue. Harcourt, upon his election, urged Vander Zalm to act on the matter as Municipal Affairs minister. Vander Zalm decreed that a new referendum had to be held requiring a 60% majority. He also wanted to personally approve the wording of the referendum and appoint a commission to set up the ward boundaries if the referendum passed.

Vander Zalm's contention that a referendum for wards in Vancouver needed a 60% majority was upheld in Victoria. Critics noted the Social Credit Party itself had received less than 60% of the vote in obtaining power. In November 1982 the voters of Vancouver voted to approve a ward system of representation, but only by a margin of 57%.

Naturally Mayor Harcourt resented Bill Vander Zalm's meddling in civic affairs. He also resented Vander Zalm's role in forcing the ALRT transit system onto Vancouver. "The Czar has once again moved to centralize power on himself and keep the burden of taxes on the serfs," said Harcourt in 1983.[2]

Like two boxers testing one another with words before a match-up, Harcourt and Vander Zalm had tested one another on several occasions prior to 1984.

After the surprise victory of Bill Bennett's Social Credit in May 1983, Bill Vander Zalm was looking for a route back into politics in 1984. Asked if he was hoping to see himself back in the fray, he said, "Yes, definitely. Not federally, though I have been asked a number of times to do so. I love Canada, but I don't really care to live on an airplane between here and Ontario. But I would like to become involved again provincially, and maybe even locally. I enjoy local politics very much."[3]

In January Vander Zalm sold his sprawling Burnaby garden shop, Art Knapp's Plantland. "This frees me up for whatever I want," he said, "and politics is one of those things."[4]

He openly speculated in January about his chances of beating Mayor Harcourt, saying it "would be a tough fight."[5] The president of the Non-Partisan Association (NPA), Brian McGavin, had already cited Alderman George Puil and Vander Zalm as possible candidates. Vander Zalm told the press he was prepared to sell his six-bedroom Port Kells home and move to Vancouver if he chose to run.

He said he wouldn't make a final decision for at least two months.

It took him a lot longer than that.

Vander Zalm felt it wouldn't be necessary to worry about whether or not Vancouver voters would view him as an outsider. He admitted he was lured towards the mayor's job by the challenge of promoting Vancouver during Expo 86.

Mayor Harcourt quickly sensed the possibility of labelling Bill Vander Zalm a carpetbagger. "If he wants to move into Vancouver I think he should earn his spurs and maybe run for parks board and learn something about Vancouver."[6]

The candidates were in training even before the promoters had time to announce the bout. Vander Zalm shaped up for a fight by joining the Citizens Against No-Fault Automobile Insurance, resting up in Palm Springs, and making speeches in the Lower Mainland. In February he outlined an eight-point blueprint for change and a return to "true free enterprise," for the New Westminster Chamber of Commerce.

Vander Zalm suggested:
1. banning unions from businesses employing fewer than fifty workers;
2. banning secondary picketing;
3. changing labour laws to make unions "more democratic";
4. scrapping the Senate;
5. fixing election dates for governments;
6. taking major issues to referendum;
7. implementing a constitutional right to "free and unrestricted trade";
8. banning government deficits, unless approved by referendum.

"We have too much big business and too little small business," he said. "Governments no longer serve the people, we serve them. The labour force no longer controls its unions, its unions control them."[7]

Although these policies were in tune with Social Credit theories, Vander Zalm nonetheless said in March that, if he ran for mayor, he would prefer not to run on the coattails of the civic Non-Partisan Association or the Social Credit party. "I favour being an independent," he said. "But, on the other hand I realize that when you're involved in an election, you also have to realistically consider how you're going to get the most votes."[8]

Again, Harcourt delivered a quick jab at his undeclared opponent. "He [Vander Zalm] will just be running for the farm team of Social Credit."[9] The farm team reference was an unintentional double entendre, underlining a potential city boy/country boy fight. And the fight would be held in the city.

As the Socred who had jumped ship, Vander Zalm was in a position open to ridicule. The *Province* newspaper held a contest to name the proposed rapid transit bridge that would link New Westminster and Surrey in 1989. The winning entry was the Van Der Span.

Ironically, Vander Zalm would also be impeded by his former membership in the government. Bill Bennett was using the first year of his new term in office to push through harsh legislation. Clearly Vander Zalm, the former Social Credit cabinet minister who told *Easy Living* magazine in 1983 that he was really the founder of restraint, would be identified as the Socred candidate, while Harcourt, who had already run for the NDP provincially, would be identified with the NDP.

Between the re-election of Social Credit on May 5, 1983, and the adjournment of the legislature on May 16, 1984, many events on the provincial scene served to hamper Vander Zalm's popularity. The government terminated the jobs of 400 provincial employees, fired Human Rights Branch director Hanne Jensen, eliminated the Human Rights Branch, invoked closure in the legislature for the first time since 1957, used closure a record ten times to cut off debate on Bill 3, announced layoffs for 300 to 400 more public employees, introduced a budget that cut funds to all ministries and eliminated grants to students, announced plans to fire 2,000 public employees and introduced back-to-work legislation for pulp and paper workers.

This was the political backdrop for Operation Solidarity, centred in Vancouver, which gathered the largest protest demonstration ever assembled on the grounds of the Victoria legislature on July 27, 1983 and also rallied 40,000 anti-Socred demonstrators at Empire Stadium on August 10, 1983.

Clearly there were already battle lines drawn between Vancouver and Victoria. Harcourt would be the Vancouver candidate in the November 17 mayoralty race. Vander Zalm could only be seen as the Victoria candidate.

But Vander Zalm kept himself in fighting trim. While disassociating himself from anti-Semitic views held by some members of the federal Social Credit party when he addressed the BC chapter of the party, Vander Zalm criticized Canada's banking system.

"Many people liken the banks to someone who gives out an umbrella and then takes it away when it rains.

"Everything in Canada is geared to bigness. Big business, big government and big unions. There's no help for the little individual."[10]

In July NPA officials conceded 49-year-old Bill Vander Zalm was no further committed to running for the mayor's job on the NPA slate then he had been at the beginning of the year. "Vander Zalm won't run unless he's absolutely confident he can win," said the previous NPA mayoralty candidate, Jonathan Baker, "and at the moment he's still not confident."[11]

The NPA tried to persuade former BC Liberal leader Gordon Gibson to run against Harcourt. They also tried for former Vancouver mayor Art Phillips. Party campaign chairman Gordon Campbell was reduced to looking for high-profile business or community leaders who had not run for elected office before.

Vander Zalm was busy arranging for the visit of Pope John Paul. In June he had said he would not make a decision about running for mayor until after the pope's departure. Meanwhile, according to *Sun* columnist Marjorie Nichols, Vander Zalm was commissioning an informal summer poll, a poll whose results predicted he would lose a mayoralty race. The pope departed on September 20, 1984.

On September 25, 1984, Vander Zalm said he would "sit tight"[12] for a week to ten days before making a decision. Delegates at an NPA nominating committee meeting the night before were told Vander Zalm would only accept a nomination if it could be demonstrated he had widespread support.

Concluded veteran Vander Zalm-watcher Nichols: "Vander Zalm desperately wants to be premier of BC. A stint in the mayor's chair would keep his name in the lights until he can leap back into the legislature. But Bill Bennett, the chap who currently warms the premier's chair, is on the verge of calling a couple of by-elections. There are currently vacancies in Vancouver East and Okanagan North. Vander Zalm won't run in Vancouver East because he can't win and the Okanagan Socreds already have a candidate.

"Here's Vander Zalm's dilemma. What if Bennett decides to add a couple more by-elections to his list? What if there is a vacancy in, say, Vancouver-Point Grey? I think you get the picture. I also figure that Bill Vander Zalm laughs himself to sleep at night with his little head resting on his scrapbooks filled with all that free publicity."[13]

But the real expert on Bill Vander Zalm knew best. Lillian Vander Zalm said the challenge of being mayor during Expo 86 was making the NPA nomination particularly attractive. "Unless something really drastic happens," she said, "Bill's going to run for sure."[14]

Lillian was right. But first Bill Vander Zalm told the NPA they needed to deliver a petition of signatures to convince him he could win. He would wait two weeks to see which way the wind was blowing. When told of the Please Run, Bill petition, Harcourt happily quipped, "I thought political primaries were held only in the United States."[15]

On October 3, ten months after first publicly toying with the idea, Bill Vander Zalm officially announced his candidacy for mayor of Vancouver. "I will run a positive campaign and concentrate on the business of how to use Expo 86 as a catalyst

for job creation and economic development," he said. "I don't intend to answer allegations from the other candidates."[16]

When Harcourt learned that Vander Zalm was announcing his candidacy from his newly-purchased Bota Gardens in Richmond (soon to be renamed Fantasy Garden World), he prophetically commented, "He's going to run in fantasyland."[17] A poll of 494 Vancouver voters at the beginning of October showed Harcourt with 50% voter approval, whereas Vander Zalm had only 20%.

Vander Zalm's campaign manager was Jack Lee. His campaign chairman was Lynn Paterson. His two aides were Myron Laka and Jim Pavich. His musical director was Juanita Vander Zalm. She wrote and performed a campaign song to the tune of the Battle Hymn of the Republic.

> Vancouver, gem of the Pacific,
> All of us know you're terrific,
> The message of your beauty all the world will span
> With William Vander Zalm.[18]

Vander Zalm pledged to find a new home in the "terrific" city of Vancouver. He eventually rented a home in the Southlands district, at 3296 West 38th Avenue, for $1,700 a month. He said he was only renting the house for two months at a time while he and Lillian searched for an appropriate Vancouver home. "I suppose some people are speculating that I'm doing this for political reasons," he said. "I don't play games. I want to live in Vancouver. I spend most of my days here now and the Surrey house is too big for Lillian and me."[19]

Vander Zalm admitted he was an outsider coming into the ring. But, as he had done in previous election campaigns, he justified his candidacy with a desire to eliminate red tape and to create a healthier governing atmosphere. "I think it is sad for Vancouver that we are viewed by other areas of Canada...as a very left-of-centre council."[20]

A few days later he said, "There are a lot of people in Vancouver who don't realize what sort of council we have here in Vancouver....If elected mayor, I would want a free-enterprise council with me, but if somehow a couple of commies came in, I'll work with them."[21]

Vander Zalm's use of the term "commies" clearly polarized the race. Mayor Harcourt quickly said nuclear disarmament should be at the top of the list of civic election issues. Vander Zalm had been cheered by the NPA when he criticized Vancouver council for its 1982 vote on nuclear disarmament, its plebiscite on cruise missile testing and its 1983 decision to declare Vancouver a nuclear-weapons-free zone.

"This is one of the most deadly and difficult elections we have ever faced," Harcourt lectured the Longshoremen's Union. "Some people don't like the fact that we are having a referendum [on the cruise missile] or that Vancouver is the peace capital of the world."[22]

Harcourt quickly backed his opponent into a corner, manoeuvring him into a position where he appeared to be arguing against peace.

Vander Zalm had expressed his opinion on nuclear arms in an interview at the end of 1983. He said, "I firmly believe that our best opportunity to negotiate with the Soviet Union for disarmament is to be at least as strong as they are. Otherwise, we lose the ability to negotiate. I am not opposed to the test sites [on the Canadian prairies]. We are not an island unto ourselves — we're part of North America. We couldn't escape from our partnership with the United States even if we wanted to. We are both too dependent on each other."[23]

Vander Zalm lost the round on peace to a slicker puncher. Harcourt, a 41-year-old former storefront lawyer, was the first opponent Vander Zalm had faced who could outspeak him in the clutch. "We feel peace is the pre-eminent issue of our time," said Harcourt. "Either you sit in your bomb shelter and eat your beef jerky and wait for the bombs to drop, or in your own way participate in bringing about a balanced nuclear disarmament."[24]

Vander Zalm began punching without discipline. In a 15-minute televised debate on BCTV he criticized the disappearance of "colour and stature"[25] from the mayor's office. He said Harcourt was negative and failed to uphold the decorum of office. Some of his jabs entirely failed to connect. "He [Harcourt] has been stumbling along and he's been fortunate, the city has been fortunate, that someone else has filled in the void but now the time has arrived that other people cannot nor will not fill in the void."[26]

When Vander Zalm and Harcourt were guests on Dave Barrett's radio program, Vander Zalm described an arrangement between the city and Shaughnessy Estates as a "payoff." In June the city had accepted $500,000 for social housing from Joseph Segal, a developer who had overbuilt his condominium project. The four condominiums at 37th and Granville had been built larger than specified. Instead of forcing the developer to tear down the units, Harcourt's council had chosen to penalize the developer financially.

The "payoff" charge riled Harcourt, who continually referred to Vander Zalm as "the candidate from Surrey."[27]

"That's a bunch of garbage," Vander Zalm said. "I could teach you more than you could ever get to know, young fellow."[28]

Ignoring the nonsensical nature of this remark, Harcourt retorted, "Thou dost protest too much, Bill."[29]

To re-emphasize his secure position, Mayor Harcourt afterwards threatened to sue Vander Zalm for slander over the "payoff" charge. Harcourt was scoring left and right. He even got some help from the right-wing NPA aldermen.

Three NPA aldermanic candidates, Don Bellamy, David Levy and Phillip Owen, disagreed with Bill Vander Zalm's position that a plebiscite on cruise missile testing was "useless."[30] Then the NPA cited the threat of an 18% property tax hike due to ALRT construction as the number one issue in the campaign. The NPA tried to lay the blame for a potential homeowner's tax increase of $125 to $150 on Harcourt. Apparently they had forgotten that the chief architect of the high priced ALRT system was not Harcourt (who had criticized ALRT at its outset as "an economic time bomb"). The man who gave Vancouver ALRT was none other than their mayoralty candidate, Bill Vander Zalm.

Vander Zalm and Harcourt went head to head in a slanging match over ALRT during an all-candidates meeting before 200 people at the Trout Lake Community Centre. The issue was how to avoid paying for ALRT, how to ensure the provincial government did not push the economic burden onto Vancouver's shoulders.

"It will take a lot of negotiating," said Vander Zalm. "But I ask you, who do you think will be better able to negotiate with Victoria, Bill Vander Zalm or Mike Harcourt?"[31] Harcourt used the issue as a chance to boast the city's triple-A credit rating, saying that rating was now threatened by a transit system for which Bill Vander Zalm ought to be held accountable. "The financing of the ALRT is a time bomb that was set up by Bill in the late 1970s, and how can you trust him now to defuse the time bomb he set off himself?"[32]

The challenger struggled to find an issue with which he could score. Harcourt, the incumbent who lived in modest Fairview Slopes, based his campaign on "peace, cooperation, civic stability and vision."[33] That didn't leave much room for Vander

Zalm, living in a rented luxury home across from Point Grey Golf & Country Club, to find an opening.

When Vander Zalm said the vote on the ward system was not binding because it was a plebiscite rather than a referendum, Harcourt's assistants checked with city legal manager John Mulberry and found the city charter made no distinction between "plebiscite" and "referendum." Vander Zalm then cried "dirty tricks," arguing that Harcourt's communication assistant Jane MacDonald and his executive assistant Shirley Chan should not be used to help with Harcourt's campaign. "In essence, they're robbing the taxpayers," said Vander Zalm. "To do it on their own time is fine but to campaign on taxpayers' time is just dirty tricks."[34]

In reply, Harcourt countered, "If Bill Vander Zalm had the good grace to apologize for all the mistakes he made [in politics] he'd be on his knees in Stanley Park for 2½ hours."[35]

Vander Zalm stopped attacking Harcourt directly and went back to former adversaries. He called for a complete probe of civic grants. In particular he was concerned about the $150,000 given in the preceding decade to DERA, the Downtown Eastside Residents Association. This did not win him any votes from the 3,500-member DERA organization, which represented many destitute citizens on the city's east side. If anything, the charge served to mobilize people's advocacy groups against him.

Vancouver wasn't Surrey. By November 12, the *Province* officially editorialized, "We support the election of a free enterprise majority on Vancouver City Council." But the *Province* endorsed Harcourt over Vander Zalm. In mid-November NPA alderman Don Bellamy bluntly called Vander Zalm's anti-Communist statements "a bunch of crap."[36]

Unable to interest the media in his charge that city council's left-leaning majority had squandered $18 million on the Cambie Street bridge project (by not allowing BC Place to pay half the cost), Vander Zalm hired a phone computer service to deliver a brief recorded message in his favour.

In his campaign literature for the Chinese community, Vander Zalm called the Harcourt/COPE (Committee of

Progressive Electors) coalition on Vancouver council a "divisive, do-nothing bunch." This could not disguise the fact that Vander Zalm had run a divisive, do-nothing campaign. He was reduced to saying his vision of Vancouver included something called a "FREE ECONOMIC ZONE status for this city, like Hong Kong and Singapore."[37] He also promised to "ensure the EXPO NORTH GATE gets built, strive for a solution to the CHINATOWN PARKING PROBLEM, assist in CHINA-TOWN BEAUTIFICATION programs."[38]

The voter turn-out for the November 17 election neared the 55% high set back in 1934. Harcourt took 62% of the vote. The loss for Vander Zalm was dubbed "embarrassing." The *Sun* said he was "trounced." Vander Zalm did not phone or meet with Mayor Harcourt to concede, as is customary.

Vander Zalm said his own defeat was not as upsetting as the re-election of COPE alderman Bruce Yorke, who narrowly beat out NPA's Phillip Owen for the tenth and final aldermanic seat. "My biggest disappointment was when [the voters] had a choice on the 10th spot between a good Christian businessman or a Communist, they chose the Communist. . . .

"If this country is going to be governed by people who are affiliated with Communists, I'm getting out. I'll keep going till I get to the last bastion of free enterprise."[39]

But the battle between Vander Zalm and Harcourt was not the end to Vander Zalm's poor showing.

On the eve of the election, Vander Zalm addressed Vancouver's Chinese community. Hoping to gain the votes of the city's multi-cultural mosaic, he had endeavoured to express his respect and love for Orientals. In this speech he inadvertently remarked that the Chinese, Koreans, Vietnamese and the Filipinos looked alike to him.

It was a minor gaffe. Vander Zalm is, for the most part, an engaging public speaker who does not rely on notes. He had simply to apologize if anyone took offense at his suggestion that all Orientals looked the same. But when letters began to appear in the newspapers, chastising him for his off-the-cuff remark, he chose to defend himself.

On November 25 in the *Province* there appeared a letter from William N. Vander Zalm of Surrey. He wrote that the actual statement he remembered making was:

"Lillian and I have no regrets about this election. It was a wonderful experience. I've long had many Chinese friends but we really came to love them during this campaign. Also, we tend to group so many in our Oriental communities as Chinese but we came to know that there are numerous strong ethnic groups. The Koreans really fought for me, as did our Filipino community. . . . Then there was the strong support from the Greeks, the Italians, the Polish. . . and the list goes on. We have so many wonderful ethnic groups."

Further to this statement, Vander Zalm wrote, "It is enough to make all good people fed up with politics and leave it to the wishy-washy or to those who go into hiding when elected, if every time something is said it is quoted out of context. It is then made worse by those responding and who get a headline in your paper.

"Strange I should have to defend myself or even bother to, but you see I have many good friends in the Chinese community and I would like to keep it that way."[40]

In fact, Cable 10 had videotaped Vander Zalm's address. Here is the transcript of his actual remarks:

"I said tonight earlier when I was contemplating as to what I might say in addressing you that I wouldn't begin mentioning names because unfortunately when you begin to mention names you are bound to leave out some individual or group of individuals who should be thanked. So I promised my colleagues that I wouldn't, and Lillian that I wouldn't start singling out people or groups. But I have to tell you I fell in love with our Chinese community—I just think they're the most wonderful people—and as I fell in love with the Chinese, I began to realize that perhaps, though they looked alike, there was another wonderful group—the Koreans, and the Vietnamese, and they were super, as well as the Filipinos. Just [a] fantastic lot of people."[41]

Once again the King George Highway Hospital Syndrome struck Bill Vander Zalm. Embarrassed by the *Province*, who revealed the contradictions between what Vander Zalm claimed he had said and the truth, Vander Zalm attacked the *Province* just as he had previously attacked the *Sun*.

"The Province has become an embarrassment to me," he wrote in a letter to the editor March 18, 1985. "Day after day, I see ridiculous misleading headlines followed by the first-section pages and realize what a terrible disservice your paper is to BC.

"Each day there is another twist to the same headline. March 11 it was 'READY TO KILL.' I know that many potential investors must be scared away from BC when seeing such headlines. They do not realize this is the sensation-seeking 'new enquirer' of BC—The Province."

On election night challenger Pretty Boy Vander Zalm had appeared almost jubilant, behaving almost as if he had won his bout with Hammerin' Harcourt. But four months later, this letter was evidence that Bill Vander Zalm, underneath his smile, was really a sore loser. Two years later his tone had changed again. In a conversation with me after he became premier, Vander Zalm commented, "People generally thought well, he must be terribly depressed about that. No. See I have another philosophy and that is, if you do your best, and you do what you believe is right, then regardless of how it turns out, it's intended or meant to be that way, and it'll come out later on that it was [meant to be]. I don't call it fate. It's not fatalism. Fate means it happens regardless of what you do. What I'm saying is that if you do your best, and work hard, but believe in what it is you're doing and carry on that way, then regardless of what the outcome [is], it's meant to be. So when I became involved in that city election, at the end of it, I just said, 'Hey, it's been a great experience, it's been a lot of fun, I've met a lot of great people and all of this was meant to be. It's part of something. And I'll find out many years from now as to why it really was.' I was meant to lose. Because if I hadn't lost, I wouldn't be where I am today."

10

FANTASY GARDEN WORLD
Coming Up Tulips

"It would appear that since its original conception in November of 1978 that the 'Bota Gardens/Fantasy Garden World' project has gone through a metamorphosis."

R.V. Switzer
Director, Richmond Permits &
 Licenses Department
February 4, 1986

If a Martian landed in British Columbia and asked to be taken to our leader any time on a weekend during the latter months of 1986, he would be gratified to realize he was being directed to a place called Fantasy Garden World.

Fantasy Garden World is the lovely, tacky and bizarre tourist attraction that is Bill Vander Zalm's prime business interest. Fantasy Garden World is where Bill Vander Zalm and his wife Lillian could be found — living in a mobile home — at the beginning of 1986, working long hours to develop their new kiddies' amusement park and European village complex. Fantasy Garden World is also where Premier Bill Vander Zalm could be found on weekends towards the close of 1986 — still living in a trailer with Lillian.

As the Ricardo Montalban of BC politics, Bill Vander Zalm has built a Fantasy Island in Richmond that doubles as the secondary capital of British Columbia. On weekends Fantasy Garden becomes the political headquarters of BC. Trade unionists, business leaders and private citizens with a beef have

all been welcomed to Fantasy Garden to bend the premier's ear
or cry on Vander Zalm's shoulder on Saturdays and Sundays.
They come to the garden just as visitors on the popular television
program *Fantasy Island* come to a magical island, hoping to get
their wishes granted, hoping to have their fondest dreams come
true.

There's even been a movie filmed there. Bill Vander Zalm told
me that in the spring of 1985 he began a starring role in
Sinterklaas Fantasy, being made by Corporate Concepts of
Vancouver. It's a story about a man who comes to Canada from
Holland as a small boy, does "pretty well" in the plant business
and becomes involved in politics. The Anna Wyman Dancers
and the Vancouver Boy's Choir are featured in scenes filmed at
Fantasy Garden World in which the hero, strolling through his
flower gardens, daydreams about his youth and about the Dutch
Santa Claus. Suddenly he finds himself transported back to
Holland — by a rainbow — and becomes the Sinterklaas of his
dreams, riding around the country on a white horse.

Vander Zalm says he was approached with the idea by
producer Keith Christie, who plans to market the film as a
documentary to the CBC and other networks. At the present
time production is halted — mid-rainbow — until the premier can
find time for a trip back to his homeland to complete the movie.

When Vander Zalm announced his candidacy for Vancouver
mayor, he did so from Fantasy Garden in Richmond — outside
the city limits of Vancouver but well within range of free
advertising for his enterprise. He also announced his bid for the
Social Credit leadership from Fantasy Garden. The premier of
British Columbia appeared in the *Globe & Mail*, grinning,
riding on the engine of a miniature fantasy train. When Vander
Zalm was planning to buy the castle the Dutch government set
up in downtown Vancouver as a centennial exhibit, he said he
hoped the publicity attendant upon transferring the huge
structure from downtown Vancouver to Richmond would create
several days of free publicity on local media.

The 8.5-hectare (21-acre) site of Fantasy Garden World at
10800 No. 5 Road in Richmond is almost half filled with

commercial development. The major and original attraction—
not built by Bill Vander Zalm—is the botanical garden itself.
Although created by the property's previous owner, John Massot,
the general public has the impression that Bill Vander Zalm
originated the impressive show garden. Vander Zalm does little
to refute this misconception. "There's not that many good
gardeners," Vander Zalm said when explaining the difficulty of
finding a buyer who could keep it going, "Well, I shouldn't say
there's not many good gardeners. There's not as many quite as
good as Bill Vander Zalm."[1]

Fantasy Garden World is more than a $7-million-plus
investment for Premier Bill Vander Zalm. In a sense it is a
reflection of Bill Vander Zalm's character.

"I like things organized," he says, "I like things neat."[2] The
pathways are scrupulously tidy. There is not a single weed to be
found. The Vander Zalms' Fantasy Garden plantation employs
several men of East Indian extraction who weed the grounds and
hose off the footpaths. They work more than eight hours a day.
They get paid $8 an hour. No overtime. "He's a very nice man,"
one of them says, "He likes very much cleaning."

Just like in the *Fantasy Island* TV show, the paternalistic
landlord of this domain has a loyal sidekick—his wife Lillian. In
fact, he told me it was Lillian who came up with the name
Fantasy Garden World. " You know we had dreams of it being a
very major attraction, and we wanted it to have a name that had
a broad appeal. Like Disneyland or Disney World or something
like this. I think perhaps that's where it came from in part. And
the whole idea of a fantasy was part of the thinking. We wanted
to have not only a garden but a children's park and surprises and
a village that was a little cookie-like. So I can't recall just how it
came about, but it was Lillian who picked it." And it's often
Lillian who answers the phone to those who call Fantasy Garden
World seeking the ear of the premier. "No, I'm sorry, Bill isn't in
right now. This is Lillian. Is it something I can help you with?"

With September dew on the grass, early in the morning, just
before the elderly American tourists arrive to drift aimlessly
amongst the plants with their cameras unsheathed, leaning over
and dutifully reading the labels on the flowers, peering into the

small white chapel for hire, waiting for the tea shop to open, the botanical garden is indeed a lovely place to be. Here nature is respected and controlled, colourful and perfect. The countless varieties of flowers and shrubs are impeccably ordered and tended.

It's only manmade touches that spoil the peaceful, Eden-like atmosphere. There are small signs here and there, admonishing the guests to behave properly. Please Take Nothing But Pictures, Kill Nothing But Time, Leave Nothing But Footprints.

Aphorisms about plants hang from the limbs of tiny trees. Sure enough, Joyce Kilmer's "Trees" can be found over by the red Oriental-style gazebo. "I think that I shall never see, A poem as lovely as a tree." Nearby is a place called Little Mountain with another sign. The hillock, guests are informed, has an elevation of 4,457 mm.

There are tiny bridges, a Dutch clock tower with chimes, a delightful little tea room, benches, more bridges, some ponds, a windmill and a splendid array of flowers. The plants are all tagged with their common and Latin names. This allows the would-be gardener to know what type of plant he or she might want to purchase later.

When John Massot first planned his Bota Garden Centre in 1982, as Bill Vander Zalm has noted in a deftly-written letter to the Agricultural Land Commission (ALC), "the idea was to create a learning centre for the horticulturists or hobbyists locally as well as an attraction for tourists from all over the world. We hold to this concept and continue to expand on this very worthwhile goal by carefully continuing the labeling process of trees, shrubs, bulbs and flowers and designing in a way that will allow the home hobbyist to create a similar display in their own garden."[3]

The reason the plants are labelled in Fantasy Garden is also because it's part of the original agreement with the ALC. To win a zoning concession, the garden was touted as an educational facility. "We are also proposing to hold regular gardening clinics or seminars in the new conservatory and the meeting room of the proposed new restaurant-souvenir complex," wrote Vander Zalm in 1985.[4] If the ALC turned down Vander Zalm's zoning

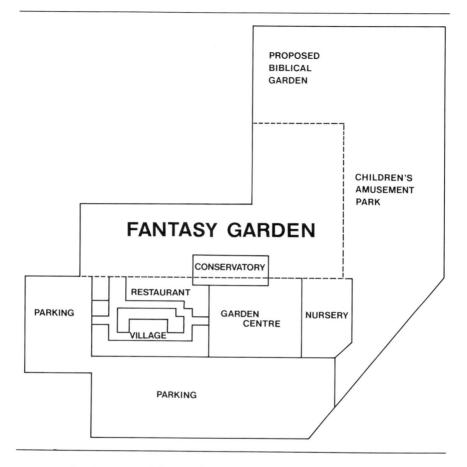

proposal, they would not just be turning down a commercial enterprise, they would be discouraging an important institution of horticultural learning.

"The conservatory and meeting room, as well as the inner plaza of the restaurant-souvenir complex will also be available to BC garden clubs for competition and displays."[5] Unfortunately the best-laid plots of gardeners and politicians can oft-times go astray. By September of 1986 any indications to the casual visitor that educational programs were offered at Fantasy Garden, or would be offered, were extremely difficult to find. No doubt Vander Zalm plans to rectify this situation when construction of his new conservatory and restaurant-souvenir complex is completed.

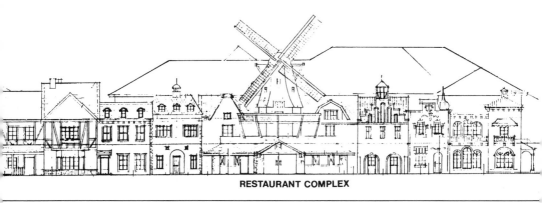

RESTAURANT COMPLEX

After stating his altruistic intentions to the Agricultural Land Commission in 1985, Vander Zalm added two lines more. "Neither Mr. Massot nor ourselves have, so far, been as successful as we must be in attracting tourists because we lack certain facilities."[6] Although there has been a confusing lack of clarity as to what those certain facilities would be, a number of tourist-oriented attractions were added to the complex during 1986

Fantasy Garden's frontal facade boasts an enormous windmill atop a European-styled "village,"a mini shopping centre which Vander Zalm, contrary to his original undertakings, wanted to lease out to other proprietors. Richmond Council bent over backwards to accommodate Vander Zalm, applying to the Agricultural Land Reserve to have Fantasy Garden World excluded from the Reserve.

Behind this shopping-mall-with-a-difference is a cavernous glassed-in restaurant. "Our restaurant provides for entertainment and the opportunity to watch things being made as well as a chance to eat it or take it home," Vander Zalm says. "This is not unusual as many restaurants provide this same service as well as 'take-out.' Our restaurant complex however is fashioned to be similar to such facilities as the Nut Tree Restaurant between Sacramento and San Francisco on Highway 80 in the United States."[7]

Alongside the 200-foot-wide village complex is a 195-foot-wide Art Knapp's Plantland store. Bill and Lillian Vander Zalm have a joint venture arrangement with Frank Van Hest, owner of

GARDEN CENTRE

the Art Knapp's store in Steveston, to operate this outlet. Leased to Van Hest, as operator, this store gives Fantasy Garden World a sliding-scale percentage of gross sales. The Vander Zalms struck a deal whereby they receive 6% on the first million in sales each year, 5% on the second million, 4% on the third million and 3% on all sales above that. Hest agreed to pay the cost of the building, plus site preparation work and various development charges. Arrangements may have been made for Van Hest's tenancy before Vander Zalm received clearance from the ALC to rent out property, according to Richmond alderman Harold Steves.

Next to the large store is an unnamed amusement park. This kiddies' playland can be seen from Highway 99 bordering it. Hundreds upon hundreds of vehicles pass the site each hour.

This banal amusement compound for small children looks like it was designed by an insurance agent (Please Do Not Climb On The Train. Thanks!) and an accountant (Visit Our Toy Store And Gift Shop). There is a tiresome pony ride with several listless little creatures forced to tread monotonously forward in sawdust, tethered to a turning wheel with metal spokes. There is a mound of leftover fill converted into a goat hollow. There is an automated mini-windmill that turns relentlessly. There is a makeshift Noah's Ark with nothing inside but a tape-recorded story ("The Ark floated for six months. Finally on the seventh month . . .").

There is no fun. There is no imagination. Walt Disney would weep.

A glossy tourist brochure advertises a stocked trout lake. There is a tiny basin. For a price, children can dangle a line. Rod rental, one ticket: 15 minutes. Each fish caught: $2. Someone has scrawled an official warning sign at the Fantasy Fishing Hole: Must take fish caught, extra bait 25 cents. The picnic tables are cement.

Parents try to persuade their children to try some of the pokey rides, the cornball attractions. But nobody's heart is in it.

The mind rebels. Never mind that this Bill Vander Zalm has bent rules for the advancement of Fantasy Gardens or, as minister, denied money to handicapped people on welfare, or sold his soul to the media. *This* is serious. The Fantasy Garden amusement park may look good from the highway at 60 m.p.h. with a miniature train tooting around its perimeter. But up close, this playground is a wasteland of uninventive hucksterism, so wholesome it's sterile, so unoriginal it's frightening. Seven million for this! screams the brain.

The other developed area in Fantasy Garden World, behind the 10-foot-high hedge surrounding the garden, is the unfinished biblical theme park. In a letter dated April 12, 1986, Vander Zalm wrote, "The Fantasy Garden World Project, in brief, is an established but improved botanical garden with a newly added Biblical Garden which features Biblical plants and fifteen life-size statue scenes depicting the Life of Christ."

In fact, the biblical garden remained unfinished and unopened to the public in October 1986, with no landscaped "biblical" plants in evidence. Vander Zalm appears to have put his efforts into completing the European Village shopping centre complex, leaving the inspirational statues of Jesus, obtained from the Block Brothers 108 Ranch, out in the cold.

About the only thing fantastic about Fantasy Garden World — beyond the beautiful botanical garden created by John Massot — is the story of how Bill Vander Zalm managed to get his tourist trap built on agricultural-zoned land in the first place.

In the beginning, there was the NDP. During the socialists' reign in power for 1,200 days, from August 30, 1972 to December 11, 1975, barely three weeks into their first legislative term, Premier Dave Barrett's cabinet passed an order-in-council designating large sections of farmland "frozen." The Land Commission Act was introduced into the House on February 22, 1973. Developers predictably howled. The NDP held its frozen ground.

Although it was initially viewed as controversial in the early 1970s, this legislation to ensure that sprawling urban populations did not blacktop the means to feed themselves was quickly emulated around North America. Ontario followed suit in June 1973. Prince Edward Island did the same in March 1974.

Vindicated, the NDP maintained their resolve. So when it was discovered that land bought in Richmond by the Insurance Corporation of British Columbia from BSM Holdings for $550,000 was in the Agricultural Land Reserve (ALR), ICBC was quickly dissuaded by Richmond MLA Harold Steves from building an ICBC claims centre on good farmland.

The land in question was located at the corner of Steveston Highway and No. 5 Road. The freeway connecting Vancouver and Seattle bordered the property to the east. To the west was a subdivision. To the south was a gas station. Technically the land was in a corridor clearly designated for agricultural use only, so the NDP decided to use the prime farmland for allotment gardens.

Richmond townhouse and apartment dwellers used the land to grow vegetables in small, separately tended plots. The NDP was replaced by Social Credit in 1975. As the composition of the Agricultural Land Commission changed over the years, so would the fate of the 8.5 hectares change.

The land was sold by ICBC in 1978 to John Massot's Bota Gardens. ICBC took a $99,000 loss on the deal when the new owner obtained the deed for $451,000.

Massot tried for some time to obtain permission for commercial operations on the land. His proposal for a commercial garden with a tiny garden shop and tiny restaurant was tabled in November 1981. It was not until January 1982 that he succeeded in getting permission to build a botanical garden with an incidental restaurant and gift shop. A new zoning class was created for the land, Agricultural II, which would later be applied to golf courses in the Agricultural Land Reserve.

The spring of 1982 also saw the "unfreezing" of 132 acres of Prince George farmland owned by the co-campaign manager of Labour minister Jack Heinrich's 1979 election race, Ted Moffat, against the wishes of the local mayor, the local planner and the Agricultural Land Commission itself. The Environment and Land Use Committee of the Social Credit cabinet was increasingly becoming a major arbitrator of agricultural land use appeals.

In March of 1983 Richmond Council, in conjunction with the Land Commission, granted Bota Gardens owner John Massot a one-year permit under the Soil Conservation Act to fill a portion of the property to prevent drainage problems for agricultural purposes. In August and in September of 1983, Massot also received — unbeknownst to Richmond Council at the time — permission directly from the Agricultural Land Commission to commence fill operations for non-agricultural reasons. These permits from the ALC alone allowed Massot to expand a 0.6-hectare parking lot to 1.6 hectares.

Harold Steves, now a Richmond alderman, maintains that the Richmond Council might not have approved the permits for an expanded parking lot if they had known in 1983 that the property was not going to be used for agricultural purposes (i.e. a garden only). At the time, standard procedure for property owners with land in the ALR was to first apply to the municipality involved for permits to place fill on the property. The municipality forwarded the application to the Land Commission, where it was approved or rejected. The Land Commission returned its findings to the municipality for final approval.

The bypassing of Richmond Municipal Council for a permit to dump fill for a parking lot was the thin edge of the wedge. This technical break with routine was not an issue in 1983 because John Massot never began expanding the parking lot. But Bill Vander Zalm did, a year after the permits were issued.

In July 1984 Bill Vander Zalm purchased John Massot's botanical garden for about $1.7 million. Massot, through Bota, took $760,000 of the purchase price as a mortgage on the property. The property was to become security for a $2-million line of credit from the Canadian Imperial Bank of Commerce to Fantasy Garden World.

When Richmond municipal officials were driving by the Bota Gardens site in the fall of 1984, they saw tons of cement and asphalt-strewn rubble being piled on the farmland. According to the original landfill permit issued to John Massot and approved by Richmond Council on March 7, 1983, valid for one year from the date of issue, the fill could contain no construction debris or other deleterious materials. In order to ensure this was the case, all fill had to be inspected and approved by a soil specialist prior to its being placed on the property. In order to facilitate scheduling of a soil inspection, a minimum of five working days notice was required before using fill from any uninspected and unapproved source. The placement of the fill had to be in accordance with the soil placement application under terms set by the Soil Conservation Act and was the responsibility of the applicant.

"The land is probably destroyed," said Steves, "I doubt it could be recovered for agricultural purposes." Upon discovering that the new owner was using a former owner's year-old permit to dump non-agricultural fill with some sort of permission from the Land Commission, Richmond Council requested a report from their staff on October 22 as to how this manoeuvre had been okayed without their knowledge.

By this time the former NDP MLA Steves had gone public with his indignation, and Bill Vander Zalm was also officially in the running for mayor of Vancouver. "Everything's been done above board," said Land Commission agrologist Brian McBride.[8] But the requested report from Richmond municipal officials took much longer than expected. The report was not received until after the Vancouver mayoralty election, on February 6.

Vander Zalm began to come before Richmond Council for permission to erect minor auxiliary buildings — an ark, a gazebo, a railroad, a railroad station. The Richmond planners discovered that Bill Vander Zalm was very persuasive when describing what constitutes an auxiliary building. The A2 zoning required that buildings be owned and operated by Vander Zalm.

By the summer of 1985 Vander Zalm was making his pitch for a large restaurant. The land was still clearly zoned agricultural. To help convince the Agricultural Land Commission Vander Zalm said, "A venture such as ours is a tremendous benefit to British Columbians."[9]

The inspiration to build their own tourist restaurant, equivalent to one the Vander Zalms had visited during a California vacation, had only one drawback. The zoning previous owner John Massot had received allowed only for a snack bar to keep the kiddies from getting hungry while families toured his botanical garden, not for a large commercial enterprise which would be a traffic draw in its own right. Vander Zalm had to twist the arms of the Agricultural Land Commission and Richmond Council — and bulldoze his way over legal obstacles — to erect his dream restaurant on land clearly zoned for agricultural use.

"John Massot obviously created the impression that a small restaurant to serve those already on the premises was really what was required," Vander Zalm wrote, "and thus a 'Bill's Eatery' or 'Lil's Take-out' could be permitted while a more tourist-oriented facility could be in question.

"We are convinced that such a facility as we propose will not only serve those already in the garden but also provide an alternative for spending some time and enjoying one's visit should the weather, as it so often does, turn suddenly bad."[10] Did the churlish land commission want to leave tourists out in the rain? Did it wish to crush Bill Vander Zalm's master plan to heighten the common man's awareness of things horticultural?

Vander Zalm had notified the ALC that Fantasy Garden World was "definitely here to stay."[11] He had said he "would prefer to work in close cooperation with you and the Municipality for the benefit of all British Columbians and thus seek your endorsation."[12] The statement indicated there was another route for him, apart from cooperating with the ALC. Perhaps there was an implied threat he could concentrate his formidable political talents on making trouble for them at higher levels.

Bill Vander Zalm received a tentative go-ahead for his less-than-incidental restaurant complex on December 6, 1985. The restaurant became operational in 1986, catering to large groups such as weddings. The European Village Restaurant is approximately six times larger than the original site permitted by the ALC when John Massot owned the property.

The Agricultural Land Commission was also urged to feel sorry for Bill Vander Zalm, as a private entrepreneur who charged admission, competing against public-subsidized garden operations. "Our competition, although we don't necessarily view them as such, are places like the Van Dusen Gardens, Queen Elizabeth Park, Stanley Park etc., all of which are located on land granted them at no charge and on which they pay no taxes. Also their advertising is done through the media by way of public service announcements, again at no charge.

"The private ownership makes us tremendously aggressive in wanting to so please the visitors so that they would return again and again."[13]

Excluding the original botanical gardens — which adhere somewhat to agricultural guidelines — the area for commercial developments at Fantasy Garden World appears to dwarf the originally approved commercial developments of Bota Gardens. In fact, Massot's original snack-bar-tourist-shop exemption from strictly agricultural use specified a square footage, according to Harold Steves, that could be fitted into Vander Zalm's Family Fun Park, European Village, Art Knapp's Plantland and biblical statuary park twenty times. This is what makes Fantasy Garden World fantastic.

As Richmond director of planning Ron Mann has noted, "Individually all of these projects bear some relation to the show garden theme but the combined effect is a fairly sophisticated tourist-oriented complex with a garden theme. The question to be decided then is to whether to try to curb the development by a strict interpretation of all applicable bylaws and regulations or to recognize that the development has already exceeded reasonable limits for a botanical show garden in the ALR and to remove the land from the ALR . . ."[14]

Fantasy Garden World made both the ALC and Richmond Council appear inept. How had they allowed this juggernaut developer to roll over them so easily? In plain view of a million Lower Mainlanders, Bill and Lillian Vander Zalm's personal Disneyland had sprung up in just four years on land that was supposedly being protected for agricultural use. It was clear proof that some people were better at getting the rules to bend than others.

To redeem themselves, Richmond Council at least tried to tax Fantasy Garden World as a commercial development, but Vander Zalm appealed his tax assessment, arguing— successfully—that his taxes ought to be reduced because by council's own definition he was supposed to be an agricultural operation. Wasn't that what they were telling him? It was Catch-22 in reverse. Vander Zalm hired Golden Ears Appraisal of Maple Ridge to argue his case for a reassessment in order to reduce his taxes. In a letter dated June 19, 1986 the agent for the Fantasy Garden appeal, Clark Chilton, received good news from Deputy Assessor L.G. Nelson regarding Assessment Roll No. R-030-683-001. Nelson informed Chilton that he was submitting a revised recommendation to the Assessment Appeal Board which would substantially lower Vander Zalm's taxes. Later, Chilton would make news when it appeared his (unsuccessful) application for a coveted position with the taxation department might have received unfair advantage—a patronage question within days of the Socred election win.

Vander Zalm told me, "The land was in the Agricultural Land Reserve. They wanted to leave it in the Agricultural Land Reserve, and leave the agricultural designation, but tax it for commercial. In order for land to qualify for agricultural land status, one could argue on the basis that if it's in the reserve, then it should qualify for that in any event. But that's not what the rules say. The rules say that if you produce x number of dollars from the land, that allows you to get the agricultural status. And it's relatively little. It's like $1,600."

"The ideal situation would be for me to have a commercial activity on agricultural land. If I could carry on with that front piece and everything in the land reserve, my taxes would probably be no more than possibly $25 to $40 thousand. Whereas now I know already the taxes will be more in the order of $125 to $140 thousand. Because of the designation. So the municipal council is really the one, and rightly so, who said, hey, that's a commercial use. You're not going to grow potatoes where the blacktop sits and the buildings stand, so you should be commercial. I never fought them on that."

Still an undeclared candidate, Vander Zalm told a Prince George audience on June 13 that he would definitely clear up any potential conflict-of-interest problems before joining the leadership fray. The next week in Victoria he repeated this assertion, emphasizing his view that it was not the public's interest which was at risk, but his own.

On June 18, he said, "I've got an application before the Agricultural Land Reserve and, unless I can get that resolved, I won't run. I'm not sure my business would get a fair break if I place myself in a position where I was continually being scrutinized."[15]

Vander Zalm had talked himself into a corner. He couldn't declare unless he came to some sort of resolution of the conflict problem, and he had to declare soon if he was going to at all. So he sidestepped. On June 20 he announced that he had transferred Fantasy Garden World to Lillian. Leaving the clear impression this was just an initial step which would be followed soon by something more decisive, Vander Zalm officially became the twelfth and final leadership candidate for Bill Bennett's job. He made the announcement at Fantasy Garden World in a Sunday news conference attended by Surrey MLAs Rita Johnson and Bill Reid, plus North Vancouver-Seymour MLA Jack Davis.

Two weeks later he was still acknowledging that the conflict remained a concern. On July 7 he said, "Let's face it, man and wife are one, we're together on it, and that's something I would want to address in the not-too-distant future."[16]

On July 22 as the convention's day of decision approached, he reaffirmed he would likely sell Fantasy Garden if he was chosen premier. "My assessment right now, although I could look at it later too, but my assessment right now is that I would, at some time very shortly after taking on the premiership, dispose in one way or another of [Fantasy Garden] . . .

" . . . Because whether it's in my name, or my wife's name, it's the same thing. I can't con anybody on that, now would I?" They were prophetic words.

Vander Zalm's solution to the Fantasy Garden conflict apparently was not an issue in the minds of the majority of Social Credit conventioneers at Whistler, BC. "Short of selling it or giving it away," he said, "you can't resolve the conflict. All you can do is tell people what you're doing. If I became premier . . . if there were a real expression from the public that they thought it was wrong, I would simply drop it [the application]."[17]

This was to become his position on the whole issue of conflict in the ensuing provincial election. Tell the people what you are doing and give them the privilege of judging, not some bureaucrat. It sounds very generous, but since disclosure legislation had already been brought in by a previous government (against Vander Zalm's bitter opposition) he was adding nothing new, while taking away the slight protection that was provided by the Bennett administration's policy of blind trusts. Under Vander Zalm's new let-it-all-hang-out approach would the suspected official have to respond in some way to expressed public concern, or could he just shrug it off and keep forging ahead with his conflicting businesses as long as his government could manage to keep winning elections? Vander Zalm's own actions, taking no further steps to resolve his conflict after being selected premier on July 30, seemed to indicate the latter.

On August 20 Vander Zalm began to say that he couldn't sell Fantasy Garden World even if he wanted to, at least not right away, because Lillian had become "too attached to it."[18]

"Consignment Bill" 's most remarkable victory in the construction of Fantasy Garden World occurred on August 22, 1986. That's the day the Agricultural Land Commission wrote a letter saying his commercial operations at Fantasy Garden World had been exempted from the Agricultural Land Reserve.

On August 22, R.P. Murdoch drafted his letter to the Vander Zalms regarding Parcel 1, Section 31, Block 4 North, Range 5 West, New Westminster District, Plan 72036 — otherwise known as Fantasy Garden World.

"With reference to the southern portion of the property, it is the Commission's opinion that the current state of development, as previously approved under Section 20(1) of the Act, permanently eliminates the opportunity for agricultural utilization. While it is recognized that the uses of the northern and southern portion of the land are operationally linked, the type of use and intensity of structural development within the two areas remain quite distinct.

"In light of the foregoing and in accordance with Section 14 of the Act, the Commission has allowed the exclusion of 3.8 hectares. . . For the most part the 3.8 hectare area approved for exclusion encompasses the major on site structures and parking area. . . with the knowledge that the remaining northern portion of the property and adjacent lands will be retained in the ALR."[19] The news that Bill .Vander Zalm's commercial operations were "unfrozen" and that he could progress with subletting parts of his development to tenants, reached the public on August 27, 1986. Defending the ALC's decision, the commission chairman maintained, "He didn't get what he asked for."[20]

In fact, Vander Zalm's initial application for zoning changes "was to simply deal with the part up front. . . And that was not even an application to the land commission, that was an application for zoning. It was Richmond Council which required us to make an application to the land commission." Vander Zalm had applied back in April to Richmond for more freedom to develop the 3.8 hectares which the ALC exempted for him.

In October 1986, amidst the BC provincial election campaign, the tax assessment figures for Fantasy Garden World became available. The 1984 assessment for Vander Zalm's investment had been $804,000. As of September 30, 1986, the new assessment for Lillian Vander Zalm's Fantasy Garden World was $4.95 million. With the Agricultural Land Commission's decision, the assessed value of Fantasy Garden World and its incremental developments had jumped more than $4 million. Vander Zalm, who generally tended to take a very optimistic view of the value of his assets when setting about to impress the banks or the public, had been trumpeting the Garden's value as $7 million. After the ALR exemption the *Globe & Mail* quoted him as saying it had gone up to $10 million. The awkward predicament had been resolved with a very considerable incidental appreciation in the value of Vander Zalm's property. By managing to have his land removed from the ALR, Bill Vander Zalm had put millions of dollars in his pocket. He'd paved paradise and put up a parking lot on agricultural land. But it wasn't agricultural land any more. So that meant everything was okay.

"I think that should finish it as an issue," he said.[21]

It didn't finish it. During the election campaign the *Globe and Mail* ran a story revealing that Fantasy Garden World Inc. and Vander Nurseries Inc. were in hock to the Canadian Imperial Bank of Commerce for $5.7 million. Pointing out that the CIBC "has been the bank of the province since the early fifties," the article raised the possibility of a conflict in Vander Zalm's position as both premier and Finance minister on the one hand, and private creditor on the other hand. Vander Zalm said, "I've never thought of it." Finance ministry spokesman Dick Melville said, "I just don't see any room for conflict." Others did, however. Under questioning by BCTV's Jack Webster, Vander Zalm allowed that he would consider stepping back from the Finance ministry if public feeling so indicated, again without suggesting how the public should register its feeling, or how he would decide when there was enough to act on.

The bank debt issue focussed attention on an interesting question I raised in an earlier chapter. What, really, was the state of the Vander Zalm finances at the time he became premier? He had apparently cast whatever nest eggs he had all in the capacious basket of Fantasy Garden World. How viable was this hodgepodge of hucksterism, horticulture and holiness from a strictly business standpoint? Lillian and Bill were both signatories to the bank debentures. Were they really showing the same sort of debt-equity ratio the bank would demand of thee and me for a $5.7 million loan? I'm not much of a financial analyst, but I have a brother, John Twigg, who knows what BC looks like from the perspective of a premier/finance minister, having served as press secretary under Dave Barrett, and who has spent the last ten years writing on financial matters for the Regina *Leader-Post* and *Equity* magazine. I knew he had been following Vander Zalm's progress with interest, so I asked him to cast his practised eye over the Fantasy Garden World operation and give me a report:

Fantasy Garden World hosted perhaps half a million visitors in 1986 and probably most of them walked out in a blissful daze, so charmed they wouldn't wonder how the business was being run. The plants and flowers are indeed beautiful; their artful arrangement imbues the vast site with a distinct almost magical aura. But what's the cash flow and what's the debt? Are Bill and Lillian Vander Zalm making any money? Do they pay their bills on time? Do their workers like to stay with them?

Those kinds of questions, routine in the business press, are not always asked of privately-owned companies like Fantasy Garden World Inc., and even less often are they answered. There is a right to privacy.

But when the private owner suddenly becomes a public figure, especially the premier, the right to privacy is suddenly diminished. The public has a right to know what his holdings are to be confident that the office-holder isn't using the privileges of power to feather his personal nest.

As well, there is a secondary right of the public, and that is to know something of how the office-holder runs his business, because presumably the way he runs his own shop will be like the way he'll run the government, which of course affects the entire citizenry.

When you approach Fantasy Garden as a business you generate a lot of questions. At the door you pay $4 for adults and $2 for kids, not bad for the scope of the attraction. But if you ask for a receipt you can get a strange look and then a fluttering as the nice lady cashier digs for a little book of blank forms and asks for your name. No ma'am, I want Fantasy Garden's name on the receipt to show I've been here.

Unbelievable as it sounds, Fantasy Garden World doesn't appear to keep track of its attendance. "It just all goes in as cash flow," says Juanita Moffat, the Vander Zalm daughter left running the place while Mom and Dad were out on the election campaign trail. But by pulling together bits and pieces from the public record, a fairly complete picture of the situation can be formed, though the past is a little murky on exactly where Vander Zalm made his reputed millions.

Vander Zalm in August 1986 disclosed his assets and liabilities in the normal fashion of a Member of the Legislative Assembly, just names but no amounts. He noted he probably didn't have to because technically he wasn't an MLA, but to set a good example and help sell the "open government" image, he did.

There were a few mistakes and blind leads. The City of Penticton's tax debt was listed even though it had been paid. Things like his customs broker (Milne & Craighead) and accountant (Thorne, Ernst & Whinney in Surrey) were listed with obviously ongoing accounts, and there were at least a dozen suppliers of construction materials, again ongoing. The Township of Richmond was on the list (as of July 31) but by October it was long-since paid and Richmond staff said there was never a problem.

More strange were the government creditors, including Revenue Canada Taxation from his 1985 tax return, BC sales tax, Receiver-General for employee deductions and Workers Compensation Board. While there were no amounts given, the list suggests Mr. Vander Zalm is not exactly quick to pay his debts to government. And, in the case of the sales tax, when he became minister of Finance he became responsible for collecting that debt from himself, an amusing conundrum if not a conflict of interest.

Phone calls to some of the smaller creditors almost invariably produced assurances there was no problem; Bill was a good ongoing client; if he hadn't paid a bill yet he soon would, and so on. There was an obvious desire to not say anything that might jeopardize the future.

The exception was Delta Aggregates Ltd., where owner Gary Green willingly described "a little disagreement we had with him." But when he realized what he'd done he pleaded to not be quoted. "I'm a member of the Roadbuilders Association," he protested, explaining any negative comments could adversely affect his access to future government business.

Mr. Green's tale is important because it illustrates what is apparently a recurring trait in Vander Zalm's business practices. Delta Aggregates quoted a price to deliver sand to Fantasy Garden World. Green thought the cartage was separate, but Vander Zalm thought it was included. When the invoice went in it wasn't paid. "We ended up eating half of it," Green said, indicating he and Vander Zalm ended up splitting the cartage bill. Green refused to disclose his loss. "We've made our peace with him now," he said.

Scotty Robertson, another sand supplier, had a similar problem. Robertson, a 69-year-old small independent, had a long association with the Garden: "I put the very first load of sand on that site," he said, mentioning he made $84,000 in 1978 working for the Garden's original owner John Massot, a relationship that continued through 1985 when Massot's son Dominic stayed on as the garden manager for Vander Zalm.

But when Delta came along with a lower quote on some sand, Robertson decided not to match it, complaining he was being callously shut out of the business. And when he put in his windup claim for $9,000 it was challenged, apparently because a Vander Zalm foreman thought Robertson had been showing up late.

Robertson spent several weeks gathering proof that he had indeed been on the job as required. When he confronted Bill Vander Zalm in his office, he said Vander Zalm turned and walked away. When Robertson went to the municipal hall to register a lien, the bill was finally paid in full, two and a half months later. "It screwed my whole year," said an obviously bitter Robertson.

Bill Vander Zalm's legal battles to trim costs for Fantasy

Garden World also include his refusal to pay full fees to a Langley design-consulting firm, Buckley, Graham and Kim Inc. The company provided design and other services during the construction of the Fantasy Garden conservatory. In a suit filed in August of 1986, the Langley firm claimed Vander Zalm had paid them only $24,000 and that $30,515 was still due and owing. An agreement between the firm and Vander Zalm had specified that the consultants were entitled to seven per cent of the construction cost of the conservatory. "Despite repeated demands by the consultants, no proper accounting of the cost of construction has been provided by Vander Zalm, which accounting he is obliged to give to the consultants under the agreement," the suit states.[22]

When the author of this book asked him about the suit, he said, ". . .if you're doing a lot of business, you're bound to get into that sort of thing. I also believe that if you're right, you fight it all the way through. There isn't one [legal controversy] where I thought, or where I went in thinking, I can win because of circumstance or evidence. But I really went in because I believed that I was right and that was the thing to do, to stand up to what it is that I was fighting for.

"So in the case of the engineering firm in Langley, if it costs more to fight them than what actually comes out of it in the end, fine and dandy. I want to see it through. Because it's right."

While Vander Zalm hasn't filed a defence yet, and there apparently were some construction problems on the conservatory job, that case and the two others illustrate that Vander Zalm is tight with his money and would rather go to court than pay a bill he doesn't think is fair.

His do-it-as-cheap-as-possible approach also shows up in the construction of Fantasy Garden World's Streets of Europe project, where Vander Zalm is his own general contractor, bringing in non-union tradesmen, often from the Fraser Valley. "It's a series of independent jobs,"said construction manager Don Sieber, who took over from original manager and project designer Chris Postma, whose sudden departure a month before completion was not immediately explainable.

"Nothing was spec'd out," said Sieber, indicating that

construction specifications were designed as needed, which illustrates Vander Zalm's penchant for charging ahead with projects and catching up on the paperwork later.

The do-it-cheap approach also was exemplified by a pile of small-diameter steel pipe waiting to be installed. It was plainly marked as being from South Korea. It is the same cheap pipe that Canadian steelmakers claim is being dumped in Canada, forcing Ipsco Inc. to curtail production from its Port Moody plant. It wasn't a large amount of pipe, but it was enough to make a mockery of Vander Zalm's statement he likes White Spot owner Peter Toigo because Toigo "makes his money in BC and keeps it in BC."

But such concerns are picayune compared with another creditor on Vander Zalm's disclosure, the Canadian Imperial Bank of Commerce, which appears in four different places. The Commerce is obviously "my bank" to Bill. A check at the Corporations Office reveals that the Commerce lent Vander Nurseries Inc. $700,000 in July 1984 (when he bought the Garden for $1.7 million from John Massot) and another $2 million in July 1985, which is about when Vander Zalm began an ambitious expansion of the commercial side as well as the huge biblical theme park. Meanwhile the Land Titles Office reveals the Commerce lent another $1 million to Fantasy Garden World Inc. in July 1985 and on July 16, 1986 (just after Vander Zalm decided to run for leader) it advanced another $2 million. In other words the CIBC has about $5 million invested in Bill Vander Zalm.

Another mortgage of $760,000 dating from July 1984 is held by John Massot's Bota Gardens Ltd., a situation Massot refuses to discuss.

The land title also shows $1 million owing to the Bank of Montreal in the name of Hestia Productions, which is owned by Frank van Hest, who operates the Art Knapp's Plantland on land leased from Fantasy Garden World.

There are rumours of other anonymous investors in the Garden project, possibly wealthy Dutch farmers from the Fraser Valley, but there is no evidence. There also may be unsecured personal loans that wouldn't show. But even the official list indicates that Vander Zalm is heavily indebted, with probably more than $6 million owing on Fantasy Garden World Inc. and Vander Nurseries Inc.

Seemingly Vander Zalm had a sympathetic banker. This puts a new light on a comment by supporter Bill Reid shortly after the Whistler leadership convention, intended as a suggestion that Vander Zalm understands small business, that one of Vander Zalm's attributes is that "he knows what it is to deal with the bank."

Does the Garden have sufficient cash flow to service such a debt as well as cover operating costs and pay for construction? Probably not.

There were 70 people on the Fantasy Garden World payroll in October, 1986 (after the seasonal layoff of part-timers), about half of them construction workers. There are only eight people in the garden crew, with the bulk of the regular staff employed on the commercial side doing jobs such as servicing the kitchen and three banquet halls on site.

Assuming an average of 50 employees making about $20,000 each, that gives Vander Zalm an annual payroll of at least $1 million, and probably higher because in August he referred to Fantasy Garden World having 85 employees. Taking the rough formula that wages are half to two-thirds of operating costs suggests he probably pays another $1 million a year on things like bulbs and paint.

Assuming a debt service cost of about $600,000 a year, that means Vander Zalm needs revenues of about $3 million a year just to break even — and before paying for any construction.

While Fantasy Garden World won't release attendance figures, Vander Zalm in January 1986 told the Vancouver *Sun* he expected 400,000 visitors during Expo, while Juanita said it was an "excellent" year that was above targets. If we give them 500,000 visits and assume each one was an adult the revenue is $2 million.

Fantasy Garden World of course has other sources of revenue, but they are small. The conservatory rents out for $1,200, the other halls for less, with different rates in different seasons. We'll assume 200 bookings a year for $200,000, stretching to $500,000 with catering. A popular wedding chapel on the grounds rents out for about $150 to a party of 40, with admission included. It does two or three weddings a day on weekends, in good weather. Or, peanuts.

Another source of revenue is the sliding royalty on sales in the adjacent Art Knapp's outlet, which might be worth $200,000 a year. And then there are cards and placemats and stickers and plaques with aphorisms on them. Maybe another $100,000, for a total of something less than $3 million.

Thus Vander Zalm urgently needs more commercial development to make the project viable. He needs banquets with liquor service. He needs trinket sales. And he needs more traffic. But in 1986 Fantasy Garden World was probably living on debt.

That shortage of cash probably explains why construction at the site slowed noticeably this summer. The $500,000 biblical theme park was meant to be finished by June, in time for Expo. The European village commercial development was supposed to be done by the summer but in October it was shooting for December 1, probably just in time for the Christmas retail trade. Why wasn't it done? "It was just a combination of things," said Juanita. "There were a lot of details to fit together."

One of those key details was a rezoning to take the commercial side out of the Agricultural Land Reserve. That came through from the Land Commission in August, just weeks after the Commerce had loaned another $2 million and just days after Vander Zalm became premier. Richmond Council effectively ratified the change on October 14, which was expected because it had applied for the rezoning in the first place, ostensibly to increase its tax take. (One of the Richmond aldermen was Nick Loenen, a Dutch immigrant who became Vander Zalm's successful running mate in the 1986 provincial election. Another was anti-abortion crusader Tillie Marxreiter, who became Vander Zalm's campaign manager. — Ed.)

The ALC decision triggered a 600% jump in Fantasy Garden's assessed value, allowing Vander Zalm to borrow more money, or at least giving the lender more comfort because he suddenly had more collateral, and it's possible the Commerce only made the loan knowing the rezoning was in progress. What can be said for sure is that the Commerce has carefully registered its claims. While Vander Zalm fretted about the possible negative impact of his candidacy on his business, it's possible that it actually helped him obtain the $2-million extension from the Commerce. What banker in his right mind would foreclose on a politician in mid-campaign, let alone one who could become top dog in the province?

There is an even more compelling reason why the Commerce might extend its loan to a questionably funded project and that is to safeguard its long-cherished role as the provincial government's lead bank. Shortly after Vander Zalm became not only premier but also finance minister, the province floated $130 million of debentures through the Commerce.

"That's a very lucrative account, one that one wouldn't want to lose," says one Vancouver banker, who wishes to remain anonymous for obvious reasons. "It's quite common in banking, you have a conflict between a big account and a small side business and of course you approve the loan [to the small business] even if you know you shouldn't [because of the debt-equity ratio], but I wouldn't want to be the guy handling the Fantasy Garden World account.

"Being premier may have already helped his investment," the banker went on, noting Vander Zalm's meeting halls also will have an advantage over others in attracting meetings for major corporate clients, such as companies that supply the government.

So our man Bill is a bit of a wheeler-dealer and perhaps more of an dreamer than a realist when it comes to business plans. He's the guy with the concept, and he doubles as pitchman, but his ideas can be overly ambitious, his judgement poor and his timing premature. Slap it together and get it done, don't pay any more than you have to and don't worry if you stretch the rules, just try not to break them. Unfortunately, reticence, caution and humility have not been hallmarks of Vander Zalm the businessman. He's developing an asset worth perhaps $10 million and yet his staffing is helter-skelter, his financing is piecemeal, and his planning vague.

The taxpayers of British Columbia can only hope Premier Bill

Vander Zalm will prove to be more prudent and disciplined in developing their assets. He obviously has ideas. If he surrounds himself with good advisers they might be able to keep him in bounds while harvesting his creativity. But if he gets loose and goes charging off on tangents, speaking while he thinks and not looking before he leaps? Heaven help us. Fantasy Garden World is just a little peanut stand compared with the complicated apparatus that Vander Zalm runs now.

John Twigg

Vander Zalm's lookalike grandfather Nicholas Klaas (centre) supervising sewer job in Noordwykerhout.

Bill "Wim" Vander Zalm's graduation photo from high school annual.

Veteran Vander-watcher Pat Brady at Vander Zalm family homestead in Bradner.

The "Kennedyesque" First Couple of Surrey, 1971.

Groucho-Marxists score direct hit on Human Resources minister, 1977. Paul Little photo.

Vander Zalm into his shovel act at 1978 convention, getting bids of $525.

Harcourt vs. Vander Zalm, 1984 — Round 1 to Harcourt. Peter Battisone photo.

Premier Bill Bennett congratulates the candidate he least wanted to succeed him, July 30, 1986. Heather Conn photo.

Bud Smith stuns the experts at Whistler by throwing to Vander Zalm. Gerry Kahrmann photo.

11

THE ROAD TO WHISTLER
Running on Empty

"Charisma without substance is a dangerous thing."
Kim Campbell
Socred leadership candidate

Skiers anxious to hit the exhilarating and slippery slopes of World-Cup-class Whistler Mountain are often fatally injured in their haste to travel the 90 minutes of twisting highway from Vancouver. There are frequent washouts along the way. Bridges have been known to disappear. In July 1986 the narrow, winding road claimed four more lives when a diesel-fuel tanker collided with a mini-bus on a sharp curve north of Lions Bay. Caution is advised on the Whistler road even for summer travellers.

The road to political power is also a treacherous road, strewn with bad accidents. It took the 12 Social Credit leadership hopefuls 55 days to make the trip to the resort community of Whistler for the Social Credit leadership convention at the end of July. Everybody tried to drive very carefully, or at least give the appearance of driving carefully. Everybody tried to appear sober. But there were more than a few washouts along the way. And the bridges that some of the candidates were counting on were dangerously in need of repair.

As the hopefuls declared their intentions everybody tried to drive responsibly, everybody tried to avoid running into any issues. Everybody, including Bill Vander Zalm, steered clear of specifics. Nobody got left at the side of the road. Nobody was forced to drop out of the race—not even last-place finisher Kim Campbell, who was rumoured to be running out of gas, running out of money. All the Social Credit leadership hopefuls moved in a slow caravan, jockeying modestly for position along the campaign trail.

It was a dull race for the public to watch.

The press tried its best to provide colour commentary. Reams of speculative piffle began to fill the newspapers. The overall research and analysis of the 12 ambitious candidates in the race for *le grand prix* of Bennett's job was so soft that many campaign camps eventually ended up using articles from the *Province* and the *Sun* amongst their own campaign literature.

The fifth estate was as useful as a fifth wheel. Press pundits were knocking into one another in the darkness of a news vacuum until the Vancouver *Sun* found a light switch. The light switch was a poll. Until the Vancouver *Sun* released the results of a Marktrend Marketing Research Inc. poll, most experts failed to fully appreciate Bill Vander Zalm's position as the leader of the pack. (Although Gorde Hunter and Jim Hume of the Victoria *Times-Colonist*, freelance analyst John Twigg, and former president of the Victoria Press Gallery Andy Stephen predicted a Vander Zalm win near the outset of the leadership campaign.) Even after this poll the media did not adequately gauge Vander Zalm's appeal, repeating the propaganda efforts of Vander Zalm's rival candidates who were — understandably — insisting Vander Zalm "couldn't grow" after a first ballot.

Vander Zalm was the last of the Whistler-bound Socred drivers to start his engine, declaring his candidacy on June 20. His pit crew consisted of Jack Davis, Rita Johnson and Bill Reid — none of whom were high profile or influential MLAs — and his "secret weapon" named Lillian. Jack Davis was his most important supporter, for Davis's capable North Vancouver-Seymour campaign team shifted its efforts towards helping Vander Zalm.

He made a test run in Prince George where he made some vague but noble-sounding pronouncements. He pledged to bring high moral standards based on true Christian principles to government. He pledged to restore a true measure of individual enterprise upon which government decision-making could be made, whatever that meant. He also pledged to bring to the people of BC a means by which everyone, regardless of status or philosophy, could be involved in the decision-making of the government.

Bill Vander Zalm, the positive thinker, did make one significant statement in Prince George. It was a complaint. He said the Social Credit Party of BC "has become more the party of Howe Street."[1]

"Howe Street" is a metaphor for big corporate power interests in BC. Bill Vander Zalm was clearly not the darling of the big-wig financiers; they couldn't trust such an erratic, risk-taking driver to replace Bill Bennett at the wheel of the provincial economy. The high-powered Vander Zalmobile would not receive their sponsorship.

Bill Vander Zalm was able to turn this lack of trust in his driving ability to his advantage. The Top Twenty Club (58 wealthy businessmen reputed to be the province's top suppliers of Social Credit funds) beckoned the leadership candidates, one by one, to appear for private consultations. Vander Zalm, along with Grace McCarthy, refused to go. Vander Zalm gave the impression of being above this sort of thing. He had integrity. He was going to be one candidate who refused to be a tool of Howe Street — even if Howe Street didn't really want Bill Vander Zalm in the first place.

This stand appeared convincing. The press and the public generally believed that anyone who could operate a $10-million Fantasy Garden World had to be rolling in money anyway. So money was not a consideration for Bill Vander Zalm. Principles were. He was one candidate who could afford to have high principles.

There is evidence to suggest, however, that the reason Bill Vander Zalm could later boast of running a surprisingly frugal campaign was that his financial resources were far more limited than was generally perceived. His image as a highly successful independent businessman was essential to maintain. Nothing sells like success. While he was soliciting campaign support in private, and delaying his entry to the race, he was telling the public that he was acutely concerned about possible conflict-of-interest problems and that's why he hadn't declared himself. The question arises, if Howe Street was not on Bill Vander Zalm's side, who was?

Vander Zalm's backers and helpers were not exactly celebrities in the fashionable men's clubs of Vancouver. Some of the smaller fry were Surrey constituency president Charles Steacy, Surrey architect Chip Barrett, Al Bascile, Ewald Waschke, Mike Lawrie and Charles Giordano. Campaign co-chairman Giordano was described as "head of the journalism faculty of Kwantlen College"—head of a faculty of two other teachers. Through Delta Media Services, Giordano was connected to the placement of thousands of dollars worth of newspaper advertisements, signed by unnamed "citizens proud to be British Columbians," during a 1981 by-election in Kamloops.

Campaign co-chairman Bill Goldie was a Vancouver-based management consultant and a key link to the BC Chamber of Commerce. Bill Vander Zalm was the choice of the small businessmen of BC, who saw that he was one of them, unpretentiously devoted to hard work and profit, and in favour of restricting unions from organizing in companies with less than 50 employees.

Two other prominent supporters were Richmond industrialist Milan Ilich and White Spot Restaurant's Peter Toigo. Ilich provided Vander Zalm with the use of a helicopter, although Vander Zalm says it was only used once, to travel between two meetings in a hurry. Toigo was an important economic influence and advisor, and has since become the chief fundraiser for the Social Credit Party. "Mr. Toigo is a good friend," says Vander Zalm. "He's the owner of the White Spot Restaurants and the Kentucky Fried Chickens and other interests. And I particularly like him because he not only makes his money in British Columbia, but he keeps it here."

By the time Vander Zalm finally organized some backing and entered the leadership race, he was able to criticize some of the other candidates for spending too much money. He was able to have Expo 86 chairman and Christian businessman Jimmy Pattison endorse his campaign on the grounds that Bill Vander Zalm was being financially modest, on the grounds that he was practicing reasonable restraint.

"Restraint" had been the buzzword for Social Credit under Bill Bennett during his latter years in power. By 1986 the party needed a new one-word philosophy. Upon announcing his resignation, Bennett officially ended the era of restraint. He said the party was now ready for "renewal."

The only viable renewal candidate was Bill Vander Zalm. Bennett had hoped the party would take kindly to his own unofficial favourite in the race, unelected Kamloops lawyer and Socred insider Bud Smith. But as Vander Zalm correctly surmised, Bud Smith was viewed as a sophisticated Bennett puppet, a mini-mini-W.A.C. When Toronto's *Globe & Mail* endorsed Bud Smith as its choice, Vander Zalm called it "the kiss of death" for his main renewal rival. Smith made one strong showing against Vander Zalm in Delta, but for the most part his strength lay in distant ridings of the north and the interior, places where he had developed behind-the-scenes contacts during his travels for Bennett.

The so-called grassroots of the party agreed with Bennett. They wanted renewal. But all the other main leadership hopefuls were clearly tainted by association with the recent restraint policies and closeness with Bennett, including Bennett's former principal secretary Bud Smith. Although Smith was "new," he was driving the remnants of the gas-guzzling Bennett machine. His pit crew included political wiz John Laschinger and former MLAs Peter Hyndman and Don Phillips. Smith also had Howe Street pitchman Murray Pezim looking under the hood and filling 'er up.

Grace McCarthy, Bennett's favoured deputy premier and Expo 86 organizer, tried to get good mileage out of contradictions. She criticized others for using political machines from Ontario, but then used an Ontario "Big Blue" worker, Kurt Foley, at the close of the race. In *Equity*, John Twigg viewed McCarthy as "the safe establishment candidate whom they could control."[2]

The other leading force in the race was "the haven for thinking Socreds,"[3] Attorney-General Brian Smith. Another long-serving Bennett cabinet minister, Smith was managed by Patrick Kinsella, Bennett's chief strategist and pollster. While pudgy Brian Smith was transformed into viable leadership material by the slick operator of Progressive Strategies Ltd., Howe Streeter Peter Brown kept the vehicle for big-business

Socredism well fueled and pointed it along the path Bill Bennett
had taken for years.

Smith, Smith and McCarthy were Restraint models desperately trying to disguise themselves with expensive paint jobs. The
grassroots would kick their tires at Whistler before betting on a
winner, but clearly the Vander Zalmobile had Renewal written
all over it. Bill Bennett, a man who had overseen a cabinet of car
dealers and disc jockies, hadn't foreseen how good the Vander
Zalmobile would look parked on the lot of Restraint Motors.
Bennett had quickly renamed his dealership Renewal Motors,
but again the grassroots of the party saw through the wet paint.

Fortunately for Vander Zalm, neither his opponents nor the
space-filling press bothered to dig up his assertion, made at the
close of 1983, that he himself was really "the founder of
restraint."[4]

To disassociate himself from the Bennett administration,
Vander Zalm toured the province and said Bennett's government had one standard for the government and another for the
people. He cited provincial liquor regulations. While the
average small businessman has great difficulty acquiring a
liquor license, any government enterprise, such as BC Place, is
granted a liquor license with ease. He said he would gradually
privatize government liquor stores.

To further distance himself from Bill Bennett, Vander Zalm
said he could do without polls. He himself was an expert
poll-taker. He said he could interpret public reactions more
efficiently and cheaply with his gut—more like Bill Bennett's
father. He also claimed the government had become complicated to the point of confusion. He said the basics of what was
required hadn't really changed in thirty years—since W.A.C.
Bennett's era. He charged that Bill Bennett's government had
not communicated as well as it should have.

And he was right. While other candidates refrained from
knocking Bennett, Vander Zalm got good mileage by displaying
his independent attitude.

He was also not above telling the people what they wanted to
hear. In outlying towns like Terrace and Trail, Vander Zalm
preached the need for decentralization of government power. In

Prince Rupert, where the pulp mill is perpetually threatening layoffs, he said, "Let's cut down the trees and create jobs."[5] He said there were lots of trees in British Columbia and if those trees weren't cut down, lots of them would rot anyway. "Few realize that Tweedsmuir [Provincial] Park is the size of France. Yet you can't mine it or log it. If we don't go in and cut, nature will take care of it with bug infestations and fires."[6] (In fact, the area of Tweedsmuir Park is only 9,698 square kilometres, about 2% of the area of France.) In Kamloops, where there are strong anti-Indian sentiments, he said he didn't believe the government should negotiate with BC Indians on land claims.

The grassroots of the party were hearing political music in their ears. Vander Zalm's 26-year-old daughter Juanita went further and recorded a rousing campaign song, written by musical associate Kelly Breaks, which aired during a Fantasy Garden party for 600 delegates.

"Grassroots" was the other key buzzword for the leadership race. There was restraint vs. renewal. But there was also "grassroots" vs. "machine politics." Renewal and genuine grassroots were good. Restraint and machine politics were bad. By those standards Bill Vander Zalm was looking very good indeed, although few outside his own camp seemed to see it.

He was also, it should be noted, the most physically attractive candidate. "Vander Zalm's smile would make any toothpaste salesperson salivate," noted one journalist. "It sticks to his face like a fat strip of reflector tape and gleams as if caught in the glare of high-beam headlights."[7] Media consultant Bernard Searle said Vander Zalm had the best manners for television. "Vander Zalm gives nonverbal indications that he is a man in control and will do what he thinks right," said Searle. "He also has a slight smile. . .when he speaks that makes even bad news not seem so terrible."[8]

The down-turned mouths of both Bud and Brian Smith were dead giveaways, ruling them out as inspirational men amongst the main contenders. Grace McCarthy looked like, well, an aging Queen Bee, whose official biography said she was 58. Searle said McCarthy "tends to be defensive on television, which makes her look opinionated."[9] Jim Nielsen had a bulldog look, having only recently recovered from a black eye administered by a jealous husband who had caught Nielsen conducting an affair with his estranged wife. Searle noted Nielsen displayed a poker face "that makes it seem like he has something to hide."[10] West Vancouver's John Reynolds, MLA for the area with the highest per capita income in all of Canada, looked as appealing as a sleek shark. Stephen Rogers had wit and charm to go with his rounded face and curly hair, but the silver spoon coated with Rogers Refinery sugar sticking from his mouth tended to blight the picture.

Handsome Bill Vander Zalm began to move up through the pack.

At the tail-end of the race was 39-year-old Kim Campbell, the youngest candidate, with four flat tires—she was female, intellectual, a lawyer and underfunded. Campbell also played the cello, spoke four languages, believed education funding should be increased, had studied Soviet government at the London School of Economics, was divorced (from ex-Vancouver alderman Nathan Divinsky), actually read literature (Tolstoy, Jane Austen, Dostoevsky), had accepted a Canada Council travel grant, and had grown up on the west side of Vancouver with a lawyer father and a lawyer brother. On the plus side, she had been born in Port Alberni. "Bill Vander Zalm likes to say he got his start at the end of a shovel," she said. "Well I got mine at the end of a halibut in Prince Rupert."[11] But no one took her bait. "As an intellectually-oriented person, I like to socialize with people who read the same things as I do and have a similar level of education, but I genuinely like ordinary people. I think it's very important to realize that a lot of people that you're out there working for are people who may sit in their undershirt and watch the game on Saturday, beer in hand. . . . I suppose they would find me as boring as I would find them."[12] Ex-premier Dave Barrett sniped, "[Kim Campbell] is fighting something. I don't know what it is."[13]

Vander Zalm passed her standing still.

A second-to-last also-ran was 55-year-old Saanich mayor Mel Couvelier. Born in Vancouver, happily married since age 18, he quit his accountant's job with Crown Zellerbach in 1959 to operate a general store at BC's last whaling station, Coal Harbour. A year later he bought Maplewood Poultry Processors, building the company from five to one hundred employees in 12 years before opening a fashionable clothing shop in Victoria. He entered politics at the bidding of Pierre Trudeau, became a Saanich alderman in 1974 and began the first of five terms as mayor in 1978. He had a Liberal past. Without provincial experience, Couvelier's potential Vancouver Island base of support was taken by Brian Smith, a former mayor of Victoria's Oak Bay district. "I don't think compromise is always the best solution,"[14] Couvelier said. Dave Barrett summarized, "Nobody could spell his name."[15]

Vander Zalm waved at Couvelier as he drove past, recalling him from the old days when they were both budding provincial Liberals in Penticton.

Third-to-last on the road to Whistler was 59-year-old Municipal Affairs minister Bill Ritchie. Born poor in Glasgow, he emigrated to Winnipeg in 1952, came to the Fraser Valley in 1957, and moved up the management ladder of livestock feed companies until he formed Ritchie-Smith Feeds in 1968. Now only a major shareholder, Ritchie had built the company to become the second-largest animal and poultry feed manufacturing firm in BC. Wealthy, with condominiums in Hawaii and extensive land holdings, Ritchie admired Winston Churchill and Flying Phil Gaglardi. Representing the Fraser Valley Bible Belt, he managed to secure degree-granting status for Trinity Western College in Langley in 1979. He was once accused of impropriety by fellow Socred Henry Friesen, who claimed Ritchie offered to help release Friesen's land from the Agricultural Land Reserve. The grassroots did not approve of the fact that he was recently separated from his wife of 36 years, but Ritchie made the even greater political mistake of speaking the truth about Vander Zalm. He said Vander Zalm had deserted the party by not running in the previous election. "Who was around in '83? It was not a time to be on the outside looking in, but on the inside looking out."[16]

Bill Vander Zalm was on the inside looking out of his speeding Zalmobile as he breezed by Ritchie.

The next straggler was Shuswap-Revelstoke MLA Cliff Michael, a man clearly hoping to hitch a ride to a cabinet post by hitching onto someone else's wagon. A former IWA official-turned-manager, Michael was a rural unknown described as "very sincere, winsomely humble...but has a yawnsome style. Wittily turned his low-budget campaign into a virtue."[17] His opportunism would appear in the form of green stickers he handed out saying "I'm uncommitted." A Michael sticker would not be a ticket to power, but it was the best ticket for a free drink. Michael contributed the idea of privatizing liquor stores. He chose to support Reynolds rather than Vander Zalm near the race's end, a wrong turn which detoured him directly back to Shuswap-Revelstoke without a cabinet post. But Michael proved his legitimacy as a candidate by being the only one of the 12 hopefuls to correctly foresee, and try to make a major issue of, threatened US duties on Canadian softwood-lumber exports. "The decision is going to be made on countervailing duties by the Americans prior to the middle of October. And if we don't head that thing off, we in British Columbia are going to be in bad, bad trouble," he said.[18] Barrett quipped that Michael "is a parody of Andy Warhol's 15 minutes for everybody in the sun. He's got three seconds."[19]

Vander Zalm whizzed by these four also-rans to the middle of the pack.

He was picking up delegates at local nominating meetings on a par with the previously declared leaders McCarthy, Smith and Smith. Out in the Fraser Valley, where the religious vote was fundamental to success, Vander Zalm was a strong second-place finisher in the constituencies that should have been wrapped up by their elected MLAs, Bill Ritchie and Bob Wenman. In particular, Vander Zalm needed to push Wenman off the campaign trail because Wenman's potential popularity with the right-to-life contingent of the party might cut into his own strength.

Fifth-to-last Bob Wenman was returning to BC after more than 11 years as a Conservative MP. Twenty years before, at age 26, he had been the youngest MLA elected in BC, and had learned the political game in Victoria as a two-term backbencher for W.A.C. Bennett. "W.A.C. Bennett is the paternal political figure for me and I hold a lot of his values."[20] Wenman was not tainted by Bill Bennett associations, he was dark and handsome and still married after 22 years, he was a squeaky-clean teetotaler and he had Vander Zalm's "work ethic" biases. Born the youngest of six in Maidstone, Saskatchewan, Wenman was against French TV and for capital punishment. He left the United Church of Canada because it was too liberal. He attended Langley's Christian Life Assembly. His backers were Christians such as advertising executive Peter Fassbender and a senior Amway official, Robert Schmidt. He had served in Surrey as an alderman—22 months under Mayor Bill Vander Zalm—and had only lost an election once in his career (to the NDP's Carl Liden in 1972). Vander Zalm knew Wenman was a hard-driving rival with a proven track record. Fortunately Wenman blew a tire in front of the media when he announced he stood for "Judo-Christian" principles.

Vander Zalm passed Wenman without stopping to help fix the tire. Farther up the road Wenman would choose Brian Smith's camp, not Vander Zalm's, even though supporters such as Fassbender would go to Vander Zalm.

It was a little-recognized fact that Bill Vander Zalm had quarreled with Bob Wenman in 1980. The Tory MP had wanted BC to build disposal and storage sites for radioactive and toxic materials on BC Crown Land. Municipal Affairs Minister Vander Zalm had said he'd rather live in an earthquake zone than near a nuclear power plant. Surrey citizens in Vander Zalm's constituency had been threatened by Wenman's suggestion. The two men were both pro-life candidates but Vander Zalm was anti-nuke. There was no love lost between them on the road to Whistler.

Much more public was Vander Zalm's relationship with sixth-to-last candidate Stephen Rogers.

Rogers criticized Vander Zalm for having "simple answers for everything."[21] He said, "So much of his policy is the very last thing that anybody said to him, whether it was a cab driver or somebody he talked to in the hallway. I can recall being in cabinet with him when there was just no consistency."[22] On July

21 Rogers stated that he could not serve in a cabinet under Bill Vander Zalm. Born in Vancouver in 1942, Charles Stephen Rogers was raised in Kerrisdale and attended prep schools — Athlone, Vernon Prep, St. George's — and learned to fly a plane at age 17. He became an Air Canada pilot with social affiliations at the Vancouver Club, the Royal Vancouver Yacht Club, the Royal Flying Club and the Shaughnessy Golf and Country Club. He was rich, although not all of the money was self-made. Married for 17 years, he'd been separated for 1½ years. The scion of his family's fortune, Rogers had proven himself both likable and capable since his election as a Vancouver South MLA in 1975. He'd blown the whistle on a Grizzly Valley pipeline scandal in 1977 which led to a government inquiry into land speculation. In 1979 he became Environment minister. In 1983 he was Energy, Mines and Petroleum minister and later minister responsible for BC Place stadium. He had few enemies.

"I make no apology for what we've done in the past. I don't want to disassociate myself in any way from the Bennett government. I was there and very much a part of it," he said.[23] He also made the mistake of telling the truth about Vander Zalm, saying Vander Zalm had a tendency to simplify issues. A reader of Kurt Vonnegut novels and technical aviation journals, Rogers was a sophisticated man, lost in the middle of the Socred leadership pack, who knew that life was not without complexities: he ranked as Vander Zalm's opposite.

Fortunately for Vander Zalm the smooth talking Rogers had made the major error of his political career well within recent memory. After being shuffled to the Health portfolio in February 1986, he was forced to resign over charges that he had breached the Financial Disclosures Act. He had failed to disclose a $100,000 interest in the Western Pulp Partnership, a debt to the Bank of BC and ownership of more than 30% of shares in Montgomery Investments Ltd. and Star Leasing Ltd.

Vander Zalm, rags-to-riches millionaire, didn't need a pilot's license to make it to Whistler ahead of Rogers.

Before tackling front-runners McCarthy, Smith and Smith at the convention, Bill Vander Zalm had just two more middle-of-the-pack candidates to outdo along the way.

Health and Human Resources Minister Jim Nielsen was widely regarded as a worthwhile administrator and a fighter — quite literally. The much-publicized black eye he had received from an irate husband in 1986 put a knock in his engine. Bill Vander Zalm had only to add a little sugar to his gas tank and Jim Nielsen would go sputtering to the sidelines. Vander Zalm mobilized his supporters on his home turf in Richmond and managed to take all but two of the delegates from the Richmond MLA's own riding.

To Nielsen's credit, he could never be accused of phony politicking. Asked about Bud Smith's campaign, Nielsen got off the best quote of the entire Social Credit leadership race, saying, "I didn't shovel shit in the stables for ten years to have someone else come in and ride the pony."[24] When asked about the man who called himself the Master Shoveller, Bill Vander Zalm, Nielsen was only slightly less candid. He said he would have difficulty serving in any cabinet that had Bill Vander Zalm as a premier, and he was peeved by Vander Zalm's failure to run in the tough 1983 election. "It's not unlike the defensive line of the football team getting a little ticked off with the wide receiver who is out there and never gets his uniform dirty."[25] Carrying this analogy one step further, Nielsen said Vander Zalm's uniform in the football game of politics was coated with "fantasy dust."[26]

Bill Vander Zalm left Jim Nielsen eating his fantasy dust on the road to Whistler.

John Reynolds remained.

In one way 44-year-old Reynolds was Bill Vander Zalm's most useful rival because his right wing extremism made Vander Zalm's seem comparatively mild. The journeyman salesman had been named in a CBC documentary as having links to an alleged Mafia figure. Reynolds sued but settled out of court for a promise it wouldn't be repeated. His dislike of left-wing sensibilities might be described as rabid. He begrudged the spending of government money on the annual Vancouver Walk for Peace.

Reynolds was born in Toronto, son of a Woolworth's manager who moved the family to Montreal. Reynolds finished school at age 16, worked for Woolworth's and began a long series of sales jobs. He hustled greeting cards, surgical supplies, stocks, insurance, chocolates and modular housing. In 1972 he became MP for Burnaby-Richmond-Delta. Columnist Allan Fotheringham said he had the attention span of a hummingbird. He went to battle for the Church of Scientology and former Howard Hughes aide John Meier, who was extradited to face murder charges in the US. He was once identified as the worst member of Parliament of the decade, in a *Maclean's* column with the headline, "In the world of politics, one man stands head and shoulders below the rest."[27]

Reynolds gave up attempts to replace national Conservative leader Robert Stanfield when a hoped-for list of 1,000 for his fund-raising dinner shrank to 30. He was a CJOR hotliner for three years but did not get his contract renewed. He stole the ultra-safe West Vancouver-Howe Sound seat from Bennett's handpicked candidate Mark Sager with a surprise show of force at a nomination meeting. Reynolds had been the first to jump into the race to Whistler.

Thrice married, John Reynolds favoured professionally run casinos in BC, reassuring the public that, "The Mob is not interested in going into Salmon Arm to work with charities and give them 35 percent."[28]

With John Reynolds on the track's far-right fringe, telling people what the Mafia would or would not do in BC, Bill Vander Zalm was able to make his own position look like the middle of the road. Even after Reynolds sided with Vander Zalm in the campaign's late stages, the new premier didn't invite John Reynolds to join his first cabinet.

The turning point in the Social Credit leadership campaign was July 26. Down to a few days before the vote the consensus of expert opinion was still exclusively favouring McCarthy and the two Smiths, with McCarthy taking an edge over Brian Smith as the all-round favourite. But after the marketing research firm, Marktrend, had canvassed 402 people throughout the province, the Vancouver *Sun* released results which were said to be accurate to within plus or minus 4.5% 95 times out of a 100.

The poll showed 50% of the people thought Bill Vander Zalm was best at providing strong leadership. The only other candidate in double figures was Grace McCarthy with 16.9%. The poll showed 39.1% felt Vander Zalm would be best at ending confrontation in BC. The only other candidate in double figures was Grace McCarthy with 14.9%. The poll showed 33.6% felt Vander Zalm would best represent BC's interests outside BC. The only other candidate in double figures was Grace McCarthy with 14.9% The poll showed 30.7% felt Vander Zalm was most trustworthy. Again the only other candidate in double figures was Grace McCarthy with 16.9%

Most remarkable, the candidates judged most likely to be concerned for the poor, elderly and disabled were BC's two notoriously severe Human Resources Ministers from the previous decade, Bill Vander Zalm (25.4%) and Grace McCarthy (20.1%).

A whopping 50.2% believed Bill Vander Zalm had the best chance of winning the next election. Vander Zalm was also picked by 46.5% as the favourite choice to win at Whistler. Vander Zalm led on every one of the seven "issues" questions, with Grace McCarthy a distant second in all categories.

"Holy smokes," said Vander Zalm. "That sounds fantastic. It makes me feel good. I thought it was my smile and my love of flowers that made people like me."[29]

"You would anticipate that, based on the publicity," said Bob Wenman, regarding the poll results. He drew 1.5% in the most-like-to-see-win category. "The known names do the best."[30]

Bill Vander Zalm may have been running on empty on the way to Whistler. He may have started off short of money and short of clear policies on important issues. But over his turbulent years in politics he had amassed an unsurpassed wealth of the most important currency — press attention, media booty — and that was really the most vital fuel of all.

THE PREMIER MARKET

Upstairs, Downstairs, All Around the Town

"It was a grab for power with no holds barred. The thought of being an instant premier had the candidates and their legions of lackeys lusting for victory to the point where decorum vanished."

John Twigg
Equity

Money talks. Money talked at Whistler, July 28–30.

BC government money had once bailed out the troubled ski resort of Whistler when the condo capital of Canada had been snowed under by unsuccessful private investors in the early 1980s. Now once again, in the fashionable mountain village that Allan Fotheringham described as a "shrine built to yuppiedom" and "the playground of the BMW,"[1] Socred money was talking, trying to save private investments.

For three frenzied days Socred money talked, rocked and cajoled. It also sang and it bagpiped and it harmonized and it flew overhead and it flashed electronically and it cheer-led and it sizzled and it broiled and it dressed in lederhosen and it can-canned and it poured free booze and it sent off one premier and it brought in another.

Back in 1973, some candidates for the Social Credit leadership spent well under $10,000 on their campaigns. In 1986 the twelve leadership hopefuls at Whistler were collectively approaching the $2 million mark in hoopla and helicopters and hype. The low spender for the 1986 campaign was said to be Cliff Michael, who had humbly budgeted $30,000. Last place finisher Kim

Campbell put her spending at $50,000. The second-to-last place finisher Mel Couvelier had told his supporters he wanted $100,000 in the kitty before entering the race. Campbell and Couvelier ended up sharing a tent, fending off rumours that they might drop out before the first ballot. "I will not say I cannot envision a scenario where that might be the case," Campbell said.[2] At the end of a $50,000 campaign Campbell was serving soda pop, juice and Rice Krispie squares cut into the shape of a K. Fifth-to-last competitor Bob Wenman put his spending at $80,000 before actual convention expenses.

There were no rules requiring candidates to disclose their funding levels and sponsors. Reynolds and Couvelier pledged to disclose their total spending afterwards. However it was the man who had been accused of contravening the Financial Disclosure Act, Stephen Rogers, who divulged he was spending about 40% of a "low-profile" $52,000 campaign at Whistler. Vander Zalm's spending was estimated in two published reports as $70,000 and $100,000. Initial reports said the other three frontrunners— Grace McCarthy, Brian Smith and Bud Smith—were spending in the area of $150,000 each. Millionaire businessman Jim Pattison later accused some Social Credit leadership candidates of spending between $400,000 and $500,000. Forty per cent of twelve leadership campaigns heading into Whistler was a lot of t-shirts, highballs, balloons and salmon steaks.

"It was the most fun I've had since I was a rock critic," said the *Sun*'s Vaughn Palmer. Kim Campbell staged her Whistler entrance with a kilted piper playing "The Campbells are Coming." Vander Zalm had an oompapa band, a hillbilly singer and a jukebox with Elvis and Dean Martin music. Brian Smith had an expensive song recorded, "Now the future's ours to share—Let Brian take us there," to synchronize with a high-tech light show featuring a giant green hand "reaching out" to delegates. Jim Nielsen hired a country band. John Reynolds hired a six-piece rock band. And over in Gracie's tent two can-can dancers in Klondike garb were sliding frilly garters up men's arms and extending net-stockinged legs for some inebriated men to toss hoops onto...

The average age of the delegates was 47. Their average

annual income was approximately $38,000. But the most important statistic was that approximately 700–800 of the 1,300 delegates gathered at Whistler were said to be "soft" or uncommitted. Hopes were therefore rationally high that money judicially spent at Whistler could buy a premiership.

While the rest of the province watched the premier-pickers at home on their televisions, a few thousand dinner reservations were made just in case some friends might drop over: Grace McCarthy reserved the chic Chez Joel restaurant; Brian Smith held down Umberto's and the Delta Mountain Inn; Jim Nielsen booked the Savage Beagle and the Longhorn Pub; Bud Smith took Tapley's Pub; Bob Wenman ordered a slice of the Original Pizza Ristorante; and John Reynolds reserved Nasty Jack's and the Citta restaurant.

To monitor the democratic process unfolding at Whistler, the Vancouver *Sun* alone sent almost 20 employees. Approximately 1,700 media types and political campaigners were soon alongside the 1,300 delegates in a cacophony of tuba players in lederhosen, barbershop quartets, bagpipe players, strutting majorettes, speeches and clinking ice cubes. *NeWest Review*'s Heather Conn said she felt like Dorothy, "swirled into an Oz-struck extravaganza of Social Credit craziness."[3]

Whereas the candidates on the road to Whistler had carefully observed speeding and speaking limits, the dash to the finish line shifted into outright bargaining and outbreaks of frustration in the clutch. Campbell River Mayor Robert Ostler led a delegation of 25 northern Vancouver Islanders who said they were willing to support only a candidate who promised to give them a new Vancouver Island Highway and a silviculture program employing 1,200. Over at a small blue-and-white tent stacked with beer, potato chips and a box of apples, Jim Nielsen was talking tough, saying, "We can export all the lousy negative attitudes to other socialist countries and they're welcome to them." Resentful of the swanky come-ons of others, Nielsen's campaign manager prophesied there would be a backlash against extravagant spenders. "There's such a barrage of freebies," said Gordon Dale, "I think people are overwhelmed. I don't think it impresses anybody."[4]

It impressed Allan Fotheringham. The acerbic national columnist called the Whistler bash "a political convention desperately short of humour."[5] After several field days of ogling anti-Vander Zalm women from the tonier sections of Vancouver prancing about in designer Bermuda shorts, Fotheringham tried to inject some levity by describing "their saddle shoes immaculate and their gold chains discreetly gold."[6] Meanwhile, as a political war correspondent, he also noted, "The troops of the Dutch immigrant marched defiantly in combinations that didn't quite click, secure in the belief that no welfare recipients or stockbrokers were within their ranks and the work ethic is secure and unblemished as the key to life. Lotus Land is now in the grip of those who know what the handle of a shovel feels like and think there's nothing wrong with fuzzy dice dangling from the rearview mirror."[7]

Because the Whistler convention centre was designed to hold only 1,700 people, much of the jockeying for power occurred in the village common or at tents pitched on the golf course. "In real terms, most of the dealmaking, if you will, will happen outside, other than on voting day when new alliances are formed by virtue of people dropping off the ballot," said Richard Moerman, convention organizer for Bud Smith.[8] This meant the struggle for power was literally out in the open. For three days Whistler was as chaotic as a trendy banana republic in the throes of a multi-faceted revolution.

The prime strategic location was the village square bandstand. Located near many of the posh hospitality suites, the small wooden structure was commandeered by Vander Zalm's forces. They plastered it with Vander Zalm posters and a sign giving the *Sun* poll results. Other candidates complained. Vander Zalm said he did not know how permission to use the bandstand was obtained, but he understood his workers had asked for it. "Everything we have done is out in the open," he said.[9]

Peter Adler, general manager of the Whistler Resort Association, said he didn't know why Vander Zalm had the bandstand. "It was supposed to be for everybody,"[10] he said. Whistler Alderman Paul Burrows said the bandstand was not to be rented out to anybody. Adler said he believed Vander Zalm's workers took it over and other candidate workers backed off rather than risk a physical confrontation.

Brian Smith supporters fought back by playing ghetto blasters at full volume from nearby windows, interfering with Vander Zalm's musicians. McCarthyites hung a sign from a hotel window overlooking the square listing all the cabinet ministers who supported her. John Reynolds lodged a protest. He was told the bandstand was somehow owned by BC Place. Apparently some sort of deal had been struck between the crown corporation and Vander Zalm's troops. Push was coming to shove. The other candidates surrendered to the Master Shoveller in the battle of the bandstand.

Whereas the 1973 Social Credit convention had cleanly elected Bill Bennett over runner-up Bob McClelland in one ballot, two sides at Whistler were threatening to do grievous damage to the 34-year-old Socred coalition. "From the day Bennett announced his retirement and issued his call for 'renewal'," wrote Marjorie Nichols, "it was clear there would be a knock-down, drag-out battle between the grassroots populists and the conservative ideologues in the establishment machine built by Bennett over the past five years."[11] UBC political scientist Ken Carty said, "Whether the coalition survives is the great unanswered question."[12]

Bill Bennett, the man who made the battle of the bandstand possible, wandered aimlessly around Whistler, respected but not revered. As nobody's committed delegate and nobody's hero, he was given a bizarre, $50-a-ticket send-off by 1,300 supporters on Monday night.

Like ordering out for pizza, somebody had got in telegrams from Prime Minister Brian Mulroney, US Vice-President Bush and Japanese Prime Minister Nakasone. Jim Pattison literally blew his own trumpet. Former cabinet minister Don Phillips and BC Hydro chairman Chester Johnson said Bennett had always been given a raw deal by the media. Former Alberta premier Peter Lougheed praised Bennett's role in constitutional talks and Pacific Rim development. A nostalgic audio-visual presentation gave a spotty review of Bennett's accomplishments. With all the sentimentality of a game show, the Social Credit party presented Bennett with a Kelowna-made Campion Allante 195 Socred blue speedboat. Party president Hope Wotherspoon also handed Bennett the keys to the yellow 1975 Chevrolet (originally bought by the NDP) which had been driven by the premier while in office.

A used car. "How Socred," noted John Twigg in *Equity*.[13] The 1-hour ceremony was noteworthy for its absence of heartfelt testimonies and Bennett's contention that "when I made the final decision to announce my retirement, Social Credit was leading any public opinion polls over our nearest competitor if an election had been called at that time."[14] Even Socred party faithful had to put their tongues in their cheeks with that one.

Bill Bennett was ducking out of a fight. The BC economy was a mess getting messier, with Expo layoffs and American lumber tariffs imminent. Four polls conducted by Angus Reid Associates between January and late June had shown the NDP consistently held about 48% of decided voters, compared to only 38% for the Socreds. The *Province* later carried a story on August 3 saying one Social Credit cabinet minister admitted $80,000 had been spent on a poll delivered to the premier just days before he announced his resignation, a poll indicating Bennett trailed both the NDP and the popularity of his own party.

Monday night a plane flew over Whistler dragging a banner saying Bill Vander Zalm For Premier.

Tuesday was for speeches. And for verbal stabs at enemies.

Jim Nielsen began the evening on a bitter note by saying he represented those Socreds who were not at the convention, "those shoved aside in the delegate-selection procedures."[15] The Master Shoveller had allowed Nielsen to elect only one delegate other than himself in his home riding. He took another swipe at Vander Zalm when he said, "There are no backroom boys making decisions for me, or even cutting my sideburns."[16] He warned that, "powerful forces have been unleashed to sway you, and deals have been made."[17]

Bill Ritchie was lacking in eloquence, saying, "I want to put to rest the myth that the NDP is the sole voice of the working people of this province."[18] Bob Wenman also failed to win votes, stiffly quoting W.A.C. Bennett and bashing central Canada. But the big disappointment of the evening was Bud Smith, who, in trying to waylay criticism of his inexperience, only encouraged his audience to consider it as an issue.

Cliff Michael gained the first standing ovation when he said, "I consider it a crime and a folly for our society to pay our young people up to $200 a week on UIC to produce absolutely nothing."[19] Mel Couvelier's speech was reputedly shaped by six advisers for ten days but his most memorable quote was, "I'm a town pump kind of person...Town pump democracy is not just a phrase, let's make it a philosophy."[20] Stephen Rogers was a disappointment, conveying the impression that he had already read the writing on the wall and had given up hope.

Grace McCarthy did not win friends or influence people by once more attacking her two Smith rivals. She reminded everyone that W.A.C. Bennett had risen into history by defeating "corrupt political machines that degraded this magnificent province."[21] Similarly John Reynolds was a walking advertisement for defensiveness, stressing, "The NDP can never form a government if we keep united."[22] McCarthy and Reynolds both seemed to be overly armoured Socreds, better suited to defending their party against its enemies than fighting in favour of something or someone.

Kim Campbell's positive remarks on education were followed by the ominous warning that, "Charisma without substance is a dangerous thing."[23] She received a standing ovation, a well-earned moment of recognition. Brian Smith gave what was considered by most people to be the best speech of his life. He forcefully stressed his capability and experience by saying he was the candidate best able to function as a premier on the following day.

Finally, after four hours, it was Vander Zalm's turn. The last candidate to enter the race, by coincidence, was the last candidate to speak.

Bill Vander Zalm started with unusual slowness, possibly aware of a need to downplay his own charisma. His handler Bill Goldie had maintained it would not be disadvantageous for his man to speak last, saying Vander Zalm could always rouse an audience. But after some standard shots at eastern Canada and his standard remarks about red tape, the weary audience was still not enthralled. "I won't be making any deals with anyone," he vowed, knocking the behind-the-scenes Machiavellianism of the Ontario Big Blue Machine candidates, "A cabinet post or a consulting job won't be traded. It must be earned."[24] Vander Zalm then made a direct plea for votes, the first candidate to do so. He referred to Bill Bennett's first-ballot win in 1973. "This Bill also needs the first ballot," he said.[25]

Nobody thought it was Bill Vander Zalm's best speech. Any-but-Bill factions took hope. Expert speculation that he couldn't get enough to win on the first ballot, and couldn't grow after the first ballot, gained force. It was obvious that the race was far from over.

The most important words of the evening were written, not spoken. Copies of a magazine article were slipped by Vander Zalm's camp under the doors of delegates for voters to ponder. It was a *Monday Magazine* piece written by Victoria freelancer Sid Tafler that detailed the connections of both the Smith candidates to big business lobbying interests, the sort of article that required some chutzpah and research. Of the countless articles and news reports that appeared throughout the month of July on the Social Credit leadership campaign, it was probably the most influential work of journalism.[26]

Wednesday came at last. Voting day.

The hoopla and the speeches and the Bennett farewell of Whistler will fade from significance and memory very quickly. Years from 1986 there will be two separate events talked about, gossiped about, analyzed and remembered. Both these events happened on Wednesday. The first event was the appearance of a banker in a small office downstairs at the Whistler Convention Centre. The second event, shortly afterwards, was a surprise strategic move on the convention floor.

Voting began a half hour late, at 10:30 A.M.

Overseeing the confusion on the convention floor, like a spotter in a football game, was a 73-year-old man seated alone above the in-fighting and the negativism and the placard-waving fuss. He had purposely positioned himself up high where he could see clearly just how the Boss Upstairs was going to work things out.

This was Flyin' Phil Gaglardi, the BC politician most tellingly compared with Bill Vander Zalm. According to the former Highways minister, the whole leadership race was running on empty, except for Bill Vander Zalm. "Vander Zalm and I go back a long ways," he says, "The reason I fought for Vander Zalm is very simple. Take a look at the slate of those that were running for premiership. Name one of them and the moment that you name that one try and think of five or six outstanding things that they have accomplished in their tenure of office in the provincial government. Can you find one?

"The moment that you name W.A.C. Bennett, a hundred things come to mind. The moment that you name Phil Gaglardi, a hundred things come to mind. Name one person that's a standout of anything or any consequence in the entire gamut of people that was running for the leadership.

"So I said to myself, if I'm going to help the province of British Columbia, which I'm a fighter for, then I'm going to try and see to it that a man gets there who I feel has got innovative, brand new ideas, who's not afraid of the bureaucracy, not afraid of doing things on the basis that they should be done. Even though he may make mistakes. Because the only man that never made a mistake is the fellow that never did anything.

"So I backed Vander Zalm."

Gaglardi had endorsed Vander Zalm back on July 20 in Kamloops. "I would say I was the only one of public consequence who declared himself on the side of Vander Zalm before the convention. Even before the polls." Due to a deep spiritual and temperamental affinity, Phil Gaglardi had appointed himself Vander Zalm's upstairs man. In Vander Zalm, Gaglardi recognized his own style and career in BC politics. "When I was minister of Highways, I was the best-known minister in Canada," he says. His long list of speeding convictions and license suspensions (over 30) had shown the people he was a dynamic figure who could virtually function above the law.

"There wasn't any meeting that I was introduced to that I didn't get more applause, more backing, than any other cabinet minister, outside of the premier," Gaglardi boasts.

Similarities between Gaglardi and Vander Zalm were raised by Allan Fotheringham as far back as 1977. Gaglardi had touted himself as "the roughest, toughest and most effective Welfare minister the world has ever known." He had kicked deadbeats off welfare rolls. He claimed to be the first man of Italian parentage ever to be named to a cabinet post in Canada. Born in Mission in the Fraser Valley, he had risen from humble beginnings. As Gaglardi gained political notoriety, the premier of his day had also feared the possibility that he might become the next premier.

"There couldn't be a person on God's earth more continuously maligned than I," Gaglardi likes to say. "I was continuously beaten by the press. Always. But I laughed at the press. I never even defended myself. Didn't care two hoots about what they said." Like Vander Zalm, Gaglardi was protected by a belief in his own righteousness. "A lot of people still believe to this day that Phil Gaglardi is the biggest crook that God ever gave breath to. But I wanna tell you, they're on the wrong track. Because I wouldn't be around today if I were a crook."

After Gaglardi attended Northwest Bible College in Seattle, he started preaching at Calvary Temple in Kamloops in 1946, for fifteen dollars a week, depending, as does Vander Zalm, on strong fundamentalist support in politics. Both Gaglardi and Vander Zalm also disguise a lack of any coherent political philosophy by invoking strong links between Christianity and democracy. Both men are apt to confuse their own work with the Lord's, claiming to see his hand in the coming together of an amusement park or the avoidance of high speed automobile accidents. Both are riveting speakers. "Sincerity is the most positive base for getting your point across," says Gaglardi. "I'm not a phony. I don't have brains enough to be a phony." Bill Vander Zalm has said, "I don't see myself as a political person. There's so much phoniness in politics." As well, Gaglardi and Vander Zalm are both fervent anti-communists. "In Russia you get up in the morning, Mister, and you do what they tell you," says Gaglardi.

On Wednesday as the voting started, Pastor Phil Gaglardi was high above the crowd, a political outcast who had the consolation of telling himself he was being Bill Vander Zalm's #1 upstairs man. Later that evening Gaglardi would give himself the satisfaction of walking around the streets of Whistler and having puzzled Socred delegates asking, "Phil, how did you know? How could you tell?" Perhaps more than any other person at the Social Credit convention at Whistler, Phil Gaglardi was in tune with the unsophisticated grassroots elements of the Social Credit party that would choose the winner.

In the best newspaper column written on the Whistler convention procedure itself, Vaughn Palmer of the *Sun* had outlined the mathematical facts about how hinterland constituencies would have a disproportionate say in the choice of BC's next premier. He outlined how the city of Vancouver, with a population of well over 400,000, would actually have fewer delegates at the convention than the northern half of the province, with a population of less than 200,000. Populous urban constituencies with two MLA's were not simply allowed twice as many delegates. The race was run in favour of any candidate who could appeal to non-urban delegates.

The "machine politics"/"grassroots" split at Whistler was really the urban/rural split under a different name. An intelligent and sophisticated man like Stephen Rogers, with a proven record of administrative skills without undue confrontations, was about to receive only a handful of votes at Whistler and lose his deposit. Rogers had made the political error of criticizing Bill Vander Zalm's avowed dedication to "Christian" principles, pointing out that the new premier should be someone capable of embracing the entire religious spectrum. Such rationality was anathema to the majority of delegates, who favoured simplistic views and ultra-conventional beliefs.

The religious vote at Whistler was a major force, and the Reaganistic fervour of the Social Credit Women's Auxiliary was also not to be taken lightly. Divorced or separated candidates were disadvantaged. Candidates who strayed far from Moral Majority principles were destined to be left out in the cold.

The Women's Auxiliary at Whistler distributed one leaflet claiming communists were responsible for the chaos upsetting the nation, quoting as evidence the "Communist Red Rules of Revolution" from 1919. Another pamphlet was called "Women Are the New Reality." It advised, "We must NOT create, emulate nor follow feministic viewpoints." Delegates were invited to wear buttons with a border of BC traced on them; inside the boundary was a human foetus and the words "Socred for Life."

It took an hour for 1,294 delegates to place acceptable Xs on their ballot sheets. Five ballots were spoiled. It took another hour and forty minutes before convention chairman Les Peterson read the results to the crowd:

Vander Zalm	367
McCarthy	244
Bud Smith	202
Brian Smith	196
Reynolds	54
Nielsen	54
Rogers	43
Wenman	40
Michael	32
Ritchie	28
Couvelier	20
Campbell	14

Everyone was nervous. Everyone was unsure. This was nothing approaching the first-ballot victory that Bill Vander Zalm had asked for, and was far below what observers felt he needed to stay in the race. He was ahead, but not as securely as everyone, even himself, felt he had to be.

Suddenly the future looked promising for Brian Smith. Kim Campbell, eliminated automatically, declared for Smith. Bill Ritchie, Stephen Rogers and Bob Wenman withdrew and also declared for Brian Smith. There was euphoria in the

Attorney-General's camp. His delegates, dressed in turquoise sweaters, saw the makings of a Stop Vander Zalm coalition. "Bill (Vander Zalm) can't grow," said Smith's handler Patrick Kinsella, "Everyone is coming to us."[27] Kinsella was confident and glib, as if he had planned everything perfectly from the start. Only Mel Couvelier had gone to join Vander Zalm. Cliff Michael had gone to John Reynolds. Brian Smith was clearly the stronger of the two so-called "Coughdrop Brothers."

Brian Smith, 53, had graduated from UBC and Queens, worked as a Victoria lawyer for 15 years, and become mayor of Oak Bay in 1974. A Progressive Conservative, he had turned Socred after inviting Bill Bennett to play tennis on the opening day of his municipality's new recreation centre. Smith was elected for Oak Bay provincially in 1979. Shy and solemn in public, his main weakness as a politician was his inability to gladhand. He had proven himself effective in the ministries of Education and Energy and as Attorney-General. But he had all the charisma of a dead fish.

Smith's high-powered handler, Patrick Kinsella, had the job of removing his candidate's rumpled-professor appearance, pinning up the corners of his naturally downturned mouth, and trying to make him look inspiring. With $175,000 worth of winding-up, Smith's contention that he would be there until the final ballot was no idle boast. Kinsella was banking heavily on the Whistler delegates being able to make a sensible choice and protect the monied status quo.

Unfortunately Kinsella's reputation as a fixer for the Ontario Blue Machine was seen by many as a liability for Smith, a man who enjoys reading books, listening to music, relaxing at his Gulf Islands retreat or going to the racetrack. Smith's other two problems were circumstantial. He was a lawyer and members of the rural grassroots distrusted lawyers. Second, Smith was an urbanite from Victoria, not Vancouver, so the major media outlets had not made him nearly as well known throughout the province as he deserved to be. He was an urbanite with all the disadvantages and none of the advantages of sophisticated connections.

When the first ballot results were announced, the first tears of the day were shed. Donny Reading, president of the Women's Auxiliary, cried to see Bob Wenman humiliated with only 40 votes. A more important setback, however, was John Reynolds' failure to get a hoped-for 100 votes. Marooned in a fifth-place tie with Jim Nielsen at 54 votes, Reynolds decided to scuttle a much-touted alliance that called for also-rans to back the fifth-place vote-getter. "When there's a tie, the deal breaks off," Reynolds declared.[28] The tie between Nielsen and Reynolds was the first of several lucky breaks for Bill Vander Zalm. It meant both men would stay for a second ballot, preventing an even greater migration to Brian Smith's exuberant camp.

Prior to the voting results Vander Zalm had boldly predicted he would get 500 votes on the first ballot. This prediction had quickly spread through the gathering, and it was widely agreed that over 400 votes could make him unstoppable. He had pulled a piece of paper from his pocket. "It's all right here," he said. "It's my horoscope. It says I'm going to win."[29] A Gemini, Vander Zalm told the press his horoscope predicted his charisma would help him achieve success that day. "You like what it says about charisma? And it says I'm no longer going to be second fiddle. It's about time," he said, laughing. Vander Zalm had also shown the press his notes for a victory speech. But after the first ballot, it looked as if Bill Vander Zalm was going to need more than just charisma to win.

The disappointing results placed Vander Zalm in a fiercely contemplative frame of mind. He remained in his box with Lillian, not mingling, staring with intense concentration over the heads of his swaying and cheering "V-Team" supporters. The V-team was happily waving their pink posters, but the look on Bill Vander Zalm's face was black.

He could still win. But it wasn't exactly in the stars. He would have to make some sort of deal. He might even have to swallow his enormous pride and surrender at some point to protect his future prospects within the party. One insider admitted Bill Vander Zalm had said after the first ballot that he could "live with" Brian Smith. Obviously he was seriously considering the possibility that the mountain might not come to Mohammed.

If his eyes or his spies had been sharp, Bill Vander Zalm would have known about a handshake between John Reynolds and Patrick Kinsella after that first ballot. The angry Jim Nielsen would surely go to Brian Smith; Nielsen had personally told him as much after the first ballot. If John Reynolds went to Brian Smith as well, on the strength of that handshake, Vander Zalm's only hope would be a coalition with his one-time adversary Grace McCarthy. Now, as he stared thoughtfully into space, his lips were tight.

Grace McCarthy, the woman who had rebuilt the party in the early 1970s, had the power to pick the next premier, but she lacked the support to be the next premier herself. While Patrick Kinsella was forming alliances in the convention centre, shaking hands with Reynolds and meeting with Bud Smith's campaign co-chairman Peter Hyndman, McCarthy tried not to appear downcast by her ability to be a kingmaker, but not a queen. Grace McCarthy, according to her campaign manager Isaac Moss, had "painted herself into a corner."[30] By insisting, "I won't be a part of a 'stop anybody' movement,"[31] and by repeatedly attacking the influence of Ontario outsiders (John Laschinger for Bud Smith, Patrick Kinsella for Brian Smith), McCarthy had signaled her intention to become Canada's first female premier or nothing at all. She was too battle-scarred and proud to sacrifice her principles in return for ministerial influence. She would refuse to help anyone on the justifiable grounds that it was about time one of the men in the Social Credit party finally saw fit to help her.

On the second ballot, Grace McCarthy increased only 36 votes.

Vander Zalm	367 to 457
McCarthy	244 to 280
Brian Smith	196 to 255
Bud Smith	202 to 219
Reynolds	54 to 39
Nielsen	54 to 30

Between the second and third ballot, Grace McCarthy met

Brian Smith face-to-face in the convention hall basement. She had set up the meeting with messages carried by Bob Wenman and former attorney-general Robert Bonner, her heavyweight adviser. She wanted Brian Smith to come to her. Brian Smith told her he would pass her on the next ballot. She had to come to him. She refused.

This was Vander Zalm's second lucky break. The inability of Grace McCarthy and Brian Smith to make a deal in the basement meant his increase of 90 ballots was not unsubstantial. Meanwhile John Reynolds had decided to play follow the leader and go to Vander Zalm. With Reynolds came Cliff Michael, who would later claim his movement to Vander Zalm was the key that unlocked the floodgates for the leader. Observers would not concur.

The dramatic floor-crossing of lawyer Bud Smith to Vander Zalm would be the king-making move. This would be seen as the second of Whistler's two most fascinating events.

The first of the two remarkable events that will be remembered and discussed long after 1986 was described in Vaughn Palmer's Vancouver *Sun* column of Thursday, July 31. It concerns the banker in the basement, Bill Vander Zalm's #1 downstairs man.

"The story making the rounds after the convention was over," wrote Palmer, "was that Mr. Smith made a deal to settle his campaign debts. He did spend a lot on his campaign, and losers have more trouble paying the bills than winners.

"But his advisers deny there was any deal to cover his debts, and clearly Mr. Vander Zalm was surprised when Mr. Smith appeared on his doorstep. But even if Mr. Smith was offered no deal, others were.

"One of Mr. Vander Zalm's main contributors, banker Edgar Kaiser, attended the convention and for a time held court in the kitchen in the basement of the convention centre. Several candidates were whisked in secret down a back elevator in the convention hall and ushered in to meet the chairman of the Bank of British Columbia.

"I am assured by the usual reliable sources that Mr. Kaiser was making a remarkable offer. If the candidates would support his man Vander Zalm, their campaign debts would be taken care of. One who was present insists Mr. Kaiser had his cheque book on the table.

"Incredible. But as near as I have been able to determine, none of the candidates who crossed to Mr. Vander Zalm availed themselves of Mr. Kaiser's generosity.

"Candidate Mel Couvelier, the first to cross, has no campaign debts. Nor, I'm told, does John Reynolds. And Bud Smith's camp, as mentioned, denies any deal."

This story was quickly disputed by Kaiser's lawyer Peter Stafford. Stafford said Kaiser didn't even own a cheque book. Vander Zalm's campaign manager Bill Goldie said Edgar Kaiser, although a confirmed Vander Zalm supporter, did not financially contribute to Vander Zalm's campaign.

Edgar Kaiser had come to the Whistler convention on Wednesday to help muster support for Bill Vander Zalm. According to Vander Zalm, he was unaware of Kaiser's presence in the crowd. Kaiser was not wearing his own delegate's badge, only a certification badge that identified him with the White Spot restaurant chain. Peter Toigo, one of Bill Vander Zalm's major supporters and close friends, managed the White Spot chain in BC.

Kaiser was no longer on the best of terms with outgoing premier Bill Bennett. It was in Edgar Kaiser's best interests to see Bill Vander Zalm as the next premier because Vander Zalm would be least likely to be influenced by the power-brokers who had dominated Bennett's government.

According to *Equity*'s John Twigg, the antipathy between the Bank of BC's Kaiser and Bennett can be traced directly to the British Columbia Resources Investment Corporation and its monetary and management problems.

After the share giveaway and sale that created BCRIC in 1979, the original directors (John Pitts, David Helliwell, Trevor Pilley, Jack Poole, Chunky Woodward and Maury Young—all since departed) bought 67% of Kaiser Resources Ltd. (now Westar Mining) for $670 million. "If you want to say BCRIC was suckered, you don't have to be very bright to recognize that," said International Trade, Science and Investment minister Pat

McGeer in the legislature, "BCRIC made a series of disastrous investments."[32]

The BCRIC deal with Kaiser Resources came with a commitment to pay for about 15% of some new oil and gas developments in the Brae fields of the North Sea. BCRIC's North Sea debt, despite a $186 million bail-out payment in 1985, had reached about $450 million with negative equity of another $160 million by the time Edgar Kaiser appeared in Whistler.

BCRIC was the creation of Bill Bennett, but had become a personal embarrassment and a political liability for him. The five free shares given to every British Columbian as an object lesson in the wonders of free enterprise had turned into a provincial joke. The ill-fated early decision to buy 67% of Kaiser Resources was at the heart of BCRIC's failure.

When the Bank of BC faced a liquidity crisis due to fleeing commercial deposits, Bill Bennett was not eager to help the troubled bank (created by his father and with brother R.J. Bennett still on its board) because Edgar Kaiser was the chief executive officer. According to John Twigg's story in *Equity*, "The grapevine here says that Bennett apparently threatened to also withdraw provincial deposits unless the same Edgar Kaiser was replaced as its chief executive officer."[33]

Bill Bennett did eventually help the Bank of BC by authorizing a $75 million loan. And Edgar Kaiser was shifted over to chairmanship of the bank.

Kaiser was a very interested observer at the Whistler convention indeed, even if his lawyer did maintain he didn't even own a cheque book. If the party establishment candidates — Smith, Smith or McCarthy — walked away with Bill Bennett's job, the government would be more likely to continue to bear a grudge against Kaiser for "suckering" Bennett's BCRIC to the tune of $670 million. But if Vander Zalm won?

There was a great deal more at stake on Wednesday than a premiership.

The next day Vaughn Palmer wrote, "A few paragraphs in yesterday's column dealing with the activities of banker Edgar

Kaiser at the Socred convention provoked a flurry of phone calls and a few denials.

"I've re-interviewed some of those who provided information for yesterday's account, and several other people, and here is what they say happened.

"Mr. Kaiser attended the Socred convention and sought support for leadership candidate Bill Vander Zalm.

"He met with at least two leadership candidates and a representative of a third. Two of those meetings were held in the basement of the Whistler Convention Centre, where Mr. Kaiser was installed in a small office in the kitchen. Mr. Vander Zalm's manager, Bill Goldie, escorted one of the participants to the meeting room. For at least one of the meetings, other Vander Zalm supporters were present.

"The subject of the meetings, according to several participants, was what could be done to persuade a particular candidate to endorse Mr. Vander Zalm. One participant insists Mr. Kaiser offered to pay campaign debts in exchange for support.

"But, as I said yesterday, there is no evidence that any of the candidates who joined Mr. Vander Zalm took advantage of Mr. Kaiser's generosity."[34]

No legal actions were taken in conjunction with the much-disputed "pay-off rumour" story. But Kaiser's attorney, Peter Stafford, said, "That story is without foundation."[35] Edgar Kaiser was reported to be "extremely upset"[36] by the rumour. But the *Sun* refused to retract the story. "It never got to the writ stage and it never got to a retraction stage," says Palmer. "I reported what I knew about the thing."

On Friday the *Sun* contacted seven of Vander Zalm's eleven leadership rivals. All seven denied being offered money for campaign expenses by Edgar Kaiser. But there were two major holes in the "denial list" that the *Sun* ran on Saturday. The two men who most influenced the fate of the leadership election with their floor-crossings were not contacted. John Reynolds couldn't be reached and Bud Smith was reported vacationing on Vancouver Island.

Bud Smith had added just 17 votes on the second ballot. While he had the backing of former cabinet minister Don Phillips and cabinet ministers Alex Fraser and Tom Waterland, all representatives from the interior of the province, he couldn't garner much support from non-hinterland cabinet members. Vander Zalm had the grassroots support. Bud Smith's best option after the second ballot was to make a deal.

According to Phil Gaglardi, Bud Smith didn't go to Brian Smith's camp because he was at odds with a strong Smith supporter, MLA Claude Richmond. According to *Province* columnist Geoffrey Molyneux, Bud Smith didn't go to Brian Smith's camp because of Brian Smith's reluctance to consider a move to Bud Smith, even though Bud Smith had beaten Brian on the first ballot, 202 to 196.

Bud Smith, the candidate with the largest tent and the only candidate equipped with a hydraulic lift at the base of his platform to lift him higher and higher as the voting progressed, felt that most of his supporters preferred Bill Vander Zalm as a second choice over Brian Smith. The 40-year-old Kamloops lawyer, never elected to public office, had to consider his political future. He had the endorsements of 11 riding association presidents, 7 past presidents and another past party director. For Bud Smith, Whistler could still be just a beginning.

It was 3:45, the middle of a hot afternoon, and a Brian Smith supporter was shouting, "We need Bud Smith now!"[37]

It was time for Bud Smith to take a walk. Outside. While Brian Smith's troops were working the floor, trying to swing delegates, Bud Smith entered his suite over Tapley's, where he found advisers Don Phillips, Peter Hyndman, Tom Waterland, Mike Bailey, Janice Tolley, Gregg Lyle, Zahir Meghji, John Laschinger and Tony Saunders.

Bud Smith quickly announced to his colleagues he was going with the flow, not against it. There was little time for debate. "The delegates told me they want renewal," Smith said, "and that is it."[38]

The deadline for withdrawal was minutes away. Peter Hyndman carried Bud Smith's withdrawal papers to convention chairman Les Peterson. Bud Smith carried himself to Vander Zalm.

At 4:02, Bill Vander Zalm was astonished. Almost everyone was shocked. Vander Zalm hugged Bud Smith. "Super! I'm glad you're here," said BC's next premier.[39]

The Brian Smith camp was stunned. "He said he'd never go there," said a disbelieving Tourism minister Claude Richmond.[40] "That's incredible," said Jim Nielsen.[41] "It's a shock," said campaign worker Liz Byrd, "It's unprecedented."[42] The wife of Patrick Kinsella, Brenda Jones Kinsella, said furiously, "That's the politics of bitterness. That fucker!"[43] She later said, "I'm afraid to have a drink, the bullet holes might start leaking."[44]

Some of Bud Smith's own workers were also scandalized. "I'm shocked," said Bud Smith's chief fund-raiser, Dale Janowsky, a former law partner of Smith's.[45] Peggy Smith of Kamloops said, "He [Vander Zalm] was the one man I said I'd never vote for. I think he will tear the party apart."[46]

It was all over but the shooting. Bill Vander Zalm had nervously sat tight and unknowingly allowed the divisiveness and selfishness of the other candidates to confound and defuse his opponents. He wasn't winning. The others were beating themselves. "Confusing, isn't it?" said Grace McCarthy, after Bud Smith's unforeseen move."Who can understand it? Not me!"[47]

The third ballot showed Grace McCarthy gaining only 25 votes with Bud Smith out of the race.

Vander Zalm	625
Brian Smith	342
McCarthy	305

McCarthy could still go to Brian Smith's camp and almost make it a photo finish. But she rebuked Brian Smith's messenger, Bob Wenman, and turned her delegates free. "You know you can't win," Patrick Kinsella told Brian Smith. "Yes, I know," he replied.[48] But Smith refused the suggestion from Vander Zalm's camp that they should parade over to his box and then stage a joint procession to the stage, eliminating the need for a final vote. "If the delegates to this convention want Bill

Vander Zalm as their premier," said Brian Smith, "then they have a right to elect him."[49]

Bill Vander Zalm called it "the triumph of the shovel over the machine."[50]

| Vander Zalm | 801 |
| Brian Smith | 454 |

At 8:13 P.M., British Columbia had selected a new premier. "Machines cannot take the place of grassroots," he said.[51] Lillian Vander Zalm simply said, "I need a shower."[52] Patrick Kinsella said, "He won with, what, 800 votes out of a population of 3 million. I wouldn't go to the polls on the strength of that."[53] Allan Fotheringham observed, "He [Vander Zalm] is now to be the new premier, thanks to the help at the gathering at the top of the mountain of such names as John Reynolds and Bud Smith, neither of whom will be included when the Guinness Book of World Records includes a chapter on ethics and principles."[54] Grace McCarthy recovered her smile and said, "The NDP must be eating its heart out right now."[55] Bill Bennett said, "I know he can lead this party, I know he can run a government, I know he can lead and be part of a team."[56] John Twigg observed, "It was delicious for the rank-and-file."[57] Marjorie Nichols said, "The neo-conservative Social Credit machine built by Bill Bennett is dead, the victim of a freakish head-on collision with a grassroots bulldozer driven by an unelected, rampaging populist."[58]

Money had talked enough. The public would never know how much was said and to whom. One journalist described Bill Vander Zalm as "The Cheapest Premier Money Can Buy" in a news story, but his publisher chose not to run it. The honeymoon for Bill Vander Zalm was started by the media without delay. The contrast between the former premier's insecure woodenness and the new man's confident affability made him irresistible. The press was onto a good thing. Whether or not the BC public was also onto a good thing as of Wednesday, July 30 at Whistler was of secondary importance.

The victor went back to his tent to make an obligatory thank-you speech to his workers. Off to the side of the tent stood

Bud Smith, looking as if he were unsure whether or not he had to wipe his feet before entering. The new premier didn't notice Smith. Charles Giordano spotted him and informed Vander Zalm of Smith's presence at the edge of the crowd. Suddenly Bill Vander Zalm was speaking about all those surprise supporters who had made the difference, wishing that all of them could be with him on this wonderful night.

Lo and behold, Vander Zalm suddenly spotted Bud Smith and gave him an official welcome into the tent. A good auctioneer of power never misses a bid. "We're the envy of the world," declared his campaign literature, "We've got people with know-how, oil, gas, coal, minerals, forestry, tourism, agriculture and fisheries. Now instead of being salesmen and order-takers we must become marketeers."[59]

The market garden of BC politics was open for business.

13

PREMIER VANDER ZALM
Happiness at Last

"So far, it's a piece of cake."

> Premier Bill Vander Zalm
> Vancouver *Sun*
> August 15, 1986

"I wish I could clone myself."

> Premier Bill Vander Zalm
> Victoria Chamber of Commerce
> September 5, 1986

A loose cannon on deck.
A breath of fresh air.
A crackup.
A saviour.
The first liberal leader of BC since Duff Pattullo.
The leader of the Nouveau Gauche.
As handsome and as upright as a rosy tulip.
As clear and uncompromising as cold steel.
The Man Who Would Be King.

Wilhelmus Nicholaas Theodores Maria (Wim) Vander Zalm has been called many things. And many of the things he has been called have not been complimentary.

But on August 6, 1986, at the BC Legislative Buildings in Victoria, just before 2 P.M., on a perfect summer's day, the 52-year-old Dutch-Canadian immigrant and botanical theme park operator took his ultimate revenge.

Everybody had to call him Premier.

For years he had lusted after the job. In January of 1975 — nearly one year before he was elected to the BC legislature — he said he wanted to be either Municipal Affairs or Human Resources minister, and that he would probably eventually seek to replace Premier Bill Bennett as party leader. On his way to the top Vander Zalm had endured four election defeats and a three-year exile, far from the limelight he adored, struggling with a floundering business and widely written off as a political force. Now he was back with a vengeance, the master of his former rivals. The precise moment he was sworn in must have been sweet indeed.

To appreciate Vander Zalm's often puzzling approach to power, it is helpful to recognize both the similarities between Premier Bill Vander Zalm and the first BC Social Credit premier, the late W.A.C. Bennett, and the disparities and hostilities between Vander Zalm and his immediate predecessor, Bill Bennett.

W.A.C. Bennett was born on September 6, 1900, in the small village of Hastings in Albert County, New Brunswick. W.A.C. stood for William Andrew Cecil. The name Cecil was in honour of Cecil Rhodes, the famous British imperialist. The name Andrew was in honour of Bennett's father.

Bennett was the fifth of seven children. Two didn't survive infancy. The family was poverty-stricken. The father was often absent and a poor provider. Bennett's upbringing was managed by his mother, a strict Presbyterian. The Bible was the final authority on all matters. "I have always believed in a great architect in the universe, and in the great life of Jesus Christ," he said.[1]

Bennett never completed grade nine, nor did he ever pursue further formal education. He began clerking in a hardware store, learning the ropes of a small business as a salesman. According to his biographer David Mitchell, "he had an obsession for cleanliness and neatness and dressed well above his means."[2] He suffered psychologically from lengthy periods of separation from his errant father, who served in World War I and then wandered far afield from the family home to the Peace River country.

"Because of his own unfortunate childhood," observes Mitchell, "he had resolved to head a unified and harmonious home."[3]

Bennett was ambitious from a very young age, believing he had some sort of mission in life to fulfill, but he was determined he must first gain financial independence. He studied finance and banking. By diligent saving, he managed to invest $350 in a piece of property in Edmonton. He met his wife-to-be in an Edmonton church basement. They never honeymooned. He bought and developed a failing hardware business during the Depression in the Prairies, promoting "sales," maintaining "Buy right, sell right and collect your money."[4]

He moved to BC, developed his own store, and purchased a palatial home. "He had consciously equipped himself with the twin certitudes of faith and family."[5] Now eager to enter politics, he was a compulsive optimist and an established maverick who fashioned himself as a man of the people fighting against the "big city machine." He was also a blatant opportunist, shifting political parties as it suited him. After several setbacks, he decided to join the little-known British Columbia Social Credit League in 1951.

Developed by an eccentric Anglo-Scottish engineer, Major Clifford Hugh Douglas, Social Credit was a repudiation of the economic liberalism that was in vogue after the First World War. Its founder argued that economic hardship existed simply because people lacked purchasing power. He suggested governments should issue a "social credit" — a credit note to help buy needed goods. The ideal was to serve the mass will. Rather than have political parties, people would vote on plebiscites and a few technocrats would implement policies accordingly.

"Implicitly, his system contained ominous hints of fascism and suggested the possibility, or even likelihood, of a veiled dictatorship. . . his later writings are concerned with Dark Forces and identify a deep-laid plot by Jewish financiers to enslave the industrial world."[6]

Depression-era evangelist William Aberhart, preaching politics and religion simultaneously on Alberta radio broadcasts, was the chief proponent of Social Credit in Canada. On August

22, 1935, Aberhart introduced Albertans to the world's first Social Credit government. "Alberta voted for Santa Claus," noted the Vancouver *Sun*.[7] With financial support from Alberta, Social Credit began to make inroads into BC. The early Socreds were, according to author Martin Robin, a "drab collection of monetary fetishists, British Israelites, naturopaths, chiropractors, preachers, pleaders and anti-Semites."[8]

W.A.C. Bennett joined Social Credit and ran for office. The party's advertisements said "W.A.C. Bennett Is Going To Answer the Machines." Entering a 1952 general election, Bennett said, "It is my conviction that a new, better and honest government is required."[9] Social Credit promised to return Christian principles to power and abolish a plan for mandatory hospital insurance. Using a complicated preferential ballot that never could be counted to all parties' satisfaction, the Social Credit Party eked out a controversial one-seat victory over the CCF in the 1952 election and was asked to form a minority government.

W.A.C. Bennett became premier of the province for the first time thanks to a leadership convention. He said that in order for a government to be successful it required a strong premier, a capable attorney-general and a smart minister of Finance. W.A.C. Bennett made himself Finance minister. His first cabinet was extremely weak and inexperienced but Bennett said, "They were a great team because they were all new and so they took advice well."[10]

Bennett's administrative style was drawn from his years in private business. He preached thrift. His government meanwhile proceeded to spend more money than any other in the province's history. He raised the provincial sales tax. Meanwhile he maintained his government's goal was "to secure for every citizen an unfettered opportunity to obtain, through his own initiative and enterprise, a share of the material abundance of our vast resources."[11]

Bennett, a cynical populist, won a 1956 election with the slogan, "Progress Not Politics." He was intensely political at all times. He was also a straight-and-narrow prude who urged his cabinet ministers to "stay away from women" and demanded loyalty from his colleagues. He had little interest in the arts or in culture. He once said, "The finest music in the land is the ringing of cash registers."[12] As a premier, he measured the progress of society in strictly commercial terms.

W.A.C. Bennett was a calculated headline-grabber who enjoyed dropping news to reporters directly, rather than officially announcing news in press releases. He repeatedly won elections by promoting fear of socialism and anger at eastern Canada. He was eager to restructure government and gradually stifled the role of parliament through ever shorter sessions, all-night bouts of "legislation by exhaustion" and emasculation of the house committee system. He believed in always expressing forthright opinions, according to his dictum, "You've got to stand for something, or you'll fall for anything, my friend." He frequently inferred that he was personally "plugged into God."[13]

Following his father's path as a salesman, merchant and real estate investor, W.A.C. Bennett's second son, Bill, decided to enter politics. W.A.C. Bennett ruled as a smiling, paternalistic autocrat; his son would be regarded by many as a cold, fraternalistic technocrat.

Born in Kelowna BC on April 14, 1932, Bill Bennett was the youngest of three children. An unremarkable student, Bennett Jr. was stoical, determined and forced to carry the weight of a famous father's reputation. He completed high school at age 18, dropped notions of trying to become a lawyer, and went to work in his father's hardware store. At 23, he married a nurse's aide at the local hospital. He developed small investments wisely and assumed the hereditary control of the Social Credit party in mid-1973, taking his newly retired father's South Okanagan seat. Even before his ascent to the premier's job in 1975, Bill Bennett was at odds with the charismatic Bill Vander Zalm.

In July 1974, Surrey mayor Vander Zalm, as a newly converted Socred, suggested to the media that Bill Bennett, as party leader, ought to call a provincial unity convention of all opposition parties. "Mr. Bennett must be wondering just what kind of convert he acquired for his party in Mr. Vander Zalm," said BC Conservative leader Scott Wallace, "It must be demoralizing for Bill Bennett, in light of the fanfare and publicity with which he welcomed this big name to the Social Credit cause, because it now appears that Mr. Vander Zalm is something less than the enthusiastic supporter which is expected of a convert."[14]

Dubbed Brutus Vander Zalm by the NDP, Bill Vander Zalm admitted he would like Bill Bennett's job even prior to his election as an MLA.

Upon reaching Victoria and becoming Human Resources minister, Vander Zalm instantly created trouble for Bennett by announcing that if able-bodied welfare recipients didn't have a shovel, they ought to get one, otherwise the government would start supplying them. These remarks led to an angry demonstration in front of the legislature. Protesters broke into the cabinet room and spent 45 minutes in verbal exchanges before Bill Bennett was able to defuse the situation.

Whereas Bill Bennett was a premier "who relished the complexity of issues,"[15] Vander Zalm was a man who believed, "The experts advising the government say we can't solve the problems of the province because they are too complicated. I say NOT TRUE. The basics haven't changed—only governments have elaborated and complicated to the point of confusion."[16] Whereas Bill Bennett liked to measure public opinion by costly polls, Vander Zalm believed strongly in main-streeting to gauge public moods.

The different approaches of Bill Bennett and Bill Vander Zalm prompted Bill Bennett to say, "I don't need polls to tell me what the guy in the beer parlour is thinking. I just walk down the hall and talk to Vander Zalm."[17]

Whereas Bill Vander Zalm said he hoped to streamline his Municipal Affairs department and theoretically help the public by concentrating more power in his own position, Bill Bennett was a leader who preferred to restructure government simply to help the Social Credit party, adopting controversial electoral boundary reforms which produced the so-called "Gracie's finger" issue. The best known altercation between the two men occurred after Bennett allowed Vander Zalm's proposed Land Use Act die on the order paper. Vander Zalm responded with his famous "gutless" charge.

Ten days after Vander Zalm had called the rest of the cabinet gutless, Bennett switched Vander Zalm to the Education portfolio. In September Bennett criticized Vander Zalm's work in front of television, newspaper and radio reporters, saying the one thing he didn't need any more was "political heat from any quarter."[18] The premier told reporters he intended to spend the weekend helping to draft education funding legislation. On the Monday that followed, Bennett was unable to say if Vander Zalm had participated in the weekend's work. The legislation subsequently contained provisions—such as permission for school boards to transfer capital funds into operational budgets—which Vander Zalm had opposed.

Tuesday morning, when Bill 89 was introduced, Vander Zalm did something seldom seen in the legislature. He crossed the floor and chatted briefly with NDP MLA Bill King and then talked for ten minutes with Opposition leader Barrett. "He came over to chat about it," said Bill King, "He is feeling isolated. He has been put through the meat grinder in public by the premier. He has been kicked in the teeth. He has been forced to introduce a bill that was designed by the premier. He has been betrayed."[19]

Vander Zalm was the lone cabinet minister to voice his displeasure at the way the government handled the so-called Lettergate scandal (where Social Credit party members placed phony letters-to-the-editor in community newspapers). He also objected to a BC Hydro rate increase.

Relations were further strained between Bill Bennett and Bill Vander Zalm when Vander Zalm chose not to run in the 1983 election. He called Bennett a "strong-minded person" with whom he had obviously had "disagreements." He then said BC's unemployment rate was far too high at 13% and he criticized heavy civil service layoffs. Since Vander Zalm was the acknowledged favourite amongst the grassroots supporters of Social Credit, Bennett and his colleagues were forced to tolerate Vander Zalm's frankness. "They grit their teeth," claimed Marjorie Nichols, "every time the man gives a speech."[20]

During the Social Credit leadership campaign Vander Zalm objected to Bill Bennett's style. "There was possibly too much strength with some of the people who were not elected. I think, too, the government of Bill Bennett did not communicate as well as they might have."[21] By comparison, Vander Zalm's campaign literature maintained, "Honesty and sincerity will overshadow the hurt that sometimes comes from the truth."[22]

When he became premier in August 1986, Vander Zalm allowed his King George Highway Hospital Syndrome to skewer the retiring leader. Even though Bill Bennett had swallowed his disappointment and raised Bill Vander Zalm's arm in victory at Whistler, Vander Zalm proceeded to make front page headlines by asserting that the "Sentinel Group" had far too much influence in the former government's affairs. The Sentinel Group was the umbrella name for companies owned by the Social Credit party's chief fundraiser, Mike Burns, and two former aides to Bennett, Patrick Kinsella and Doug Heal. Burns, Kinsella and Heal jointly owned Dome Advertising Ltd., which did business with the government.

"I know it's dangerous to quote rumours," said Vander Zalm, "and I'm not even quoting rumours, but the rumours have been out there and somehow there's been the connection between the premier's office or the government and people connected with the Sentinel Group, and that may be, I don't know. But I will find out."[23] In fact, there was public evidence that Patrick Kinsella had advised at least one organization to hire former MLA Peter Hyndman on a $4,000-per-month retainer basis to help draft legislation in a knowledgeable way in the hope that it might be "rubber-stamped" by cabinet.

Within an hour of taking office as the new minister of Energy, Mines and Petroleum Resources, Jack Davis said that two of Bennett's fondest mega-project dreams, Site C dam on the Peace River and a natural gas pipeline to Vancouver Island, might no longer be considered. "I question the economics of any government putting in millions into a project that would not serve exceptional needs," said Davis, a minister formerly spurned by Bennett, "We can serve those needs in other ways."[24]

In policies as well as style, the government of Bill Vander Zalm disassociated itself from the administration of Bill Bennett as soon as possible. After an inaugural speech on August 6, in which Vander Zalm pledged a new approach to government that would be "open and up front,"[25] Bill Vander Zalm proceeded to pursue a course more consistent with the 1950s populism of the cagey Bennett Sr.

Like W.A.C. Bennett when he formed his first government in 1952, Vander Zalm had a maverick persona which placed him very much alone at the helm. The captain of the Socred ship of state took on the Finance portfolio, like W.A.C. Bennett, and appointed a caretaker cabinet that featured his leadership rival Brian Smith back in as attorney-general; Grace McCarthy restored to the bridesmaid role of deputy premier; Hugh Curtis, former Finance minister, demoted to provincial secretary; Vander Zalm's old Surrey cohort Rita Johnson in Municipal Affairs and Transit; and Jack Davis, back from the grave as master of Energy, Mines and Petroleum Resources, along with most of Bennett's former choices in the their former places.

Unfortunately many of the most capable ministers from Bill Bennett's era were deciding not to work with Vander Zalm, many before and some even after he announced his cabinet. Cumulatively he was losing James Chabot, Don Phillips, Bill Ritchie, Harvey Schroeder, Jack Heinrich, Garde Gardom, Bob McClelland and Tom Waterland. Alex Fraser had cancer. Stephen Rogers was openly critical of Vander Zalm. Jim Nielsen said he was retiring to write a novel. Then Curtis, whose advice Vander Zalm badly needed in Finance, repaid the premier's slight by announcing on September 25 that he wouldn't seek re-election either. Atlin MLA Al Pasarell died in a plane crash on the way to attend a constituency nominating meeting on September 27.

Without a strong team behind him, Vander Zalm tried to keep himself in the limelight in order insure his party's victory in the election he was to call for October 22.

Vander Zalm put his best foot forward in Edmonton on August 10 when he attended the annual meeting of the ten Canadian premiers. This conference seemed more of an occasion for provincial premiers to polish their reputations than their policies. As Geoffrey Molyneux of the *Province* wisely noted, "How can they agree to 'fight to save agriculture, energy and lumber from international competition' and then endorse free trade? One's black, the other's white."[26]

Vander Zalm again improved his image as a statesman by adopting an intermediary role in the 31-month contract dispute between the 34,000-member BC Government Employees Union and the provincial government. An agreement was reached on August 20, creating the impression that Bill Vander Zalm could be a friend of labour. Provincial labour leaders were appreciative but skeptical. The BCGEU controversy was a golden opportunity for Vander Zalm to appear hospitable to unions, to create a good "first impression." Two tougher strikes with the IWA and the BC Nurses Union continued unresolved.

Vander Zalm and his wife went on a three-day whirlwind tour of Castlegar, Trail, Kimberley, Fort Steele and Cranbrook in late August. The highlight was an impromptu singalong in Kimberley, as Lillian played the accordion and Vander Zalm sang a beer-drinking song. "Are we in some sort of movie?"[27] asked a TV cameraman. In Trail, Vander Zalm played *bocce* with elderly Italian-Canadians. The premier also rode a sled down a hillside outside Kimberley. He admitted there was not much substance to his first provincial tour.

In August Vander Zalm opened a Sikh temple in Richmond wearing a white kerchief on his head and a garland of marigolds around his neck. He spoke a few words of Punjabi. His picture appeared in colour on the front page of the *Sun*. In late September he made good on an earlier promise to participate in native Indian life. He kicked off his election campaign by taking Lillian to stay overnight at the village of Gwa-yee, hosted by the Musgamagw Tribal Council at Kingcome Inlet. It was supposed to be a private study session. But somehow the urban media managed to make the trip and send back chummy photos of Lillian hugging an Indian girl. Little press notice was given to the Indian leaders' stated resolve, after the Vander Zalms left them, that they were still going to vote for the NDP.

As a political campaigner, Bill Vander Zalm cultivates a flamboyant exterior with his winning personality and good looks. In Edmonton at the premiers' conference he appeared in

the flashiest car, a cherry-red Chrysler. Attending the cabinet swearing-in ceremonies in Victoria he rolled up in a rented green Oldsmobile Cutlass. While visiting Prince George in September Vander Zalm donned a $2,500 fur coat and posed as an advertising model. (A rival fur coat company in BC, Pappas Furs, had been running an extremely successful ad campaign for several years featuring *Rocky* and *Rambo* actor Sylvester Stallone modelling fur coats.)

In one of the most penetrating studies of Vander Zalm so far written, Sid Tafler of Victoria's *Monday Magazine* once noted the extent to which Vander Zalm expertly performs for the media. "He often cocks his head disarmingly, coquettishly, and flashes his broad, toothy, amiable smile with ease. He's an unforgivable ham — photographers complain they have trouble catching him out of pose."[28]

Vander Zalm's only mistake in manipulating the media was his compliance with his handlers' advice to appear in a $200,000 TV ad campaign to assure the BC public that the deficit for Expo 86 — whatever it turned out to be — would be paid for from lottery funds. "At the rate of $6 million a month," he said on the slick ad, "the deficit will be cleared in 1988 and not by tax dollars."[29] The ad misleadingly implied the Expo deficit would be only $168 million. Expo chairman Jim Pattison concurrently estimated the Expo deficit might be around $311 million. The ad failed to mention that $140 million of lottery funds had already been allocated to Expo.

The real flaw in the ad was that it demonstrated a glaring hole in his integrity. Vander Zalm, who had promised to bring high Christian principles to leadership, had stated earlier, on the Jack Webster Show, his belief that lotteries were essentially a form of taxation on the poor. So in the television ad, he was essentially saying Expo 86 would be paid for by the poor. To avoid alienating the voters, he was willing to allow this situation to continue, even though he strongly felt it was wrong. Neither the NDP nor the media cared to unravel Vander Zalm's twisted principles and recall his pledge in his inaugural address "to do not what is expedient — but what is right."

I confronted him about this lapse in an interview, and he didn't offer a very reassuring defence. "I'm not making apologies for the ads on television talking about the after-Expo [deficit]," he said. "But when that was first presented to me, the time was booked, the arrangements had been made with the advertising agency to put it all together, all of that was done. My gut was telling me, 'I don't really need this. I shouldn't be doing it. This was arranged before my time, it's booked, but I don't really need it.' That was my gut. But I took it on anyway."

During the election campaign, while the Opposition's Bob Skelly nervously tried to concentrate on policy statements, Vander Zalm refused the Opposition Leader's challenge to debate and admittedly concentrated on his own personal style. "Style means a lot in any campaign," he said, "because it's what people see."[30] For the most part the media much preferred covering Vander Zalm's style to Bob Skelly's attempts at substance. Substance required analysis and research. Substance was dull. Bob Skelly, it was assumed, was a dull person. Bill Bennett had been a dull person. It was time for a change.

In conjunction with his extremely amiable personality and his accessibility to media, Vander Zalm did, however, present a number of proposals for change.

Following his selection at Whistler, Vander Zalm said he would examine a tax voucher system that would allow property owners to direct their taxes to either the public or private school system. He later modified this promise considerably, indicating he might just try this system in one small area as an experiment. He said he hoped to abolish some government-run agricultural marketing boards. He hoped to pay more attention to agriculture. He would sell government liquor stores to private interests, allow casinos in some BC communities where residents approved, review the province's labour code, make Crown Corporations more responsive to the public, scrutinize abortion procedures, implement more public referendums and tackle public funding for small businesses.

His most popular promises concerned liquor. He said he would continue Sunday drinking after Expo 86 was over. He also strongly hinted he would lower the prices of beer. As well, he wanted to remove taxes from restaurant meals.

With an accumulated deficit of $5.1 billion, Finance Minister Vander Zalm ordered a review of the much-debated stumpage system used by the Department of Forests to charge forest companies for timber cutting rights, due in November. In a province where fifty cents of every dollar is still generated by the forest industry, this forestry review would be crucial to the economic well-being of all British Columbians. According to the 1984–85 annual report for the Ministry of Forests, stumpage generated $187 million in revenues for the province. Increasing stumpage fees by 10% could generate an additional $20 million.

But it wasn't the prospect of an additional $20 million in revenues that chiefly prompted the stumpage review. US lumbermen were charging that BC's low stumpage fees constituted a subsidy that allowed Canadian exporters to undercut the domestic US product. For the second time in three years, they asked the US Commerce Department to impose a 35% countervailing duty on softwood imports. In an eleventh hour attempt to head off an adverse decision, expected in October, Vander Zalm went public with a proposal to voluntarily hike stumpage rates on the Canadian side. A countervailing duty on the order of 35% would cripple the industry in BC. It was much to Bill Vander Zalm's personal advantage to delay that US countervail decision, at least until after the election, and in Prince George Vander Zalm said he expected the Americans to defer their decision until the BC review was completed.

It was a bold move, in sharp contrast to the position taken by former premier Bennett, and of course, by the industry. Everyone knew BC stumpage rates were a scandal, but during the recent crisis in the industry few had been willing to criticize. Then the Americans got on the case and no loyal Canadian wanted to admit the legitimacy of the US charge lest he play into American hands. Labour and industry stood together in denying there was a de facto subsidy and even NDP leader Bob Skelly found himself in the strange position of condemning Vander

Zalm when he broke ranks to suggest, yes, maybe industry could pay a little more for the timber resource.

The economy of BC was failing badly.

Unemployment was at 12%, compared with 9.5% nationally. This was the third-highest rate in the country, behind Newfoundland and New Brunswick. More layoffs would be forthcoming with the closure of Expo 86. Labour unrest was growing, particularly in the troubled lumber industry, where an IWA strike was threatening to cost BC lumber producers upwards of $1 billion. ICBC and BCGEU workers had settled contracts but still in negotiations were 25,000 hospital employees, 11,400 pulp and paper mill workers and 30,000 teachers. Contract talks were due for ferry workers, telephone company employees and hydro workers. Jobs were scarce and getting scarcer, most notably in the province's #1 industry. Whereas in 1981, 96,000 workers helped BC forest companies export $4.8 billion worth of wood fibre products, in 1985 the export figure rose to $6.2 billion while the number of employees dropped to 78,000.

As Raymond V. Smith, chief executive officer of Macmillan Bloedel Ltd., said in 1986, "Except for BC, the North American economy has performed fairly well since 1983."[31] Smith noted the problem in the forest industry began when major BC companies were engaged in capital programs, for which they had borrowed heavily, in order to keep ahead of competition. "As interest rates soared leading into the recession," Smith says, "more and more of the industry's income was shifted to financing debt. MacMillan Bloedel alone spends $70 million to $80 million a year on interest, and other companies have faced similar burdens on their borrowings. It's a load the industry continues to carry into 1986."[32]

Lumber prospects did pick up considerably in BC thanks to a midyear turnaround reported by Canfor Corporation, Macmillan Bloedel, BC Forest Products, Weldwood and West Fraser Timber. The unthreatened bright spots in the BC economy were fishing, copper and BC Hydro. Hydro chairman Chester Johnson announced revenues surpassed $2 billion for the first time and left Hydro with a net income of $12 million for the year ending March 31, 1986. Unfortunately, while Hydro profits soared it was partly at the expense of labour, as the number of Hydro employees had been dropped from 8,205 in 1984 to 6,508 in 1986.

The dark spots were BCRIC and coal. With BCRIC shares dropping to $1.25 from a high of more than $9 when the company was started in 1979, BCRIC's chief executive officer Bruce Howe resigned his post. BCRIC had reported a $5.2 million loss for the first half of 1986 and had commenced "downsizing" the company with layoffs. "It's regrettable but that's the way it is," said Howe.[33] In the coal industry, Japanese buyers pressured suppliers to either cut prices or volume. The Quintette Mine in northeastern BC forced co-owner Denison Mines to undertake a $240.7 million "write-down," resulting in a net loss for 1985 of $157.9 million.

Overall, annual capital investment in BC had declined to $8.5 billion from $12 billion between 1981 and 1985. This drop ensued even in spite of massive government spending on Expo, Skytrain and the Coquihalla Highway. The essence of BC's financial woes were summed up by Richard Allen, chief economist of the BC Central Credit Union. "The private sector has not been the engine of growth it was supposed to be when the government implemented restraint more than three years ago," said Allen.[34]

In 1980, the number of people who came to live in BC outnumbered those who left the province by 40,000. In 1985, 7,000 more people left than arrived. Restraint was very much in disrepute. As the man who proudly claimed credit as the founder of restraint, Finance Minister Vander Zalm should have had his work cut out answering for the mess. But no one in the media thought to ask. Vander Zalm even succeeded in taming tough guy Jack Webster of BCTV with pronouncements like, "A good economy will look after all the other problems."[35] Webster, known for his bulldog approach to interviews, could not snare Vander Zalm on a single issue on the show that kicked off Webster's new late-afternoon TV program on September 2.

"We will move to consolidate and build upon the growing climate of economic renewal and confidence that is taking hold and strengthening across British Columbia," Vander Zalm said in his inaugural address.[36] "I have some innovative ideas and strategies to bring about new employment for British Columbians and the operations of the Finance ministry are closely linked to those plans,"[37] the new Finance minister later said.

Before announcing his departure from Vander Zalm's team, former Finance minister Hugh Curtis said, "it's possible. . .substance may be delivered eventually."[38] Eventually, on September 29, Vander Zalm announced an economic expansion program under which the provincial government would take over operation and promotion of Vancouver International Airport as well as become more involved with port development at Roberts Bank. The moves were suggested by a task force headed by BC Transit chairman Stuart Hodgson. The BC government hoped to somehow make Vancouver the communications hub of the Pacific, being, it was noted, an equal distance from both Tokyo and London. Vander Zalm made this announcement on a podium carrying a fresh slogan, "The New Economy."

Bill Vander Zalm's "New Economy" rhetoric was in lock-step with the neo-Reaganite utterances of the previous Bennett administration to such a degree that one reporter was moved to ask, "Isn't this the same thing we've been hearing for the last ten years?" All Vander Zalm could say was, "Well, you're hearing it again."

Vander Zalm's administration continued to make British Columbia the only province in Canada not to stop selling South African wine. His stance on South African trade revealed the extent to which Vander Zalm and Reagan were philosophically linked. Even when the federal government's external affairs department moved to terminate import permits for South African products, thereby stopping the flow of South African wines in Canada, Vander Zalm protested, repeating the Margaret Thatcher hypocrisy that such trade sanctions primarily hurt South Africa's blacks. "You won't find many white men picking the grapes or crushing the grapes in South Africa; it's all black people,"[39] he said. Like Ronald Reagan and Margaret Thatcher, Bill Vander Zalm was willing to assert that he understood what was best for South Africa's blacks better than the majority of the country's black leaders who were requesting the trade sanctions developed from a Commonwealth Conference in London in August of 1986.

Meanwhile Bill Vander Zalm's economic expansion program was inconsistent with his general policy of promoting laissez-faire capitalism. While rising to power and popularity with a much-touted belief that less government involvement in the people's affairs was best (stating, for example, that he would take a new hard line against government bailouts of financially troubled businesses) he was advocating an economic expansion program for the province in which the government would be the leading player. This contradiction did not seem to bother anyone. On September 18 he spoke to the Canadian Chamber of Commerce, saying, "Government cannot continue to interfere with the marketplace as it has for too long in this province." Eleven days later he announced the government would be at the leading edge of his New Economic Reality.

Obviously one of the problems with taking a bead on Bill Vander Zalm's personality and political philosophy is that he continually adds new pieces to the puzzle of his approach to power. It is virtually impossible for journalists to make sense of the puzzle when they are given new pieces daily. A pervasive confusion as to Bill Vander Zalm's motives in public office has naturally evolved. That confusion is easily verified. When one looks at the long list of attempts to buttonhole Vander Zalm in a phrase, he remains a two-sided jigsaw puzzle of conflicting personas.

The irrepressible good-looker of the BC cabinet.
The architect of a reign of terror.
The baby-faced Dutchman.
The Minister of Misery.
Not wishy-washy.
Insufferably blunt.

Charming, warm, aware, intelligent, sincere.

Archaic.

The most adroit media manipulator in Canadian politics today.

Completely undisciplined in the political field.

One of those Jaycee types who always remember names and take pains to punctuate sentences with them during otherwise casual conversation.

Always one quote away from political disaster.

The compleat populist politician.

The darling of the born-again rightists.

The Jumpin' Jack Flash of BC politics.

The Jimmy Swaggart of politics, the Oral Roberts of Confederation.

The Dutch Juggernaut.

The Zalm.

14

VANDER ZALM
& THE MEDIA
Some Observations

*"I knowingly say things in a controversial way that
tends to get the press."*

Bill Vander Zalm
to Robert Williamson, *Globe & Mail*
March 1, 1979

INCIDENT #1:   It's Monday morning in the Inn of the North.
The attractive woman reporter from the *Province* has lost her
earrings. She doesn't know where to find them.

Bill Kay has found them. Bill Kay is a former golf pro from
Alberta. He is also serving as Premier Vander Zalm's press
secretary, chauffeur and travelling companion. Bill is returning
the earrings to the reporter in the lobby of the hotel. He is sidling
up to her, putting his arm around her. She is pleased to get her
earrings back. She is not so pleased to be seen with the arm of
Premier Vander Zalm's new press secretary around her shoulder.

She does not tell Bill Kay to keep his mitts off. She doesn't
dare. The amicable tensions that exist between the premier's
office and the media are typified in this exchange. How close can
the press and the politicians get before it's too close for comfort
or propriety? It is a fascinating sport to watch, this cat and
mouse game where the roles switch back and forth, back and
forth. In this particular incident the media representative must
ingratiate herself. The attractive woman reporter does not
rebuff Bill Kay. She knows she is going to need his cooperation in

the coming days, weeks and months — maybe even years — ahead, and it doesn't pay to make enemies with people who can help you. Besides, he has just returned her earrings. Bill Kay has just done the reporter a little favour.

INCIDENT #2: It's Monday afternoon in the Inn of the North and International Trade Minister Pat McGeer is nervously handing over a newly prepared press release to a reporter from BCTV News, the most wide-reaching news outlet in the province. Government communications counsel Dave Laundy has arranged the meeting. There are no other mainstream reporters present.

"Do you think this is good enough for an on-camera?" McGeer wheedles. Now the power is on the other side. The political representative must ingratiate himself. McGeer waits at the seated reporter's shoulder as he quickly examines the printed information. The gist of it is that McGeer is being dispatched to attend some sort of economic conference back east. It's not front-page material by any means. But the reporter decides to be benevolent. This time. After his 60-second look at the story, he motions his cameraman to set up an item.

The reporter and McGeer scurry over to the far corner of the foyer, beside a plant, out of earshot of the only other person around. There is an aura of discreet bargaining about this conversation. But who's selling? Who's buying? Is this free trade? Who's getting the best of the transaction? Is this a scoop? Will this show the world that the man from BCTV is one step ahead of the other reporters? Will this show the world that Pat McGeer is once again a major force in BC politics?

Ten minutes later the other reporters are beckoned forward by Dave Laundy, who seems to be a very nice man doing a very competent job for all concerned. But BCTV News already has the story in hand. One is left with the impression that the reporter has just done Pat McGeer a little favour.

INCIDENT #3: It's Monday afternoon and Premier Vander Zalm is in the midst of one of the "scrums" that he seems to enjoy so much. The reporters are thrusting their microphones into his face. They are hoping to be thrown a scrap of sustenance to fill their daily quota of newsprint or airtime. Vander Zalm appears cool and in control, remarkably tolerant.

Then CKVU's Dale Robbins breaks the rules. He is asking an embarrassing question. Robbins is bringing forth some sort of statistic about people being unemployed. How is Vander Zalm's optimistic speech really going to do much for everybody out of work? Isn't he simply talking a good game? Vander Zalm is taken aback. His smiling and thoughtful countenance suddenly expresses irritation. He takes note of who asked the question, but makes no attempt to answer it.

"No comment," he says, curtly.

And that's it. The end of the item. Vander Zalm, who has pledged an open and up-front style, apparently need only answer questions he prefers to answer. None of the other reporters jump to Robbins's support, asking backup questions. In fact, quite the opposite. The rest of the scrum is probably secretly pleased to see that a competitor for news has just been shut down. Vander Zalm's response, everybody knows, is hardly one that can make it onto the evening news.

Dale Robbins has done something uncalled for and in bad taste, like someone breaking wind at a tea party. The next time he attempts to get a personal interview with Bill Vander Zalm, the odds are he'll have to line up behind the others. And all because the CKVU reporter tried to do the BC public a little favour.

And so, as Kurt Vonnegut wrote, it goes.

These three incidents, all from the same day, reveal that the relationship between media and politicians may seem highly principled on camera, but it can be rather tawdry and clumsy off camera. Everybody's in it together. And nearly everybody agrees to play by the rules. The rules are simple and very unoriginal: you scratch my back, I'll scratch yours.

This game is not pretty but it can be sophisticated. That is, the players must respect invisible boundaries and unwritten rules. If the politicians agree to make themselves available, the media must agree not to ask questions which are too difficult or challenging. Those who break the rules will pay a price. The game is dignified by the fact that the tradeoffs work both ways. If a reporter is so uncouth as to embarrass a politician he will be cold-shouldered. Similarly if Vander Zalm slips into a meeting through a back door, bypassing the press, he could pay for it in the morning. The press demands its daily feeding. And the politicians need the press.

Journalists must remain in calling-card-distance of power or run the risk of being cut off from their supply of material. That's why even ardent Bill Vander Zalm critics, such as the *Sun*'s Marjorie Nichols, invariably offer some complimentary columns about the new premier. When Bill Vander Zalm was a struggling cabinet minister, he once accused Marjorie's paper of spreading venom about him. Bill Vander Zalm as a very popular premier has the upper hand. He may choose to grant a personal interview to Marjorie Nichols or he may not. Nobody in the media wants to be left out in the cold. Overnight, personal stances on Vander Zalm are softened in the media. Despite his political record and his innumerable contradictions of rhetoric and policy, Vander Zalm has become respectable because the commentators wish to retain their own well-paid but never secure positions.

This problem of fuzzy standards in the media is complicated by the fact the political journalists and commentators see themselves as competitors against one another. Even in the silly situation where the *Province* and the *Sun* are owned by the same company and operate out of two halves of the same building, with the same presses, the facade of healthy competition is maintained to motivate excellence. In fact, competition between political reporters and critics does precisely the opposite.

Precious few journalists have the guts to risk jeopardizing their ease of access to those with power by confronting politicians with uncomfortable questions. As a result, the undisciplined "scrums" favoured by Vander Zalm actually work in his favour. He is seen to be extremely accessible. But in fact he is only accessible to hurried, simplistic questions.

The nature of Bill Vander Zalm's symbiotic relationship with the media obviously requires analysis if one is to understand fully how Vander Zalm became premier of British Columbia. Unlike most politicians, who are extremely reserved and careful in their relations with the press, Bill Vander Zalm does not play against the press, but with them. That is, he understands the voracious appetite of reporters and seems to respect it. "I like nothing better," he has remarked, "[than] for a reporter to get a front-page byline. I think, 'That's just got him a mark with the people he works for.' It's really a desire that the success I have for myself I also want for others."[1]

Bill Vander Zalm plays a mating game with the press, not a baiting game—although the jealous lover has his moments of rage. If he has any one particular genius as a politician, it is his salesman's understanding of how the media function, and his ability to fashion his behaviour accordingly. He realizes—perhaps better than many journalists—the desperate need of the professional space-fillers to provide lively news copy six days a week. And he exploits it for all he's worth.

"He says the first thing that comes to mind," Vaughn Palmer has noted, "and the crowds eat it up."[2] So, of course, do the journalists. Not only has Vander Zalm obligingly supplied journalists with over-publicized quips and pranks, taking advantage of the many years of "on-stage" experience he gained as an auctioneer; he has also proven himself to be unusually adept at capitalizing on spontaneous situations (the banana-cream-pie incident), plotting to insert himself prominently in the public eye (hoping to be mayor during Expo 86) and using media to further his private business interests (advertising Fantasy Garden World at every opportunity). Vander Zalm agrees his ability to promote himself has helped him "a fair bit. Politics," he says, "is marketing."

This is a man who, while seeking the leadership of the Social Credit Party, and therefore an instant premiership, decided to shave off his out-of-date but trademark sideburns in front of the television cameras. "I cut off 1½ inches and got four minutes of TV," he said. "I left the other 1½ inches so that I'll get another four minutes when I decided to shave them."[3]

This is a man who openly admitted he was running his provincial election campaign in 1986 on style, not substance.

This is a media Frankenstein.

Upon announcing his plans to temporarily retire as a Social Credit cabinet minister, Education Minister Vander Zalm was asked about the large share of media coverage he had garnered during eighteen years in political office. He said, "I'm going to miss that as much as the media."[4]   The *Globe and Mail's* Robert Williamson has described Vander Zalm as "an unrepentant media philanthropist."[5] Clearly those in the media have realized that Bill Vander Zalm is a media opportunist, a politician who tries to insert himself into the news as often as possible. The *Sun's* veteran reporter Hal Lieren said, "He is a man who enjoys publicity. He is unusually forthright for a politician, says what is on his mind and usually manages to say it pithily. He can usually come up with a twist of phrase, a sentence that is sure to grab a headline, or to fit neatly into the 'voicers' of radio reporters who produce hourly news tidbits with the fecundity of rabbits. At times he even seems to take a perverse delight in saying outrageous things to see what kind of reaction they produce in reporters."[6]

Far from resisting Vander Zalm's gambits for attention, the press has encouraged him to perform and to present audacious statements. "I've had good reporting," Vander Zalm said, upon announcing his sabbatical in 1983, "No complaints on that."[7]

But those who have watched his media play closely over the years have occasionally seen the happy face mask slip, revealing a quite different actor behind it. *Province* staff knowing his reputation for friendly calls offering stories on slow news days must have been shocked to read his letter in the March 18, 1985 edition saying, "The *Province* has become an embarrassment to me. Day after day, I see ridiculous misleading headlines followed by the first-section pages and realize what a terrible disservice your paper is to BC. I know that many potential investors must be scared away from BC when seeing such headlines. They do not realize this is the sensation-seeking 'new enquirer' of BC — The *Province*." The provocation for this outburst was the paper's article on his windup speech in the Vancouver mayoralty race, which accurately reported that he said Koreans, Filipinos, Vietnamese and Chinese look alike. It was reminiscent of a similar letter that accused the *Sun* of "spewing its venom" on him in 1983 after the editors refused to let him use his gardening column to advertise his own botanical garden. "I realize, and always have, your position as far as Bill Vander Zalm is concerned," he wrote. "I appreciate that was aggravated by my refusal to continue a garden column when I was told by an editor that I could write about public (tax-supported) gardens but not privately owned gardens...If one day there is only one newspaper, no election, and no need to advertise, you can probably take pride in having been responsible for it, but you will not have the means to say it."

These outbursts reveal a Vander Zalm which stands in sharp contrast to the media image we have of Vander Zalm as a sweet-natured believer in the maxim, "If you cannot say anything good about someone, don't say nothing." They suggest instead a man who secretly nurtures a considerable reservoir of bitterness against the world. This resentment as it applies to the media shows frequently in smaller ways. When explaining the failure of his cherished Land Use Act to me he put much blame on the media. "Even though most local government people were supportive of it, they [the press] searched out some of those who were opposed and they were naturally the ones who were most often quoted—there's no use getting somebody to quote that's in agreement with you so they searched out the ones that were opposed..." In the Sept. 21, 1981 letter he wrote defending his brothers against an investigation brought by the ALR, he blamed the whole problem on "a newspaper article in the Vancouver *Sun*, dated August 22, 1981,...[that] was inaccurate and biased but gave the Press little satisfaction as it appears the public may have read it for what it was. The only satisfaction the Vancouver *Sun* could hope to get from the article now is to stir your bureaucrats into badgering another taxpaying business into defending themselves against the unknown or unproven allegations of a 'mud-slinging' journalist who possibly could not make a living running a nursery because it takes honest hard work!"

What is surprising about these outbursts is their intensity, revealing a passion that is decidedly out of character and borders on the irrational. It seems to point at something deeper than mere disappointment over poor publicity. Vander Zalm's Dr. Jekyll and Mr. Hyde media personality came into clearest focus during the Pulling Wings Off Flies Affair.

On June 22, 1978 the Victoria *Times* published a Bob Bierman cartoon of BC's Human Resources Minister gleefully picking the wings off flies. The cartoon was captionless. Although the person seated at a desk in the picture was not specifically identified as Bill Vander Zalm, the likeness was apparent and it was confirmed by a tag pinned onto the subject's lapel which read "Human Resources." The minister was depicted with a demonic, highly pleased expression on his face. Vander Zalm filed a suit for damages. More than any other issue or statement in his political career, the legal battle over the propriety of Bob Bierman's caricature catapulted Vander Zalm into the national media spotlight for an extended period.

Vander Zalm's suit was against Bierman, editor Barbara McLintock and Victoria *Times* publisher Stuart Underhill. During the week-long trial in early January 1979 Vander Zalm maintained the cartoon showed him "as some monstrous person picking wings off flies. It's just terrible."[8]

Justice F. Craig Munroe, in his seven-page judgement released January 17, 1979, awarded $3,500 and court costs to Vander Zalm. This judgement prompted a barrage of press coverage from sea to sea. The publicity lasted well over a year. Writers pontificated that the freedom of the press might be jeopardized forever. Cartoonists unleashed a new string of related Vander Zalm caricatures (the first and most audacious of which was Rand Holmes' Vancouver *Free Press* cartoon of Vander Zalm ripping the arms off a cartoonist).

Political cartoonists were essential, according to right wing columnist Doug Collins, to keep politicians from becoming "even bigger pompous asses than they are now....Hell, didn't cartoonists spend years lampooning Richard Nixon as a crook? If it hadn't been for them Tricky Dickie might have found a way to stay in the White House."[9]

So much publicity was generated over the libel suit and the 1979 judgement that few British Columbians recall a BC Court of Appeal ruling by five judges that eventually overturned the

Justice Munroe decision in February 1980. This ruling by the five judges was unanimous, making it very difficult for Vander Zalm to appeal it to the Supreme Court of Canada. Vander Zalm accepted the advice of his lawyer not to.

Vander Zalm admitted to me he had regrets about the lawsuit, "in the sense that it was so unnecessary. Had the Times-Colonist simply said, 'Ya, it's bad taste, unnecessary, overdone,' I would not have pursued it. But it was their approach to it that really led me [to court]. The time came where I said to them, 'Look, if you don't give me some letter of apology, I'm going to pursue it all the way through.' And my stubbornness had me pursue it all the way through. I wasn't looking to get money from Bierman. All I was trying to get from the Times-Colonist was something, however brief, to indicate that it [the cartoon] was bad taste."

But why, given Vander Zalm's zest for cooperating with the media, his appreciation of the media's role, his own penchant for political satire, and his record of appearing invulnerable under attack, did this one particular cartoon succeed in getting under Bill Vander Zalm's skin? He had endured "venomous" verbal attacks. He had accepted a physical attack (the banana-cream pie). He had weathered an irate mob of trade unionists in his Surrey council chambers. He had seen his private property vandalized. He had more or less shrugged off threats to his family. Why did he sue over Bierman's cartoon? To Bierman "it was just another cartoon. It was Vander Zalm who made it famous."

The answer may be that Bill Vander Zalm needs the media, not just politically, but psychologically.

In a nutshell: the more political power Bill Vander Zalm can attain, the more people he can reach; the more people he can reach, the more he is able to broadcast his own opinions about his own fine nature and good intentions. Given his odd habit of continually referring to himself in the third person ("Bill Vander Zalm believes. . . . Bill Vander Zalm isn't someone who . . . ."etc.) and his repeated editorializing about his own sensitive personality ("I'm really a softie. . . . I'm not the hard-nosed, heartless type of guy that some people made me out to be. . . ." etc.) it doesn't take much of a psychologist to suggest that by broadcasting his own integrity and likable qualities, Bill Vander Zalm is really trying to convince himself, as well as the voters, that he truly is a fine human being.

Like most actors, Vander Zalm's craving for the spotlight is not merely a desire to please an audience. His desire to hold centre stage in BC politics is not born of an entirely altruistic desire to serve others, but is in large measure an egocentric desire to serve his own self-esteem. The media are essential tools for Vander Zalm to use in building a sparkling self-image of concerned goodness.

The caricature attacked Bill Vander Zalm's self-esteem on a deeply personal level, and contradicted his extensive advertising of his own good character. It is conceivable Bierman's cartoon — and to a degree, all the bad publicity he has stored away in his inner bank of resentments — exposed something to the world that Vander Zalm himself had been working most of his life to reject. Threats to his family were one thing. A well-aimed spear at his rosy self-image was something else.

Bill Vander Zalm's approach to life is based upon a consistent belief in his own good intentions. Bierman says, "He has an enormous ego. He believes he can move mountains. Whatever he decides to do, it's the will of God." He has repeatedly echoed his contention that people can't really go wrong as long as they are convinced they are doing the right thing. "My philosophy has assisted me a great deal," he says. "If a person does his or her very best, with good intentions, fairly and truthfully, then the result — whatever it is — was meant to be."[10] This juvenile approach to life keeps Vander Zalm from delving deeply into his own motivations.

The cartoon by Bob Bierman turned Bill Vander Zalm inside-out.

The cartoon by Bob Bierman reminded Bill Vander Zalm that, among other things, he was a man who had withheld federal welfare subsidies to the handicapped in 1976-77. From October 1976 until February 1977, Human Resources Minister Bill Vander Zalm had refused to pass along an extra $22.50 a month, provided to the disabled by the federal government.

Very few British Columbians, let alone Canadians, recall that on the final day of February 1977, about 100 handicapped persons were forced to assemble in front of the BC legislature to protest Vander Zalm's retention of federal monies before they could receive what was rightfully theirs. (In 1977 the poverty level for a handicapped adult on welfare was $284 a month. The disabled protesters were receiving $265 a month. The federal subsidy would have lifted their income to the poverty level. But Vander Zalm had retained the funds on the grounds that all federal monies should go into provincial general revenues and didn't come under individual ministers' budgets. He believed the matter had to be scrutinized by the opposition during budget debate before any increase could be passed along.)

As soon as the issue was unearthed—by the handicapped protesters and not by the media—Vander Zalm agreed to hand over the money.

Few politicians could have survived a disclosure that they were withholding money from handicapped welfare recipients. Vander Zalm handled the matter with ease. He upped the handicapped benefits as soon as he was found out and he steadfastly maintained he was not at fault. By adopting an I-know-I'm-right-because-my-heart-is-pure stance in any controversy, Vander Zalm was able to appear strong in the face of opposition. In this way Bill Vander Zalm made other politicians—who often tried to find reasonable middle ground on issues—appear weak and indecisive by comparison.

The case of the scorned Social Credit cabinet minister Peter Hyndman is a classic case in point.

As minister of Corporate and Consumer Affairs, Hyndman was forced to resign over questionable use of public funds, most notably a dinner washed down with four $37.50 bottles of Pouilly-Fuise, a French wine. A hospitality expense claim dated March 31, 1981 revealed that Hyndman had had dinner with four other people at Il Giardino di Umberto in Vancouver on February 20. The other people were Peter Brown, governor of the Vancouver Stock Exchange, his wife, and a Mr. P. Lind, described as a director of Ontario Hydro, and his wife. The bill was $374.57. It included four bottles of Pouilly Fuisse wine. There were other glaring problems with Hyndman's expense vouchers, most importantly a $60 business dinner with *Sun* publisher Clark Davey—which Davey said never took place.

The *Sun* went after Hyndman. The newspaper adopted an aggressive stance by picturing Hyndman as a high-living minister who guzzled Pouilly Fuisse (poo-yee fwee-say) at the public's expense. At a time when Premier Bennett was asking

British Columbians to tighten their belts, Hyndman buckled under the pressure and resigned.

Bill Vander Zalm's response to the issue is worthy of note. "I would have made up little bottles of Pouilly Fuisse," he said, "and filled them with BC wine."[11]

If he had found himself in Peter Hyndman's position, Vander Zalm would have used the squabble as an opportunity to assert his invincibility. He would have telegraphed to the public via the media that he was not a man who would kowtow to any indignation sparked by the press. What was a self-respecting provincial cabinet minister supposed to do anyway? take the governor of the stock exchange out for hot dogs?

By behaving in a guilty manner, Hyndman convicted himself in the public eye. He even paid back the money for the disputed Clark Davey dinner. Bill Vander Zalm, on the other hand, doesn't admit guilt. He might admit to making a mistake from time to time, but he never admits to the media that he ought to be held culpable for any mistake. In fact, Vander Zalm's forthright and stubborn belief in his own good intentions protects him from blame in his own mind for any disruptions he might cause. As a boy scout who is always trying to do his best, he can do no wrong.

"I try to say what I think as openly as possible," he says. "It gives me comfort. I can fall asleep at night knowing the answer tomorrow will be the same."[12]

Bill Vander Zalm's boy scout bravado in an era of pussyfooting Machiavellianism makes him stand out from the crowd. The media have been quick to reward Vander Zalm for this "up-front" and frank style, inflating non-issues into major stories, fanning sparks of conflict, leaving unappetizing stories such as Vander Zalm's retention of welfare funds to be forgotten while providing reams of coverage for Vander Zalm's more frivolous and colourful remarks.

In this way the media Frankenstein learned to walk — before long he picked up so much momentum he was running for the premiership of the province, impossible to dismantle.

Vander Zalm's remarks on Quebec, and the treatment of those remarks by the media, show how easily Bill Vander Zalm was able to become the embodiment of W.A.C. Bennett's wily maxim that a kite can't rise except against the wind.

In 1976, upon the election of the Parti Quebecois, he remarked, "If they make a decision to separate it won't cost me any sleepless nights."[13] He scandalized the liberal media establishment of that era by adding, "Adieu, Quebec."[14] He noted Quebec's separation from Canada, if it happened, would limit the number of French Canadian transients in BC.

The *Province* took Vander Zalm to task in an editorial. Typically, Vander Zalm stuck by his remarks. "I think that when I speak of borders and passports I was speaking partially in jest," he said, "but when I say it costs us money and considerable money and that there has to be separation or not separation, a change of approach, I mean that."[15] Vander Zalm essentially objected to "the charges and threats by Levesque that if the feds didn't do certain things, Quebec would separate. You can hear that for so long and then you say, 'For crying out loud, go ahead if that's what you want. You can't hold us to ransom.' "[16]

Vander Zalm denied that he was anti-French. He said he objected to the costs of bilingualism. "I'm one of those anglophones who is considerably frustrated and fed up with English and French on everything."[17] Specifically, he cited bilingual corn flakes boxes. The fuss over these opinions led Vander Zalm to clarify his stance several times, correcting what he believed was misleading reportage by the *Province*. "I'm not holding anything against the *Province*," he said. "The publicity doesn't bother me."[18]

Vander Zalm said he was happy about the result of the Quebec election because it would bring about a quicker settlement of Quebec's problems. He said he felt Quebec would not separate. He said he was essentially fed up with "All the talk, and of course now there is a Senate committee going to travel around the country to convince people that unity is the thing. They are going to drag this thing out forever."[19]

Although many British Columbians agreed with Vander Zalm's opinions, the media objected to Vander Zalm's lack of statesman-like diplomacy, which only strengthened Vander

Zalm's integrity in the eyes of the public. Making some more mileage on the issue, Vander Zalm gave an interview to a French language TV crew in Vancouver on November 16, 1976, and proceeded to autograph a box of cornflakes.

It was much better for Human Resources Minister Bill Vander Zalm to be under attack for remarks on Quebec than to be under attack for his policies in human resources. "The things I say are probably what a lot of people are thinking," he noted. "Other politicians would like to talk that way but they wouldn't dare because they think they'll get a lot of heat and flak."[20]

In 1979 Vander Zalm was back in the national headlines with still more "controversial" comments on Quebec.

While attending a regional Social Credit convention in Williams Lake, BC Municipal Affairs Minister Bill Vander Zalm sang a song in which he indirectly referred to Premier Rene Levesque as a "frog." To the tune of "On Top Of Old Smoky," he performed a lighthearted satire.

> There once was a Liberal
> By the name of Trudeau
> He came like a saviour
> Tho' why we'll not know
>
> I promise you nothing
> Just trust in my lot
> This promise he kept us
> Cause nothing we got
>
> We faced unemployment
> For lack of good jobs
> But work was a no-no
> Best suited for slobs
>
> Pierre said we'll fix it
> There's buildings not full
> We'll all work in Ottawa
> Or retire in Hull

The problem persisted
Pierre didn't nap
And just for good measure
Gave LIP, LEAP and CRAP

We now needed money
To pay for those bills
The press started printing
Those 50-cent bills

He needed distraction
A political fog
And out of the East
Came the sound of a frog

Bilingual the key word
French is what it takes
You'll get your lessons
From a box of cornflakes

It cost us billions
The East blew its nest
Trudeau said forget it
We'll take from the West

We again need a saviour
Any other will do
Someone to direct us
Yes, even Joe Who.

Originally, when Vander Zalm performed the song around Christmas, he had sung a different seventh verse. "He needed distraction/ A political cheque/ When out of the East/ Came Rene Levesque." In his Williams Lake version Vander Zalm ad-libbed the "frog" reference.

The Federation des Franco-Colombiens was reportedly enraged by this racist slur and was considering legal action. Human Rights branch director Kathleen Ruff and BC Human

Rights chairman Margaret Strongitharm reportedly disapproved. And BC broadcaster Laurier LaPierre said the minister's use of the word "frog" was not a laughing matter and that he would ask his lawyers to consider the launching of a class action suit against Vander Zalm.

"I think the majority of people think it rather comic that there should be such an enormous amount of publicity and coverage over what started out as a rather humourous thing," Vander Zalm said.[21] Although he said he would be willing to apologize face to face to anyone who might be offended by the frog reference, he steadfastly maintained the term "frog" was not meant in any way as a slight against French Canadians or Quebeckers or anyone else.

The Edmonton *Journal* published a cartoon of Vander Zalm pulling the legs off a frog. The Vancouver section of the Jewish

"It's a fun thing, don't you see"

Peoples Order issued a news release citing the Social Credit's abysmal record regarding racism.

Bill Vander Zalm, meanwhile, said most of the phone calls and letters to his office supported him. He blamed the media for giving widespread publicity to his remark. "It seems obvious that some people continue to keep this issue alive, making an even bigger mountain from a molehill," he said, in a letter to a lawyer for the Federation des Franco-Colombiens. "I am sure I need not again remind you that the word was used in the context of a humourous song at a relatively small gathering in Williams Lake — hardly the media capital of the world."[22]

Although Liberal Senator Jean Marchand took the anti-Liberal song as a major blow against confederation, an amused Rene Levesque met BC Premier Bill Bennett at a first ministers' conference and quietly asked Bennett to slip him a copy of the lyrics. Later a Quebec delegation at a municipal affairs conference asked Vander Zalm to perform the song.

Vander Zalm had the "racist" issue in clearer perspective than the media which, no matter how they hammered away on the matter, kept spelling Bill Vander Zalm's name right. "Some people think those of us who come from other countries are immediately upset by every little remark. I think that's just a little bit small,"[23] Vander Zalm later noted, taking refuge once again in his innocent pose as an ordinary common-sense guy who stands out because he dares to speak what everyone thinks.

Looking at the enormous coverage given to Vander Zalm's off-the-cuff comments over the years, and the often paltry coverage of his hurtful actions, one can conclude that Vander Zalm's manipulation of the media has worked enormously to his advantage. It is hard not to feel that there is something sadly amiss in the way the media, for its part, has allowed this to happen.

15

INTERVIEW
Face to Face

"I prefer to talk about what's still to be done rather than what we did."

Bill Vander Zalm
Campaign literature, 1986

This is an interview with Premier Bill Vander Zalm recorded on the morning of September 13, 1986.

TWIGG: As a new premier, this must be a fascinating time for you. Do you feel the job is changing you?

VANDER ZALM: I can't say it's changing me, no . . . [I'm] maybe more cautious than I used to be when I was a minister, although I'm not so sure it's caution [so much] as having found my niche, so to speak. I guess I was very frustrated at times when I was in a minister's portfolio because I knew what I wanted to see done, or what I thought had to be done, and to think that somehow because of bureaucracy or just the approach of government, it couldn't be done, that bothered me. Whereas now, of course, being in the top spot you can get it done if you want to see it done. So I feel I'm enjoying this more than any job I've had in government.

TWIGG: Have you ever thought about why it is you're so attracted to power?

(seven-second pause)

VANDER ZALM: No. I don't know. I guess perhaps, you know, I was sort of brought up from a very young age to get things done, to finish whatever it was I was doing. I suppose it's a part of your character if you want to lead or be at the leading edge of things all the time, then obviously that comes through the rest of your life. So I don't know. I guess it's just perhaps a part of my character, my nature, and it's a little of my upbringing as well.

TWIGG: You've described yourself as being "very Dutch" once. Has it ever occurred to you that this might put you at odds with English sensibilities? In that the Netherlands and England have been trading adversaries for centuries?

VANDER ZALM: No, I'm very Canadian. I'm not very Dutch. I'm very Canadian. But I've always said that if a person sort of runs down his homeland, and doesn't really appreciate where it is he came from, and the customs and the cultures he was born with, then he'll not make a good Canadian. Because he could develop that same disrespect and lack of interest in Canada.

TWIGG: I raise that question because this year you were quoted as criticizing the "totally antiquated British parliamentary system of government."

VANDER ZALM: That is correct. I'm still of the opinion that sooner or later the system is going to have to be changed. It is antiquated.

TWIGG: Would you change it to more resemble the American system?

VANDER ZALM: Well, I think we have the advantage in Canada of being able to adopt the best of both. Maybe if we could go back to square one and pick some system, and I had some say in it, and [if] I could pick some system from some place in the world, I'd probably end up with the Swiss. I think they perhaps have got the closest to what might be the type of ideal government — where people appear close to it and where there appears great trust. I think the Swiss really have the best of it. But whether we could ever get our people to go back that far now and change that much of the system, I doubt it.

We could, however, gradually bring a little more of the American democracy into the British parliamentary system. We can do it in little ways. We can begin almost immediately. We can get television into the house [legislature] to bring a little sanity into the proceedings by having it exposed more publicly. That's just a small move towards some change. We could go to referenda to allow for democracy to creep in just a bit more. We can go for a greater degree of decentralization. We consider what we have now — a sort of a hodgepodge and a lot of rule from Victoria and a lot of regulation from Victoria — and decentralize into some of the regions. So there are things that we can do within the existing system that will bring us closer to a more democratic process.

Twigg: Do you recognize the many similarities between yourself and W.A.C. Bennett when he was first premier? And that there are many parallels in his life, as well?

Vander Zalm: Well, I don't know what all of the parallels [are]. But I think perhaps one of the things that we really have in common is that he could respond, he could feel what. . .

Twigg: He sent up trial balloons, too?

Vander Zalm: Ya. He had a way of finding out what the wish of the people [was]. He could feel it, he had a good gut feel for that sort of thing. And I believe — as a matter of fact, I know, from past experiences — that I can feel it in my gut what it is people are wanting, or what it is a group is seeking, or where it's at. So there's a great similarity that way.

You know I used to see W.A.C. Bennett when I first became involved provincially. I used to see him come down the corridors in the parliament buildings for those first few months. After that, we didn't see a whole lot of him anymore. Because I don't think Bill [Bennett] particularly wanted to have him involved in the process there. But whenever I saw him he'd stop and he'd say, "Bill," — that's me — "I got a piece of advice for you." He said, "Please." *(whispering)* "Stay in the middle!" *(no longer whispering)* "Don't go too far to the right. Stay in the middle." And he said that all the time.

Twigg: Those words are coming back to you now?

Vander Zalm: It wasn't just the once. It was often. He repeated it every time I saw him. It was the same message. "Bill, you're going to go places. But stay in the middle. Stay in the middle."

He perceived me as being a bit right wing at the time, I think. And he didn't think that's where I belonged. So he kept telling me to stay in the middle. I think the perception of me being right wing was probably in part because of my approach to work, my work ethic. That was [probably] where it came from. Plus the fact that I came into government and immediately got into Human Resources. I had to sort of turn one very permissive attitude, as evidenced by my predecessor, Norman Levi, to where we really had to tighten up and change it. And it had to be done very quickly. And much of what I was able to accomplish in Human Resources was not by tough laws or hard lines — although it may appear that way it was really because of attitude. A changing of attitudes.

But what really created this perception, or this image of me then, is something that I feel so strongly about now, and always have. The sort of image people develop about you happens not over a long time, it comes from when you first meet them. It's like you never get a second chance to create a first impression. And if you meet somebody, and you're seen to be happy and smiling and pleasant, that's how people remember you, even if afterwards you're not that way. Similarly, when you come into politics, if you come in hard-line, knocking, firing people and all that sort of thing, that's how you're perceived from ever on.

TWIGG: But you didn't come into politics in Victoria. You came into politics in Surrey. You had a reputation already for hard-line policies in Surrey.

VANDER ZALM: *(agreeing)* Mmm-hmm.

TWIGG: The reputation followed you to Victoria. You were not an unknown entity when you arrived in Victoria.

VANDER ZALM: No, . . . what's really sustained me through all of this, through this whole long period of politics, and what people consistently, constantly mention when they see me, is, regardless of whether they're NDP or Socred, Liberal, Conservative. . . they say, "Well, you know, we don't agree with what you say, or we don't always agree with what you say, but we trust you because we know you're not afraid to say it." And I think that's what they remember best. In other words, there's a trust. I think it's worth a great deal.

TWIGG: You were saying in Prince George that you admired [Premier] Grant Devine because he could condense a problem down . . .

VANDER ZALM: He can. He's a great orator. He can just take a very difficult problem and condense it to a couple of sentences. And you understand and you feel good with it. That's a problem in government. That's a problem people have. I have a problem with it because I'm perhaps inclined to be impatient. I want to see things done very quickly. But you see it so often. People send letters, ten pages, twelve pages. Poor people, they don't know what they're doing. I mean, they lose by that.

TWIGG: There's a difference between the admirable quality of being direct, and the sometimes admirable quality of being able to simplify something. Some people say you have a tendency to want to simplify [too much] . . .

VANDER ZALM: That's true.

TWIGG: . . . what could be, in fact, complex situations.

VANDER ZALM: Ya. You see, but, that's my beef. That was my beef in government, when I was there before. I haven't had that problem yet, because I think the people I work with know where it is I'm coming from and they're beginning to adjust accordingly. Now whether that's good or bad, I don't know. But I'll tell you, I used to have a lot of problems with that when I was in government because I always had the impression that the bureaucrats and the specialists and the people who were writing reports and doing the studies were purposely going out [of their way] to make it look complex.

They would give you rafts of reading when really the bottom line could have been given to you in a few sentences. And I always had the impression that it was to their advantage to make it complex. And I was always of the opinion — still am, for that matter — that the basics don't change, you know. The problems perhaps seem to be more complex but the basics of it don't change. If you can take a complex problem and somehow reduce it to its roots, it's not that difficult to solve.

TWIGG: But some problems *are* complex.

VANDER ZALM: Some problems are complex, okay. *(Laughing)*

TWIGG: You have identified your greatest weakness as "a soft, soft heart." How has that ever led you to do things against your better judgement?

VANDER ZALM: I can't give you specifics on that. But I could be convinced at times to do things simply because, you know, I can't stick with the hard lines, so to speak. So I'm not the hard-nosed, heartless type of guy that some people made me out to be. I don't know if it's a weakness, in any event. It may not be a weakness.

TWIGG: You've also said that whenever you've compromised your belief[s] in government at the urging of others, it's backfired. Can you give me some examples?

VANDER ZALM: This happened a number of times during the various portfolios I held where ministry people, through their reports, or through their convincing me, would have me take on a particular approach, or make a particular policy statement, or any number of things like that. If it was contrary to what I really believed in, or what my gut told me it should be, I had problems with it.

A better example — and I'm not making apologies for the ads on television talking about the after-Expo [deficit] — but when that was first presented to me, the [advertising] time was booked, the arrangements had been made with the advertising agency to put it all together, all of that was done. My gut was telling me, "I don't really need this. I shouldn't be doing it." This was arranged before my time, it's booked, but I don't really need it. That was my gut. But I took it on anyway.

TWIGG: Okay, I want to ask your gut something. On September 2nd, on Jack Webster's program, you said you agreed wholeheartedly with Jack Webster that lotteries were essentially a tax on the poor. At the same time you're on television assuring the people of British Columbia that the deficit for Expo 86 is going to be taken care of by lotteries.

It necessarily follows that, from a logical point of view, you are saying to the people of BC that the deficit for Expo 86 is going to be taken care of by the poor people of BC.

(Silence)

Why some reporter hasn't asked you this, I don't know.

VANDER ZALM: It's amazing, yes. *(Pointing his finger at interviewer)* Good question! I'm glad you're not reporting today.

TWIGG: You can't just point a finger and say, "Good question." You have to respond to that!

(Silence)

Because as a man who says he's going to bring the highest Christian principles to government, it's, I think, a very un-Christian policy to make the poor people pay for the $1.5-billion-dollar government party.

VANDER ZALM: I don't like lotteries, never did. But you know it's a fact of life. They're with us. The same people who I think are being taxed through the lottery process, because they're continually going into the store to spend their last five bucks on lottery tickets, are the ones that would scream loudest, and cry foul, if somehow Bill Vander Zalm or his government came along and took all those machines out of corner grocery stores. So, you know, I'm in that bind.

TWIGG: *This* is a complex situation.

VANDER ZALM: It's there. I don't like it. It's a fact of life. It's one of those things that you somehow have to accept because it appears to be the will of the people.

TWIGG: Given the fact that you believe that's how they function, then it's not particularly moral to make the poor people pay.

(Silence)

So you're going to have to do something about that.

VANDER ZALM: I don't know what you can do. You can't, like I say, you can't take the lotteries away from the people now. They're obviously wanting it. Because they're spending more and more every year on lotteries. And the very people that you're trying to save from the lotteries are the ones that are spending most of the bucks.

TWIGG: Do you regret any of the policies that you've had in the past in retrospect? Such as that incident where you were withholding the federal welfare subsidies from the handicapped? In retrospect, that doesn't look very good in the history books. Are there things that you've done that you would have done differently?

VANDER ZALM: Ya, there are things. When you're a minister, of course, you're not the final say in what it is that gets done through government. Mind you, in a government, you can't always do all the things you'd like to see done in any event. I just mentioned the lottery thing. I don't like lotteries. But because public opinion says we want lotteries, you don't want to...I'm not one to go against all that public opinion. And it appears to be pretty evident throughout the whole of British Columbia, the nation for that matter [that people want them].

Similarly, often times there are actions required in government that you take because of the bigger picture. Whether it's lack of finances, or whether it's because it fits better with policies as they exist elsewhere in the government, or because you're being told by your colleagues in government that's how it's to be done, you can't always get exactly whatever it is you'd like to see. There has to be room for compromise. So you may not like it, but you live with it, because you appreciate that the system makes it thus.

TWIGG: Since I asked that question, I may as well move on to a few other harder ones...You were involved in a case against a man named Albers in '79, and you lost the Bierman cartoon appeal case, and you had that long-drawn-out fight with the King George Highway Hospital. Now there's a Langley consulting firm which is involved in a suit against you. As someone who once wanted to be lawyer, do you think there's a part of you that enjoys these legal battles?

VANDER ZALM: No.

TWIGG: You sure get into 'em.

VANDER ZALM: Well, that's because if you're doing a lot of business, you're bound to get into that sort of thing. I also believe that if you're right, you fight it all the way through. There's isn't one of those you mention where I thought, or where I went in thinking, I can win because of circumstance or evidence. But I really went in because I believed that I was right and that was the thing to do, to stand up to what it is that I was fighting for.

TWIGG: It's interesting that [you're now saying] you're willing to take principle beyond monetary concerns...You once described yourself as being quite stubborn. Do you have any regrets at all about the whole Bob Bierman case? in retrospect? Because if anything generated a lot of press, that did.

VANDER ZALM: I spent a lot of time on that. I won the first round. I lost to the Appeal Court. I got a fair bit of satisfaction knowing that as far as the first case, I had a good hearing, as did the other side, and the judge, after seeing and hearing all the evidence, decided in my favour. The Appeal Court, on the other hand, really went on points of law.

TWIGG: As Human Resources minister you trimmed over $100 million from your budget in one year, and then as Municipal Affairs minister you selected the ALRT transit system which British Columbians will be paying for for 30 years.

Does it strike you as strange that on one hand you would be an extreme fiscal conservative, and on the other hand you would be criticized for choosing a system which is more expensive than more conventional systems which could have been used?

VANDER ZALM: 'Course I don't agree. I know it's a very costly system, the Skytrain. But I still maintain that it would have cost more to put in the conventional system.

TWIGG: Did you or [White Spot owner] Peter Toigo call Edgar Kaiser and ask him to come up to the Social Credit convention?

VANDER ZALM: No. Didn't know he was there. But I don't have

any problems with Edgar Kaiser. As a matter of fact, he's going to serve on the Vancouver-as-an-International-Finance-Centre Committee. I don't have any problem with him. I don't think he was that involved in our campaign in any event.

TWIGG: These are questions that I think the press should ask you. So you're getting them...Did you use Milan Ilich's helicopter during the Social Credit leadership?

VANDER ZALM: Ya.

TWIGG: Olga Ilich is the chairman of the Richmond advisory planning committee. She's also the property development manager for Progressive Construction, the Richmond company that has a three-quarter interest in a large block of land in the Terra Nova area of the Agricultural Land Reserve. And the Richmond Council has now voted to bypass the Agricultural Land Commission and go directly to cabinet for permission to exempt Terra Nova from the agricultural zoning for a housing development.
  Do you see any conflicts potentially in this situation?

VANDER ZALM: Between myself and...?

TWIGG: For either. Olga Ilich. Or yourself.

VANDER ZALM: No. Olga Ilich only advises, along with others, the council. The council then decides. One could look for conflicts in anything and everything.

TWIGG: You said, "I knowingly say things in a controversial way that tends to get the press." You're a good promoter and a good marketer. How much do you think your marketing of yourself in the media has helped you get to the top of BC politics?

VANDER ZALM: A fair bit. Politics is marketing. Promoting British Columbia. Getting economic development. That's marketing. Running a Fantasy Garden is marketing. Much in life is marketing. *(Tapping on the table to emphasize his point.)* Even a strong marriage involves a degree of marketing.

TWIGG: You've got to tell me more about that one. Explain that.

VANDER ZALM: Well, you know, marketing requires that you sort of bite your tongue. Think things through. Look at the bigger picture. Know what's ahead. There's much more to marketing than simply going out and saying I've got an ashtray to sell, it's made of glass and it's $4.95 and you should buy one. It depends on what you're marketing, too, as to what's the involvement. But ya, even a good marriage requires a bit of marketing. Life is marketing.

TWIGG: Your second cousin, Pete Warmerdam...

VANDER ZALM: Holy smokes! You've done your research well.

TWIGG: He says, "One thing about the Vander Zalms, when there is an opportunity, they seize it." The other thing he said about you which is really interesting is that, "Bill will always look at the light instead of looking at the dark."

VANDER ZALM: Ya.

TWIGG: That really interests me. Because there's some potential danger in that. If someone is always optimistic, always looking at their best intentions, it follows that one can become ignorant of one's baser motives — which we all have. And so it occurs to me that it's possible in your concentration upon your self-perception of the guy who's going to ride the white horse, the guy who's always optimistic, that you may miss some of the darker areas of life. In yourself.

Have you ever thought about that?

VANDER ZALM: Ya, but then you see you don't ever have perfection. There's no such thing as a perfect world or a perfect person or perfect circumstances. I mean, no matter what it is, it's got its lighter sides and its darker sides. You're either in a world of optimism or in a world of pessimism. Well, I suppose you could be a bit of both, too. The ideal would be one who could be optimistic but yet keep in mind that if perhaps things didn't work out quite as you had anticipated then the result would be something else. In other words, always to have that balance.

TWIGG: You see I worry that you might be naively optimistic. To an abnormal degree.

VANDER ZALM: I am, by nature, very optimistic. I find it

difficult to be a pessimist. Or to really perhaps assess the darker side of things. That could be. That could be.

TWIGG: Because do you know why? Do you know what made me think about this? Your admission that you don't like to look at the darker side of things obviously goes back to the fact that when you were a small boy in Holland, and the Nazis occupied your town for five years, those were very dark times. And one could theorize that you are, to a large degree, functioning in reaction to those very dark times.

VANDER ZALM: To some degree. Because even when I refer to those times, I don't refer to them as dark times. Knowing they were. I'm still, you know, looking at what the brighter side of it was and saying, "Ya, but during those times we did have order." And things were principled.

TWIGG: And obviously there were horrible things going on.

VANDER ZALM: That's right. That's right. No, you're very perceptive. I agree. That's the optimism coming through. But I don't think that's bad!

THE MORNING AFTER

An Afterword by Howard White

Soon after Whistler Vander Zalm began disavowing plans for a 1986 election. He wanted time to put his own stamp on the government, he said. In early September he told the author of this book, "Well, yes, there is an opportunity to go in and win. But I think that opportunity would still exist in May or June. As a matter of fact, the opportunity might even be better then. Because a lot of people, at least history tends to tell us when we look at Miller and Getty and Turner—that it doesn't pay to go immediately after you've just been chosen leader because you tend to carry the baggage from your predecessor. And that maybe you're better to wait and establish your own record. History tells us that.

"And I'm not afraid of establishing a record. Because I think there's some great things in the offing. Some difficult times. I know I can tackle them. I feel I'm aware what needs to be done, budgetary-wise and program-wise, and legislatively I've think I've got a good program in mind for the next year. So I'm confident in my own head that I could go in May or June and do as well, if not better, than what I would do right now."

Having just finished an expensive leadership convention that was not in the 1986 budget, the party was short of money. But the polls showed Vander Zalm's rejuvenated Socreds 21 points ahead of the NDP, and the more Vander Zalm denied it, the more obvious it became this was a chance the famous Vander Zalm opportunism could not resist. On Wednesday, September 24th, he gave the minimum 28 days notice for a provincial general election to follow on the 22nd of October.

The election campaign was an anticlimax. A month shorter

and nowhere near as suspenseful as the leadership contest, the only question it posed was how thoroughly the Vander Zalm juggernaut would flatten NDP forces under a faltering Bob Skelly. Skelly, an ex-teacher first elected to the legislature in 1972, had been a compromise choice for leader when favourites Bill King and David Vickers became deadlocked at the NDP's 1984 leadership convention, and he had struggled in the role from the first. Dave Barrett had been criticised for lacking the old fire in his latter years as NDP leader, but Skelly was so much milder yet that party supporters were soon comparing him unfavourably with Barrett. With Bill Bennett's re-election master plan coming to a climax in the simultaneous completion of Expo 86, the ALRT, the Coquihalla Highway and the new Alex Fraser Bridge across the Fraser River, all ballyhooed to the limit with government advertising, it seemed the NDP needed something special in the way of inspiration in order to stay in the race, and Skelly wasn't looking special.

The funny thing was, of course, that none of Bennett's great works could overcome the deepseated distrust and animosity his eleven years of cold, calculating and disaster-prone rule had built up in the electorate. He had fought with almost everybody in the neighborhood, and now there was no one left to support him. Where a belated preference for taking the political high road had not worked for Barrett because voters could remember his own street fighting phase too vividly, it did work for Skelly. With Expo half over, the NDP was still comfortably ahead in the polls and it seemed the most expensive election build-up in Canadian history had been for naught. The voter preference for Skelly's calm, reasoning option was so strong there seemed, as of June, 1986, no way the NDP could lose this one.

Then Bennett resigned.

There has been no shortage of speculation about whether Bennett was pushed or staggered off on his own, but no one has seriously suggested he actually foresaw and planned the revival of Socred fortunes that would follow. The leadership win by his old nemesis Vander Zalm was certainly not sought by Bennett. If he'd had his way the job would have gone to Bud Smith or Brian Smith, the two most likely to continue the Bennett regime in practice, and neither of those would have had the great advantage in charisma that proved the deciding factor in Vander Zalm's subsequent defeat of Skelly. Skelly's lack of charisma had never been an issue in his role as Opposition leader under Bennett, because Bennett didn't have any either. Neither did either of the Smiths. Running against them, the issue of leadership style, which Skelly was not able to escape from while running in Vander Zalm's shadow, would not have played a part in the election. If Bennett had his wish and placed Bud Smith in the leader's job, Skelly likely would have shown up as the more experienced and confidence-inspiring of the two on the campaign trail, rather than the bumbling, unappealing figure he appeared beside Vander Zalm.

Moreover, as Bennett's close colleagues, neither the two Smiths nor Grace McCarthy, the other establishment favourite, could have distanced themselves sufficiently from Bennett to escape his taint. The voter desire for renewal would very likely have remained on the side of the NDP, and the Bennett resignation would not appear the master stroke it did to some after the Vander Zalm sweep. Neither the caucus nor the party establishment supported Vander Zalm, so none of them could take credit for his success; it is unlikely any of the candidates they favoured could have withstood the strong NDP surge in the last days of the election campaign when the electorate, awakening from the Vander Zalm spell, sliced his lead from 21 points to 5.

The only one who can claim to have judged the political tides of 1986 correctly from the outset is Bill Vander Zalm himself. From the time reporters started calling him the morning after Bennett's resignation, his moves were calm, confident and unfailingly on target. His long delay before declaring his leadership candidacy built up media suspense and kept the free publicity coming his way at a time when he had no money to buy any. His energetic stumping around the province in Milan Ilich's helicopter established him in the hearts of crucial rural delegates at a time when the front runners were alienating the grassroots by hobnobbing with Vancouver plutocrats.

He started with no cabinet support, no budget, no media

credibility as a serious contender, and facing a potentially disastrous controversy in the Fantasy Garden zoning conflict, but managed to turn all his problems to advantages. The lack of cabinet support he used to bolster his image as an outsider, a fresh face who best filled Bennett's own prescription for renewal. The lack of budget he used to depict himself as the soul of modesty, basing his campaign on genuine human contact while others drew the wrath of Jim Pattison for spending big bucks on distasteful US-style hoopla. The lack of editorial approval he ignored as usual while using his talent for headline-grabbing to keep his and Lillian's smiling faces constantly on the front pages. And by inviting the public to share in his ethical dilemma concerning Fantasy Gardens he turned the issue into a prime-time melodrama that played to top ratings throughout the summer and fall, gaining him yet more publicity others couldn't buy. His starring performance emphasized his stature as a successful businessman who was ready to steer the provincial economy with a practiced hand. Lillian's supporting role subtly emphasized the fact most of Vander Zalm's opponents had less than exemplary marital histories. The "Bill and Lil Show" didn't hurt attendance back at the Gardens, either.

Listening to his "gut" instead of polls and exercising political discipline far more mature than anyone expected, Bill Vander Zalm made the highly-paid Socred braintrust at Whistler look like a pack of amateurs, but even after winning the leadership few political insiders had taken the full measure of Vander Zalm's newfound strategic prowess. Many NDP advisers and supporters were openly rooting for a Vander Zalm win at Whistler because they were so firmly convinced he was a political stumblebum who would immediately disgrace himself and become a liability in the next election. There were many sage predictions of the Social Credit Party's complete demise, to be brought about by Vander Zalm's inability to keep peace among Bill Bennett's coalition of Tories, Grits, nouveau riche opportunists and aging W.A.C. Bennett worshippers. Even following the province-wide wave of "Vander Mania" set off by his dramatic grassroots defeat of the big money machine at Whistler, the NDP was slow to perceive just what they were up against; in fact, even after being trounced at the polls Oct. 22, many in the NDP remained secure in the conviction Vander Zalm fluked into office with unfair help from the media and would be soon revealed as a straw man, presenting the Harcourt-led NDP with easy pickings in 1990. But Vander Zalm didn't stumble. On the contrary.

Vander Zalm's strategy in the provincial election was as simple as it was bold: he would steal Skelly's position. Why not? It was obviously what people wanted. He would present himself also as a non-confrontational candidate who could usher in a new day of conciliation and cooperation that would surely revive the good life British Columbians had left behind in the seventies. Good times just around the corner. Milk and honey. This put him in the awkward position of running against his own party's record, but more than that, against his own record. It led to a strange spectacle in his first few days as premier. Here was a man who had just swept into power on a wave of popular acclaim, spending all his time assuring reporters not that he would continue to be the same old Bill they had come to know, but that he would become an entirely different person. The right-wing extremist was gone. The scourge of the poor, of the underprivileged, of ethnic minorities, was no longer operative. The new guy loved everybody. It was a lot to swallow, but Vander Zalm set about to prove it by making generous settlements in the longstanding BC Government Employees Union dispute and the nurses' dispute, then showing his empathy for the working man by declaring his support for a dollar-per-case reduction in the price of beer. Interrupting his packed campaign schedule to honour an earlier commitment to spend several days at the Gwa-yee Indian Reserve at Kingcome Inlet added further lustre to his halo, and obscured the fact he wasn't taking a position on Indian demands.

Vander Zalm couldn't lose. Since he was expected to revert to past form at any time and start lashing out at minorities, he got positive press simply by *not* doing it. He got more ink for shaking the hand of the Gwa-Yee chief and saying "Nice weather today" than Skelly did for announcing he would end the province's century-long opposition to the recognition of Indian Land

Claims. There was nothing mysterious about Vander Zalm's approach. He was flying his kite against the wind again. In the sixties when everyone else was preaching tolerance, he preached intolerance. Now that he was expected to preach hate he was preaching love. The media went crazy for it. It was as simple as "man bites dog" and yet Vander Zalm was the only one who seemed to know about it. It shouldn't have worked as easily as it did, because everyone knows a grown man with a history of self-serving demagoguery doesn't change into a Mahatma Gandhi overnight, at least not just for the convenience of winning an election. But Vander Zalm displayed a talent for pleading his case on television that had a direct appeal to viewers' hearts which put one in mind of Ronald Reagan (a comparison Vander Zalm enjoys). Vander Zalm's "Trust Me" appeal was so compelling he soon had veterans like Liberal Party President Iona Campagnolo and *Sun* columnist Marjorie Nichols swearing he was a true Liberal at heart and the new milk-and-honey Bill was the real Bill, revealed at last.

"The preliminary evidence," Nichols wrote,"is that what we see is what we're going to get. . . a smiling optimist who believes that the powers of persuasion can move mountains."[1]

Historically, it is a fascinating thought that the strategy Vander Zalm was using to dazzle 1986 voters came directly from W.A.C. Bennett, who marked him for great things if he would only "go to the middle."

Skelly found his position as the conciliatory candidate so thoroughly usurped he was forced to change strategy and go on the attack against the usurper. But the crowd doesn't like to see its favourite criticized, and Skelly looked terrible making jokes about losing his voice because he ate "the wrong kind of tulip bulbs for lunch," and later suggesting that Vander Zalm, who got in hot water by telling reporters he sent Lillian home to do the laundry, "washes his own socks and he does it in his own mouth." The NDP campaign whipped up a series of TV ads showing a two-faced Vander Zalm changing his tune on issues such as schools and the role of women, and a more effective later series featuring man-in-the-street interviews with voters who distrusted the new milk-and-honey-Bill. Coming at a time when

Vander Zalm's interventions in the IWA strike and the countervail issue were backfiring and his mother-in-law was saying she didn't think he'd make a good premier, this last ad campaign was no doubt partly responsible for Vander Zalm losing ground in the polls and falling behind Skelly on the question of voter trust.

One of the things that made even the most cynical political observers consider the possibility that Vander Zalm had somehow managed to work a basic change in his personality was the new maturity he had brought back from his three-year sojourn in the political desert. The old impatience which had moved him to say he would rather see Quebec separate than wait for a resolution of their differences, and to announce that there was massive welfare abuse without waiting for investigation results that eventually contradicted him; the old volatility that led him to fight with Grace McCarthy for disagreeing with him on no-fault insurance and to call the cabinet "gutless" for backing off on his Land Use Act, now seemed to be replaced by a willingness to take the long view, have confidence in his own strategy, and wait for the people's verdict. Rather than strike back at Skelly directly, Vander Zalm made a show of being generous to his floundering opponent while subtly heightening voters' doubts by emphasizing the importance of strong leadership in the campaign. When the polls showed the NDP's well-prepared emphasis on issues was making strong headway in the closing weeks, pressure increased on Vander Zalm to lift the gag he'd placed on Socred candidates early in the campaign, and let them debate issues. He was roundly abused for ducking a public debate with Skelly, a challenge that must have tempted him sorely, but he kept his head and held to his initial conviction he could steal this election without having to pay the price in promises and commitments. Instead of taking the NDP's bait he used the threat of a shrinking Socred margin to fire up his own troops for an all-out effort on E-Day.

Appearing happy and loose in an election eve interview, Vander Zalm gave CBC-TV anchorman Bill Good Jr. a sealed envelope predicting a majority Social Credit win with 47 of BC's 69 seats. Within an hour of the envelope being opened at the

closing of polls the next day, computer projections showed Vander Zalm's guess to be good within 2 seats. With a few close races still up in the air, the totals were Socred 49, NDP 20.

Bill Vander Zalm had rescued the Social Credit party from impending defeat and produced a strong mandate to continue. But he had done more than that. He had purged the caucus of its tired faces, at the same time avenging himself on his former detractors in cabinet. He had thrown off the much-resented dominance of the "Ontario machine" typified by super-hack Patrick Kinsella. He had shown the Daddy Warbucks types of the "Top Twenty Club," who had owned a "first mortgage" on the party under Bennett, that he could do it without them, restoring the party to its populist, petty-bourgeoise roots. He had demoralized the opposition. And best of all, he had avoided tying his hands with firm campaign promises and set policies. He could start off with a blank slate.

On his first try, Vander Zalm had crafted the kind of victory most leaders spend their lives dreaming about.

The "most unusual premier Canada has produced since Rene Levesque" was now for real. The Alice-in-Wonderland atmosphere that had bewitched British Columbians since Vander Zalm cast his spell at Whistler was over and the province began to collectively blink its eyes and ask itself just what had happened and just who this new fellow sitting in the premier's chair was.

Liberal party president Campagnolo hailed him as "the first Liberal premier of BC since Duff Pattullo." Veteran Vancouver alderman Harry Rankin called him a "right-wing, redneck populist." His friend and adviser Pete Toigo insisted he was a man without an ideology who only needed to be told what people wanted so he could do it. The NDP insisted he was a neo-conservative ideologue with a secret agenda all of his own, which voters would soon discover to their woe. An elderly Alberta woman ran up to him at the First Ministers Conference in Edmonton and declared, "You're the kind of Socred we used to have in this province!" Throughout the rest of the country people just shook their heads and said "BC has done it again!"

To have been in public life as long as Vander Zalm has and still keep people so confused is in itself an accomplishment. Certainly there was much more consensus about Pierre Trudeau after he'd been around twenty years, and it was not to his advantage. It goes without saying Vander Zalm is a bit of an enigma, which is not a bad thing to be if you are a politician. Certainly, he seemed more of a puzzle after his resurrection in 1986 than he did during his career in cabinet, when many would have put him down as redneck demagogue with limited scope. The new, mature Vander Zalm added a whole new set of clues which seemed to hint at something greater, whether for good or ill, than first thought. But it seems safe to say that time will not show him to have changed, but only to stand more revealed, and the personality that is revealed will not contradict the one we have known, but confirm it.

The Liberal Vander Zalm seems easily dispensed with. Apart from the fact he sought power under Liberal colours briefly long ago, there is little in his history that bespeaks a liberal temperament. His church ties and fundamentalist personal morality, affecting issues like abortion, religious schooling, equality of the sexes, racial tolerance, sexual tolerance, subsidies to business and sanctity of the major park system, are anathema to liberals, and suit him better to the company of the kind of back-bench Conservatives who sponsor bills calling for restoration of capital punishment and abolition of metric measure. But the Conservative Party is the party of the old-money establishment and Vander Zalm is a grassroots politician, not an establishment one. His loyalty is with the small businessman who belongs to the Lions Club, not the tycoon who belongs to the Terminal City Club. Bill Bennett had established a cozy relationship between the party and the moneybags of Howe Street, but this support diminished under Vander Zalm, leaving the party in a financial pinch following the 1986 election. Vander Zalm's talk of hitting the forest giants with higher stumpage rates made it clear he was not in tune with Howe Street at all. Of course that could change rapidly, as Campagnolo pointed out.

Charges that Vander Zalm is a right-wing extremist can't be dispensed with quite as readily. One problem is his relationship to the Federal Social Credit Party. Although not a member, Vander Zalm has gone out of his way to maintain links with the Federal Social Credit Party despite its increasing extremism during the last ten years. After then-Premier Bennett and other cabinet ministers had renounced the federal party in 1978, Vander Zalm went on record saying he didn't think the federal party should be written off. According to a Canadian Press report on May 12, he backed the federal leadership's aim "to rid the country of abortionists, homosexuals, and unscrupulous bankers."

"I don't disagree with those particular attitudes," Vander Zalm said. "I have to concur with the majority of things [party leader Lorne Reznowski] said...I think there are probably a lot of people, particularly now, that support that type of philosophy and favour a strengthening of the family unit."

Following a year of controversy over the racism issue in 1984, only 35 people saw fit to attend the annual convention of the federal Socred's BC chapter in Vancouver. Among the faithful was Bill Vander Zalm, sharing the speaker's platform with federal party Vice President Jim Green. Green spoke in defence of party member Jim Keegstra, who lost his job for teaching Alberta school children that the Holocaust was a hoax, and warned that "the world's major financial powers are controlled by people who support the Zionist conspiracy." In his speech to the gathering Vander Zalm said Anti-Semitism was "not at all the party's view," adding somewhat lamely, "at least not to my knowledge," then proceeded to criticize Canada's banking system and attack "big business, big government, and big unions."

At the party's federal convention in 1986, a motion was passed supporting the Botha regime in South Africa. During the 1986 election in BC, Vander Zalm took a stand opposing the Canadian government's sanction against South African wine, claiming sympathy for black workers. During the period of grace while the sanction took effect, the BC Liquor Control Board stockpiled quantities of South African wine. Later, on November 7, Vander Zalm set off a South African Action Coalition protest by agreeing to receive South African Ambassador Glenn Babb. After the meeting Vander Zalm flew one of his trial balloons suggesting BC might enter into a $100-million prefab housing deal with South Africa. The balloon drew fierce fire from the province's liberals, including lumber union head Jack Munro, who speculated such talk could wind up making BC "the laughing stock of the free world." During the election, Victoria lawyer Doug Christie, who had defended both Ernst Zundel and Jim Keegstra on charges of disseminating hatred against Jews, announced that his Western Canada Concept Party would support Vander Zalm.

It is difficult to say what such associations really mean in terms of Vander Zalm's personal politics. Some would seize them as proof of his fundamental extremism, while others would dismiss them as the innocent venturing of an irrepressibly optimistic salesman type who is willing to talk to anybody. The latter is certainly the simpler explanation, and we are bound to accept the simplest explanation that works. But one can accept it and still ask, is this "life-is-marketing" ethic adequate? It is unsettling to have a head of government who has been known to rub elbows with some of the most dismaying elements in Canada's public life. We should be able to expect aspirants to high office to clearly distance themselves from groups which deny history's most ghastly act of genocide and openly endorse the regime at the focus of the world's struggle against racism. To be seen in a context which may lend credence to such groups may only be an error in judgment, but there may be times when much will depend on our leader's judgment.

The one label that sticks to Vander Zalm is the one on which he and Harry Rankin both agree: populist. A populist is a kind of a loose cannon on the ship of state's deck—it can end up pointing in any direction. The original Social Credit League that began under Bible Bill Aberhart in the thirties was a populist movement—and so was J.S. Woodsworth's Canadian Commonwealth Federation, the forerunner of the NDP. The thing that makes a populist leader is his independence from traditional established interests: corporate business, organized labour, the church, the military, the throne. He holds power by virtue of a direct relationship with the people that bypasses traditional channels, and by making deals with traditional power blocks. Populist movements sometimes spring up around single issues, such as the agricultural crisis of the US midwest in the late 1900s or of the Canadian prairies in the 1930s, or the religious fundamentalism in the US today. Often populist administrations spring up around charismatic strongmen such as Huey P. Long or Juan Peron. These leaders sometimes have no overriding aim apart from preserving their own power, and play one faction off against another while keeping the masses loyal with chicken-in-every-pot schemes like Long's "Share-the-Wealth" giveaway, Aberhart's "basic dividends" or W.A.C. Bennett's "Homeowner Grants." Vander Zalm's cheaper beer shows a clear, if somewhat infantile, grasp of the tradition.

Much in Vander Zalm's early and late history locates him in this strongman-populist tradition. It is significant that when Alan Twigg asked him why he sought power he paused as if he'd never thought of it before, then answered, "I don't know." In cabinet he was the ultimate "hands-on" minister, giving full rein to his "exaggerated take-charge complex" within days of appointment. His emphasis throughout the '86 election campaign on strong, charismatic leadership at the expense of open debate and his clearly paternalistic "trust me" appeal are disturbingly reminiscent of the anti-parliamentary tendencies of populism.

The 1986 election campaign itself was centred on Vander Zalm's personality to a extent seldom seen even in these image-worshipping times. The only two issues which played a major role in the campaign, the US lumber tariff, or as Vander Zalm liked to call it, "The Countervail," and the several labour disputes that arose, were personally appropriated by the premier, as if no other cabinet ministers existed. When a reporter asked the premier why he seemed to be displacing his own labour minister, who lost his seat by 500 votes and could have used some good exposure, he said only he would "have to be talking to the minister about that." It was the old take-charge impulse, now raising the possibility he would carry his centralizing proclivity to new extremes as premier. Once the humiliation of the NDP was complete, he announced that he would give his cabinet "strong leadership" and not hesitate to "look in" to make sure ministers were doing what was right for the people of BC. The strongman populist often assumes he embodies the will of the people, and can intuit their interests.

An incident which occurred immediately following the election gives some insight into the Vander Zalm method. The United Fishermen and Allied Workers' Union, backed by the Sunshine Coast Regional District and others, had been calling for a moratorium on the granting of licences for private fish farms, which had been proliferating at an alarming rate for two years. The Bennett administration had been backing fish farms against all opposition and Jack Davis had promised more growth under Vander Zalm, but the UFAWU's Bill Procopation sent the premier a telegram restating the union's moratorium demand anyway. The telegram arrived in Victoria October 20 while Vander Zalm was away campaigning and his secretary Dorothy Sage wrote Procopation a short, neatly typed reply saying that the premier would be looking into the matter after October 27.

But when Procopation received this reply there was a handwritten note across the bottom: "Dear Bill, (I'm back) I've asked the ministry to put a hold on licences until I have a chance to get more info. [signed] Bill." When the amazed but jubilant UFAWU contacted the ministry official in charge for details of this unexpected breakthrough, he had never heard of any moratorium and angrily vowed he was opposed to the idea.

Another official, who had worked under Vander Zalm in Municipal Affairs, sighed, "I hope we're not going to have to go back to looking in the papers every morning to see what our ministry is doing."

Vander Zalm's impatience with bureaucracy underlay his writing of the ill-fated Land Use Act in 1981, which slashed the red tape involved in seeking approval for developments, but centred so much discretionary power in the minister's hands NDP critic Jim Lorimer called it a "fascist document." Vander Zalm brushed these concerns away, saying it was not centralist. But he also said, "I feel that democracy has been interpreted to mean that somehow you could make things more democratic by spreading out or diluting the responsibility of any one person. My type of democracy would require a lot less government."

His impatience with due process extends to the legislature itself. In conversation with the author of this book, Vander Zalm reaffirmed his oft-stated belief that "the British parliamentary system is obsolete" and clearly indicated his desire to restructure it, although his explanation of just what he would do to it tailed off in vague praise for the Swiss system of government. During the campaign he promised to make government more "open" by televising debates in the House, putting more issues to referendum and extending the committee system. Most observers would welcome televised debate, although it could end up increasing Vander Zalm's already immense advantage with the media. Likewise, everyone who cares about the health of parliamentary democracy in BC would have to applaud any revival of the house committee system, which all but died out under 33 years of Social Credit government. But the real question is whether or not the process of forcing the legislature into an increasingly peripheral role will continue as it did under

Bennett father and son, whose main strategy in dealing with it was one of avoidance.

Vander Zalm has not distinguished himself as a parliamentarian, either. His impatience with opposing viewpoints and his deep, abiding aversion to the political left do not make him a likely candidate to reverse the Bennett tendency to govern by order-in-council and to restore parliamentary debate to its central place in government. He is not noted for skill in debate himself, in spite of his penchant for musing about major policy change before TV cameras. He tends to have a hard time putting together a logical string or holding a consistent train of thought while on his feet, falling back on Babbitt-like cliches about the sanctity of free enterprise and the evils of creeping socialism. His habit in government has been to hoard authority, not to share it, and to do differently would be to go against the most ingrained traits in his nature.

Closely looked at, his "open government" proposals do not necessarily promise improvement in the role of the legislature. Vander Zalm's willingness to talk does not translate as willingness to change his mind; in promoting his Land Use Act he talked to everybody but gave in to few. Increased use of referenda may well prove to be a means of circumventing bipartisan debate, adding little more to the democratic process than Bill Bennett's frequent use of polls. And a leader who cultivates a habit of dialoguing with the public via television is not the same as a leader who respects the public's right to be represented fairly in a democratically run legislature. An anti-parliamentary populist can cultivate intimacy with the people to democracy's cost, and so might Vander Zalm. Sometimes he seems to be preparing to carry out the whole function of parliament inside his own head. It may well be he will succeed in making the public more aware of the political process, and more involved, the way Barrett did in government, but it seems very unlikely he will take an interest in making government more democratic. One can take the interest he has shown in improving BC democracy as a hopeful sign, but it would be more in keeping with his past political history to do the opposite, and in the name of efficiency, chip away at the democratic safeguards built into that parliamentary system of government over the past 700 years.

On a more specific level, it is unlikely Vander Zalm's lifelong identification with small business will diminish. He is a former head of the BC Chamber of Commerce and his campaign adviser, Bill Goldie, has more recent association. The small business people of the petty bourgeoisie are the rock upon which his power is based and give him one of his greatest advantages heading into office: the opportunity to take an independent line with the big corporations that dominate the BC economy. But we have seen his own interest has been in development, and it is likely his best efforts will be aimed at clearing away the sort of regulatory impediments that frustrate projects like Fantasy Gardens, while businesses that require more thoughtful kinds of help, like seed money and market development, may fare less well. The side of his personality that might appreciate the role of cultural industries, for example, would appear to be as absent as if it had been surgically removed.

In Surrey Vander Zalm became a hard taskmaster to his fellow developers once in office, transferring his loyalties to the new job in hand, but that didn't always happen in later postings, such as Municipal Affairs. The Agricultural Land Reserve will find its perilous existence more perilous, as will the Islands Trust. More will be heard of logging and mining in major parks, and offshore oil exploration, unless Vander Zalm's trial balloons get shot down resoundingly, and even then, he may just keep sending them up again. His new level of super-municipal government, the county system, will no doubt be tried, as will the voucher system of allotting educational funding, along with a host of other bright ideas he hasn't had yet. Whatever happens, there will be a lot of action under Vander Zalm, because he is a doer, and he likes to change things in big ways.

Vander Zalm did, of course, inherit a flat economy. But he can not be blamed for it, and in that way it can be safer than taking on a booming economy just in time to have it bust, as happened to Barrett. His worst problems could be of an internal kind. He is off to a bad start on the conflict-of-interest question. Because they usually don't begin with great personal wealth, it is a common story with populists to become embroiled in business scandals, and Vander Zalm's private business activities could lead him into deeper conflict, but not necessarily. There is a tradition in BC politics for the families of leading politicians to build major business enterprises without getting in trouble, and if Vander Zalm can't figure out how it's done he will find a good adviser in his admirer Phil Gaglardi. A trickier question is, can he depend on his followers to be as discreet? By his own actions he has already served notice the administration is open for business, and there could well be a few among his supporters who will translate the message too liberally. And while Vander Zalm may have escaped fealty to Howe Street for the time being, he has racked up some political debts with special interests who gave him strong support during his re-entry into politics. One of these is his defender on Richmond Council and campaign manager, Tillie Marxreiter.

Marxreiter is an anti-abortion and anti–sex education activist who, as a Richmond school board member in 1975, helped create a national sensation by supporting the banning of a juvenile novel called *Go Ask Alice*. As a leader of Richmond Concerned Parents she was active in having a sex education program, begun under NDP education minister Eileen Dailly, discontinued. On municipal council she supported Vander Zalm's Fantasy Garden rezoning and the controversial application to rezone the rich Terra Nova farmland for residential development. The application was sponsored by another of Vander Zalm's political creditors,the Ilich-owned Progressive Construction. Marxreiter helped organize both the early delegate support in Richmond that put Vander Zalm's leadership bid in gear and played a key role at Whistler. "We take a lot of credit (for Vander Zalm's success)," she says. By backing the winning horse from the time he was still a longshot, Tillie Marxreiter has assured that her brand of fundamentalism will have an inside track in the premier's thinking.

Whether Vander Zalm continues to succeed the way he succeeded in 1986 will depend to a large extent on whether he gives in to the temptation of right-wing strongman politics, or whether he continues to listen to the ghost of W.A.C. Bennett whispering in his ear, "go to the centre, Bill, the centre." He can do a lot wrong as long as he doesn't break up the Liberal-Conservative-Socred coalition, because the NDP has shown no proof it can win against a united front of

free-enterprise voters. One thing that is sure is that the man who crafted the dream victory of 1986 has the political skills to be around for a long time. His enemies hope that his shallowness and mental disorganization will soon expose him as unfit, but they perhaps overrate the importance of these faults in a political leader of the 1980s. Vander Zalm has already been compared to Ronald Reagan. He could stay around another twenty years and become one of those colourful regional legends that make a permanent mark on the national psyche, like Maurice Duplessis or Joey Smallwood. He's got the potential.

W.A.C. Bennett was right about that.

NOTES

Chapter 1. NOORDWYKERHOUT

1. Vancouver *Sun*, Oct. 15, 1984.
2. Ibid., April 12, 1976.
3. Ibid.
4. Ibid.
5. *Vancouver*, April 1983.
6. Vancouver *Sun*, October 15, 1985.
7. Ibid., October 15, 1984.
8. Ibid., October 17, 1986.
9. Ibid.
10. *Vancouver*, April 1983.
11. Published by McGraw-Hill Ryerson, 1980.
12. Henri van der Zee, *The Hunger Winter* (Jill Norman & Hobhouse, 1982).
13. Ibid.
14. Vancouver *Sun*, October 15, 1984

Chapter 2. FAMILY MATTERS

1. Vancouver *Sun*, October 15, 1984.
2. Ibid., April 12, 1976.
3. Ibid.
4. *Maclean's*, September 8, 1986.
5. Helen Colijn, *Of Dutch Ways*, Dillon Press, 1980.
6. Vancouver *Sun*, October 15, 1984.
7. *Easy Living*, December 14, 1983–January 17, 1984.
8. Ibid.
9. Ibid.
10. Vancouver *Sun*, October 15, 1984.
11. Philip Sheffield High School annual, 1952.
12. Ibid.
13. Vancouver *Sun*, October 15, 1984.
14. *Globe & Mail*, March 1, 1979.
15. *Vancouver*, April 1983.
16. Vancouver *Sun*, August 9, 1986.
17. Vancouver *Courier*, April 12, 1979.
18. Vancouver *Province*, August 3, 1986.
19. Vancouver *Courier*, April 12, 1979.
20. Vancouver *Province*, August 3, 1986.
21. Vancouver *Courier*, April 12, 1979.
22. Ibid.
23. Ibid.
24. Ibid.
25. Ibid.
26. Vancouver *Province*, October 17, 1986.
27. Vancouver *Sun*, August 9, 1986.
28. Ibid.

29. Vancouver *Courier*, April 12, 1979.
30. Ibid.
31. *Metro Magazine*, September 29, 1977.
32. Vancouver *Sun*, August 9, 1986.
33. *Metro Magazine*, September 29, 1977.
34. Vancouver *Sun*, August 9, 1986.
35. Vancouver *Courier*, April 17, 1979.
36. Vancouver *Sun*, August 9, 1986.
37. Ibid.
38. Vancouver *Province*, August 15, 1986.
39. Vancouver *Sun*, August 9, 1986.
40. Ibid., July 18, 1986.
41. Ibid., April 12, 1976.
42. Ibid., March 23, 1976.
43. Ibid.
44. Vancouver *Province*, October 19, 1986.
45. Stan Persky, *Bennett II*, New Star Books, 1983.

Chapter 3. BUSINESS MATTERS

1. *Monday Magazine*, November 26–December 3, 1982.
2. Vancouver *Sun*, October 6, 1981.
3. Edmonton *Journal*, February 10, 1979.
4. Vancouver *Sun*, March 14, 1978.
5. Ibid., June 14, 1982.
6. Ibid., January 23, 1984.
7. *Vancouver*, April 1983.

Chapter 4. ASSUMING POWER

1. Vancouver *Sun*, December 8, 1969.
2. Vancouver *Province*, December 8, 1969.
3. *Monday Magazine*, November 26–December 2, 1982.
4. *Vancouver*, April 1983.
5. Vancouver *Sun*, April 12, 1976.
6. Ibid.
7. Speech, January 5, 1970.
8. Vancouver *Province*, December 1, 1971.
9. Ibid., January 22, 1972.
10. Vancouver *Sun*, July 18, 1986.
11. Vancouver *Province*, March 6, 1975.
12. Ibid., October 3, 1970.
13. Ibid., March 31, 1971.
14. Ibid., June 2, 1971.
15. Ibid., May 23, 1972.
16. Ibid., May 28, 1974.
17. Speech, January 5, 1970.
18. Speech, January 4, 1971.
19. Ibid.

20. Ibid.
21. *Metro Magazine*, September 29, 1977.
22. Vancouver *Province*, May 4, 1972.
23. Campaign literature, May 1972.
24. Ibid.
25. Speech, January 8, 1973.
26. Vancouver *Province*, March 1, 1973.
27. Ibid., May 11, 1973.
28. Ibid.
29. Vancouver *Province*, September 25, 1973.
30. Ibid., November 27, 1973.
31. Ibid., November 29, 1973.
32. Ibid., December 4, 1973.
33. Ibid., December 5, 1973.
34. Ibid., December 11, 1973.
35. Ibid.
36. Vancouver *Sun*, August 26, 1975.
37. Vancouver *Province*, May 15, 1974.
38. *Maclean's*, August 11, 1986.

Chapter 5. HUMAN RESOURCES

1. Vancouver *Sun*, December 15, 1982
2. Press conference, September 18, 1974.
3. George Woodcock, "Playing to the People," *A George Woodcock Reader*, edited by Doug Fetherling, Deneau & Greenberg, 1980.
4. Lorne J. Kavic and Garry Brian Nixon, *The 1200 Days: a Shattered Dream*, Kaen Publishers, 1978.
5. *Metro Magazine*, September 29, 1977.
6. Ibid.
7. Ibid.
8. Ibid.
9. Vancouver *Express*, May 4, 1979.
10. Vancouver *Sun*, December 23, 1975.
11. Vancouver *Province*, December 23, 1975.
12. Vancouver *Sun*, December 23, 1975.
13. *Monday Magazine*, November 26, 1982.
14. Ros Oberlyn, Vancouver *Express*, May 4, 1979.
15. Ibid.
16. Stan Persky, *Bennett II*, New Star Books, 1983.
17. *Globe & Mail*, October 12, 1977.
18. Ros Oberlyn, Vancouver *Express*, May 4, 1979.
19. Vancouver *Province*, February 18, 1977.
20. Ibid.
21. Vancouver *Sun*, April 12, 1976.
22. Ibid., October 17, 1977.
23. Vancouver *Province*, December 23, 1975.
24. *Globe & Mail*, March 1, 1979.
25. *Metro Magazine* September 29, 1977.
26. Vancouver *Sun*, April 12, 1976.
27. Vancouver *Province*, April 3, 1976.
28. Ibid.
29. Ibid., November 26, 1977.
30. Ibid.
31. Ibid.

32. Ros Oberlyn, Vancouver *Express*, May 4, 1979.
33. Stan Persky, *Son of Socred*, New Star Books, 1979.
34. *Metro Magazine* September 29, 1977.
35. Stan Persky, *Bennett II*, New Star Books, 1983.
36. Allan Fotheringham, *Saturday Night*, 1975 (quoted in *Bennett II*).
37. Stan Persky, *Bennett II*.
38. Ibid.
39. Ibid.
40. Ibid.
41. Ibid.
42. Ibid.
43. Ibid.
44. Ibid.
45. Ibid.
46. *Metro Magazine* September 29, 1977.

Chapter 6. MUNICIPAL AFFAIRS

1. Vancouver *Courier*, March 1, 1979.
2. Ibid.
3. Vancouver *Sun*, August 14, 1980.
4. Vancouver *Province*, January 13, 1981.
5. *Vancouver*, April 1983.
6. Vancouver *Sun*, December 2, 1981.
7. Ibid.
8. Ibid.
9. Vancouver *Province*, September 19, 1980.
10. Vancouver *Sun*, December 2, 1981.
11. Ibid.
12. Vancouver *Province*, July 30, 1982.
13. *Easy Living*, December 14–January 17, 1984.
14. Vancouver *Sun*, December 15, 1982.
15. Vancouver *Province*, January 13, 1981.
16. Ibid., October 5, 1980.
17. New Westminster *Columbian*, June 18, 1979.
18. Ibid.
19. Vancouver *Province*, December 6, 1980.
20. Vancouver *Sun*, October 1, 1977.
21. *Globe & Mail*, May 17, 1984.
22. Vancouver *Province*, January 13, 1981.
23. *Vancouver*, April 1983.
24. Vancouver *Province*, May 23, 1982.
25. Ibid.
26. Ibid.
27. Ibid.
28. *Globe & Mail*, May 17, 1984.
29. Ibid., May 19, 1984.
30. Ibid.
31. Vancouver *Province*, April 14, 1985.
32. Ibid., December 12, 1985.

Chapter 7. EDUCATION

1. Vancouver *Province*, August 11, 1982.
2. *Canadian School Executive*, March 1983.

3. Speech to the Coquitlam Chamber of Commerce, August 12, 1982.
4. *Jack Webster Show*, BCTV, September 21, 1982.
5. Vancouver *Province*, September 12, 1982.
6. Ibid., October 20, 1982.
7. BCTV, August 30, 1982.
8. Vancouver *Province*, September 12, 1982.
9. *Vancouver*, April 1983.
10. Victoria *Times-Colonist*, September 21, 1982.
11. Speech to Victoria Chamber of Commerce, February 16, 1983.
12. *Early Edition*, CBC Radio, February 17, 1983.
13. *Gary Bannerman Show*, CKNW, August 30, 1982.
14. *Early Edition*, CBC Radio, February 17, 1983.
15. Victoria *Times-Colonist*, September 21, 1982.
16. *Jack Webster Show*, BCTV, January 3, 1983.
17. Victoria *Times-Colonist*, September 21, 1982.
18. *Jack Webster Show*, BCTV, January 3, 1983.
19. Vancouver *Province*, September 12, 1982.
20. BCTV, August 30, 1982.
21. Ibid.
22. *Vancouver*, April 1983.
23. *Gary Bannerman Show*, CKNW, February 25, 1983.
24. CBC Radio, September 27, 1982.
25. *Jack Webster Show*, BCTV, September 21, 1982.
26. Victoria *Times-Colonist*, September 21, 1982.
27. *Monday Magazine*, December 2, 1982.
28. *Gary Bannerman Show*, CKNW, October 11, 1982.
29. Ibid., August 30, 1982.
30. *Jack Webster Show*, BCTV, September 9, 1982.
31. Victoria *Times-Colonist*, September 21, 1982.
32. Vancouver *Province*, September 12, 1982.
33. Ibid., August 11, 1982.
34. Vancouver *Sun*, July 18, 1986.
35. Speech at Social Credit nominating convention, Delta, September 30, 1982.
36. Speech at BCSTA Seminar, August 26, 1982.
37. *Canadian School Executive*, March 1983.
38. Stan Persky, *Bennett II*.
39. Vancouver *Province*, October 20, 1982.
40. Ibid., February 6, 1983.
41. Ibid., October 20, 1982.
42. Ibid., September 12, 1982.
43. Ibid., August 19, 1986.
44. Vancouver *Sun*, November 24, 1982.
45. Ibid., April 2, 1983.

Chapter 8. ON SABBATICAL

1. Vancouver *Sun*, April 2, 1983.
2. Ibid..
3. Vancouver *Province*, April 3, 1983.
4. Vancouver *Sun*, April 2, 1983.
5. Ibid., April 2, 1983 (Denny Boyd column).
6. Ibid.
7. Vancouver *Province*, April 3, 1983.
8. Ibid., January 22, 1984.
9. Ibid., April 4, 1983.
10. Vancouver *Sun*, April 2, 1982.
11. Ibid.
12. Vancouver *Sun*, October 11, 1984.
13. Ibid.
14. Ibid.
15. Vancouver *Province*, March 21, 1984.
16. Vancouver *Sun*, November 24, 1984.
17. Ibid.
18. Campaign literature in bid for mayor of Vancouver.
19. Vancouver *Sun*, February 8, 1984.
20. Ibid.
21. Ibid.
22. Vancouver *Province*, September 14, 1984.
23. Ibid., September 19, 1984.
24. Ibid.
25. Ibid.
26. Ibid., September 20, 1984.
27. Ibid.
28. Ibid.
29. Vancouver *Sun*, July 18, 1986.
30. Victoria *Daily Colonist*, May 9, 1979.
31. Vancouver *Province*, August 1, 1986.
32. Vancouver *Sun*, July 18, 1986.
33. Hansard, June 9, 1982.
34. CKNW, August 11, 1982.
35. Hansard, June 9, 1982.
36. Vancouver *Sun*, January 22, 1986.
37. Ibid.
38. Ibid., March 1, 1986.

Chapter 9. VANDER ZALM VS. HARCOURT

1. *Globe & Mail*, April 25, 1984.
2. Vancouver *Sun*, January 10, 1983.
3. *Easy Living*, December 14–January 17, 1984.
4. Vancouver *Sun*, September 27, 1984.
5. Ibid., January 23, 1984.
6. Vancouver *Province*, March 4, 1984.
7. Ibid.
8. Ibid.
9. Ibid.
10. Vancouver *Sun*, June 11, 1984.

11. Vancouver *Province*, July 26, 1984.
12. Vancouver *Sun*, September 25, 1984.
13. Ibid., September 27, 1984.
14. Vancouver *Province*, September 27, 1984.
15. Ibid., September 28, 1984.
16. Ibid., October 4, 1984.
17. Vancouver *Sun*, October 3, 1984.
18. Ibid., October 18, 1984.
19. Ibid., October 20, 1984.
20. Vancouver *Province*, October 4, 1984.
21. Vancouver *Sun*, October 18, 1984.
22. Ibid.
23. *Easy Living*, December 14–January 17, 1984.
24. Vancouver *Province*, October 11, 1984.
25. Ibid., October 16, 1986.
26. Vancouver *Courier*, October 17, 1984.
27. Vancouver *Sun*, October 16, 1986.
28. Ibid.
29. Ibid.
30. Vancouver *Province*, October 29, 1984.
31. Ibid., October 30, 1984.
32. Ibid..
33. Ibid., October 21, 1984.
34. Ibid., October 26, 1984.
35. Ibid., November 5, 1984.
36. Ibid., November 16, 1984.
37. Vander Zalm's Vancouver mayoralty campaign literature.
38. Ibid.
39. Vancouver *Sun*, November 19, 1984.
40. Vancouver *Province*, November 25, 1984.
41. Ibid.

Chapter 10. FANTASY GARDEN WORLD

1. Vancouver *Sun*, August 15, 1986.
2. *Vancouver*, April 1983.
3. Letter, May 6, 1985.
4. Ibid.
5. Ibid.
6. Ibid.
7. Ibid.
8. Vancouver *Sun*, October 24, 1984.
9. Letter, May 6, 1985.
10. Ibid.
11. Ibid.
12. Ibid.
13. Ibid.
14. Report to Richmond Council, June 16, 1986.
15. Vancouver *Sun*, June 18, 1986.
16. Ibid., July 22, 1986.
17. Ibid., July 5, 1986.
18. Ibid., August 22, 1986.
19. Ibid.
20. Ibid., August 27, 1986.
21. Ibid.
22. Ibid., August 28, 1986.

Chapter 11. THE ROAD TO WHISTLER

1. Vancouver *Province*, June 22, 1986.
2. *Equity*, September 1986.
3. Ibid.
4. *Easy Living, December 14, 1983*–January 17, 1984.
5. Prince Rupert *Daily News*, July 10, 1986.
6. *Maclean's*, August 11, 1986.
7. Heather Conn, *NeWest Review*, article to be published.
8. Vancouver *Sun*, July 24, 1986.
9. Ibid.
10. Ibid.
11. Vancouver *Sun*, July 5, 1986.
12. Ibid., July 3, 1986.
13. Ibid., July 27, 1986.
14. Ibid., July 17, 1986.
15. Ibid., July 27, 1986.
16. Ibid., July 15, 1986.
17. Ibid., July 30, 1986.
18. Ibid., July 19, 1986.
19. Ibid., July 27, 1986.
20. Ibid., July 7, 1986.
21. Ibid., July 22, 1986.
22. Ibid.
23. Ibid., July 14, 1986.
24. *Maclean's*, July 7, 1986.
25. Vancouver *Sun*, July 23, 1986.
26. Ibid.
27. *Maclean's*, July 7, 1986.
28. Vancouver *Sun*, July 24, 1986.
29. Ibid., July 26, 1986.
30. Ibid.

Chapter 12. THE PREMIER MARKET

1. *Maclean's*, August 11, 1986.
2. Vancouver *Sun*, July 29, 1986.
3. Article to be published.
4. Vancouver *Sun*, July 29, 1986.
5. Vancouver *Province*, July 3, 1986.
6. *Maclean's*, August 11, 1986.
7. Ibid.
8. Vancouver *Sun*, July 26, 1986.
9. Ibid., July 28, 1986.
10. Ibid.
11. Ibid., July 31, 1986.
12. *Maclean's*, August 11, 1986.
13. *Equity*, September 1986.
14. Vancouver *Sun*, July 29, 1986.
15. Vancouver *Province*, July 30, 1986.
16. Vancouver *Sun*, July 30, 1986.
17. Vancouver *Province*, July 30, 1986.
18. Vancouver *Sun*, July 30, 1986.
19. Ibid.
20. Ibid.
21. Ibid.
22. Ibid.
23. Ibid.

24. Vancouver *Province*, July 30, 1986.
25. Vancouver *Sun*, July 30, 1986.
26. Sid Tafler, "Power and Privilege," *Monday Magazine*, July 17, 1986.
27. CBC Television, July 30, 1986.
28. Vancouver *Sun*, July 31, 1986.
29. Ibid.
30. *Maclean's*, August 11, 1986.
31. Ibid.
32. *Equity*, July/August 1986.
33. Ibid.
34. Vancouver *Sun*, August 1, 1986.
35. Ibid.
36. Ibid.
37. Ibid., July 31, 1986.
38. *Maclean's*, August 11, 1986.
39. Vancouver *Province*, July 31, 1986.
40. Vancouver *Sun*, July 31, 1986.
41. Ibid.
42. Ibid.
43. *Vancouver*, October 1986.
44. Vancouver *Sun*, July 31, 1986.
45. Ibid.
46. Ibid.
47. Ibid.
48. *Equity*, September 1986.
49. Ibid.
50. *Maclean's*, August 11, 1986.
51. Ibid.
52. Vancouver *Province*, July 31, 1986.
53. Ibid.
54. *Maclean's*, August 11, 1986.
55. Vancouver *Sun*, July 31, 1986.
56. Ibid.
57. *Equity*, September 1986.
58. Vancouver *Sun*, July 31, 1986.
59. Vander Zalm's 1986 Social Credit leadership campaign literature.

Chapter 13. PREMIER VANDER ZALM

1. David Mitchell, *W.A.C. Bennett and the Rise of British Columbia*, Douglas & McIntyre, 1983.
2. Ibid.
3. Ibid.
4. Ibid.
5. Ibid.
6. Ibid.
7. Ibid.
8. Ibid.
9. Ibid.
10. Ibid.
11. Ibid.
12. Ibid.
13. Vancouver *Sun*, August 16, 1986.
14. Vancouver *Province*, July 4, 1974.
15. Vancouver *Sun*, August 1, 1986.

16. Vander Zalm's 1986 leadership campaign literature.
17. Vancouver *Province*, August 3, 1986.
18. Vancouver *Sun*, September 29, 1982.
19. Ibid.
20. *Vancouver*, April 1983.
21. Vancouver *Sun*, July 18, 1986.
22. Vander Zalm's 1986 leadership campaign literature.
23. Vancouver *Sun*, August 15, 1986.
24. Ibid.
25. Ibid., August 7, 1986.
26. Vancouver *Province*, August 14, 1986.
27. Vancouver *Sun*, August 27, 11986.
28. *Monday Magazine*, November 26, 1982.
29. Vancouver *Province*, September 3, 1986.
30. Vancouver *Sun*, September 27, 1986.
31. *Equity*, January/February 1986.
32. Ibid.
33. Vancouver *Sun*, August 15, 1986.
34. *Maclean's*, August 11, 1986.
35. *Jack Webster Show*, BCTV, September 2, 1986.
36. Vancouver *Sun*, August 7, 1986.
37. Ibid., August 14, 1986.
38. Vancouver *Province*, August 1, 1986.
39. Vancouver *Sun*, September 27, 1986.

Chapter 14. VANDER ZALM & THE MEDIA

1. *Globe & Mail*, March 1, 1979.
2. Vancouver *Sun*, July 14, 1986.
3. *Maclean's*, August 11, 1986.
4. Vancouver *Sun*, April 2, 1983.
5. *Globe & Mail*, March 1, 1979.
6. Edmonton *Journal*, February 10, 1979.
7. Vancouver *Province*, April 2, 1983.
8. Vancouver *Express*, January 17, 1979.
9. Vancouver *Free Press*, January 17, 1979.
10. Vancouver *Sun*, October 15, 1984.
11. *Monday Magazine*, December 2, 1982.
12. Vancouver *Sun*, July 5, 1986.
13. *Maclean's*, August 11, 1986.
14. Vancouver *Sun*, November 14, 1976.
15. Ibid., November 16, 1976.
16. Ibid.
17. Ibid.
18. Vancouver *Province*, November 19, 1976.
19. Ibid.
20. *Monday Magazine*, December 2, 1982.
21. *Globe & Mail, February 7, 1979.*
22. *Vancouver Express*, March 7, 1979.
23. Vancouver *Sun*, November 15, 1984.

THE MORNING AFTER

1. Vancouver *Sun*, October 25, 1986.

BIBLIOGRAPHY

Cohn, Angelo. *The First Book of Netherlands*. Franklin Watts, 1962.

Colijn, Helen. *Of Dutch Ways*. Dillon Press, 1980.

Collier, Basil. *The Second World War: A Military History*. William Morrow & Co., 1967.

Fetherling, Doug, ed. *A George Woodcock Reader*. Deneau & Greenberg, 1980.

Fotheringham, Allan. *Collected & Bound*. November House, 1972.

Hart, B.H. Liddell. *History of the Second World War*. Cassell, 1970.

Horn, Michiel, and David Kaufman. *A Liberation Album*. McGraw-Hill Ryerson, 1980.

Kavic, Lorne J., and Garry Brian Nixon. *The 1200 Days: a Shattered Dream*. Kaen Publishers, 1978.

Koning, Hans. *Amsterdam*. Time-Life Books, 1977.

Magnusson, W., W.K. Carroll, C. Doyle, M. Langer, and R.B.J. Walker, eds. *The New Reality*. New Star Books, 1984.

Mitchell, David. *W.A.C. Bennett and the Rise of British Columbia*. Douglas & McIntyre, 1983.

Morley, J.T., N.J. Ruff, N.A. Swainson, R.J. Wilson, and W.D. Young. *The Reins of Power*. Douglas & McIntyre, 1983.

Persky, Stan. *Bennett II*. New Star Books, 1983.

Persky, Stan. *Son of Socred*. New Star Books, 1979.

Snyder, Louis L. *The War: A Concise History*. Julian Messner, 1960.

Tomes, John. *Blue Guide Holland*. Ernest Benn Ltd., 1982.

Utrecht State University. *A Compact Geography of the Netherlands*. Ministry of Foreign Affairs, The Hague, 1974.

Van der Zee, Henri A. *The Hunger Winter*. Jill Norman & Hobhouse Ltd., 1982.

INDEX